COMING TO PEACE
WITH SCIENCE

Bridging the Worlds Between Faith and Biology

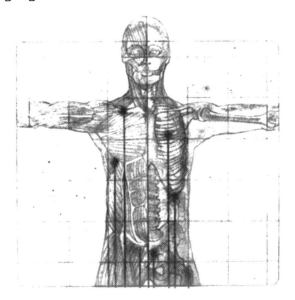

DARREL R. FALK

Foreword by Francis S. Collins

InterVarsity Press
Downers Grove, Illinois

InterVarsity Press
P.O. Box 1400, Downers Grove, IL 60515-1426
World Wide Web: www.ivpress.com
E-mail: mail@ivpress.com

©2004 by Darrel R. Falk

InterVarsity Press® is the book-publishing division of InterVarsity Christian Fellowship/USA®, a student movement active on campus at hundreds of universities, colleges and schools of nursing in the United States of America, and a member movement of the International Fellowship of Evangelical Students. For information about local and regional activities, write Public Relations Dept., InterVarsity Christian Fellowship/USA, 6400 Schroeder Rd., P.O. Box 7895, Madison, WI 53707-7895, or visit the IVCF website at <www.intervarsity.org>.

Design: Cindy Kiple

Images: Gary Kaemmer/Getty Images

ISBN 0-8308-2742-0

Printed in the United States of America ∞

Library of Congress Cataloging-in-Publication Data

Falk, Darrel R., 1946-
   Coming to peace with science: bridging the worlds between faith and
   biology/Darrel R. Falk
     p. cm.
   Includes bibliographical references and index.
   ISBN 0-8308-2742-0 (pbk.: alk. paper)
   1. Creation. 2. Evolution (Biology)—Religious
   aspects—Christianity. I. Title.
    BS651.F35 2004
    231.7'652—dc22

2003027937

P	20	19	18	17	16	15	14	13	12	11	10	9	8	7	6	5	3	2	1
Y	20	19	18	17	16	15	14	13	12	11	10	09	08	07	06	05	04		

To my parents, Lawrence and Isabelle,
who lovingly showed me a living faith and a
sweet peace I could never forget,

To my church family at
Syracuse Immanuel Church of the Nazarene, 1977-1984,
who showed me that the world of faith
was still relevant to a science professor, and

To my wife, Joyce,
whose patient and loving support
throughout the circuitous journey enabled me
to find my way to the bridge that led back home.

CONTENTS

FOREWORD

OBSERVERS NOTE A WRESTLING MATCH taking place in our materialistic society: the naturalistic worldview, which embraces the tools of science as a means of understanding the world, versus the spiritual worldview, which seeks to determine truths about God and faith. Many conclude that the natural worldview is winning.

After all, science has achieved many triumphs, from determining the natural laws that govern all objects in the universe to discovering the principles that govern all living organisms and mapping the sequence of the human genome. Yet despite the intellectual satisfaction of these achievements, thoughtful people still have eternal questions that science is unable to answer: "Why am I here?" "What happens after I die?" "Is there a God? Does he care about me?"

Polarizing influences abound, locking these worldviews in seemingly irreconcilable conflict. Some evolutionary biologists cite growing evidence from the fossil record and DNA analysis to argue that evolution proves there is no God. In the process they commit the logical fallacy of using natural laws to exclude the supernatural.

Religious fundamentalists, perceiving an assault on their faith from evolutionary theory, cite an ultraliteral reading of Genesis to insist that the earth is only a few thousand years old, and God created all species out of nothingness.

Tragically, earnest seekers confronted with these extreme expressions of the two worldviews feel obligated to choose one or the other, missing out on the deeply satisfying harmony of science and faith in a personal God experienced by many scientists, including myself. Particularly at risk are those who, having been taught young-earth creationism by well-intentioned families and churches, ultimately become exposed to overwhelming scientific data supporting evolution and an old earth. Faced with unreasonable demands on their logic by sincere teachers of their faith, is it any wonder that many sadly conclude that they cannot believe in a God who would ask them to deny the truth?

It is especially to those seekers that Darrel Falk speaks in this remarkable book. With clarity and skill honed over many years as a widely admired teacher of biology, Falk presents evidence from cosmology, geology, paleontology and genetics to make a compelling case for an ancient earth and the relatedness of all life forms. Most important, however, he presents a loving Creator God who used the mechanism of evolution to create living things, including the human race. The seemingly random process of evolution, which admittedly requires rejection of an ultraliteral reading of Genesis, is not random to God. He is not limited by space and time, and the ultimate appearance on this planet of sentient creatures with whom he could have fellowship was never in doubt.

Falk points out compelling reasons that this harmonization of science and faith is inherently reasonable and does not lead inevitably toward denial of the essential truths of Christianity. Thus the synthesis proposed in this book, referred to by theologians as theistic evolutionism, is not a convenient, after-the-fact scientific apologetic but an entirely consistent and logical stance. I believe even St. Augustine would have embraced it.

God is the greatest scientist. Surely he is not threatened by our efforts to understand the natural world. Surely he does not expect us to disbelieve the facts that science is gathering about the wonderful beauty and order around us.

This book should provide wonderful comfort to earnest seekers who have concluded that faith requires a rejection of science, or that science requires a rejection of faith. It should also be carefully read by church leaders who, in their sincere attempts to defend the faith, ask seekers to disbelieve a massive body of evidence that supports gradual creation.

Skeptics of science can be reassured that life makes sense, and the methods of science can be trusted. Those fearful that science requires a descent into atheism will be reassured by the vibrant Christian spirituality evidenced in Falk's narrative. The deeply satisfying harmony of science and faith, as demonstrated in Falk's life (and which I am fortunate to say operates in my own), should be a source of great encouragement to those who have grown despondent in their quest.

Francis S. Collins, M.D., Ph.D.
Director, National Human Genome Research Institute,
National Institutes of Health

PREFACE

MANY BOOKS ABOUT THE ACTION OF THE CREATOR written over the past forty years have used metaphorical language that draws from the field of engineering. God is frequently referred to as a designer, as though he designed and built living creatures in a manner analogous to how we humans construct a building or a piece of equipment.

Metaphors, by definition, draw upon human experience. As we try to picture the activity of God, our image of God at work is constrained by our own inability to adequately imagine that which we have not seen.

Regardless of whether proponents of design arguments maintain that creation occurred in six twenty-four-hour days or over millions of years, they frequently find themselves at odds with much of the scientific world. A huge gulf has come to separate the world of faith from the world of scientific reasoning. True, the world of science is highly agnostic. Almost by definition, its purpose is to try to explain the events of natural history in nonsupernatural terms. It searches for rules and laws of regularity to explain the existence of everything and does so in a manner that purposely excludes the intervention of the supernatural. Indeed, were it to include the exploration of divine activity, it would not be science—at least not as science has been practiced over the past 150 years.

On the other side of the chasm exists the realm accessible by faith. Again, almost by definition, it exists through a whole different approach to the universe. Here, there is a commitment to the principle that the supernatural is just as real as the natural. Indeed, on this side of the gulf, people live, move and have their being in the belief that at the heart of existence, including most vividly their own, all is grounded in the supernatural. It is this transcendental Presence that set in place the rules scientists study, and it is this same Presence that can suspend those rules anytime, anywhere.

Far too often society—especially North American society—finds itself on one side of the gulf or the other, and it is becoming increasingly difficult to find a bridge between the two sides. This is one of the great tragedies of today's culture. On one side, that of the world of faith, is life in the Presence of the Creator—a life rich in meaningful fulfillment and heartfelt joy. On the other side exists the study of nature—the study of what the Creator has made—in all of its aesthetic majesty. Oh, that there were a bridge that would take the people who love the detailed study of nature to the other side to see and experience the beauty of the world of faith! Similarly, would it not be wonderful if there could be a bridge to take people of faith into the detailed world of nature, a world created by the God they love?

Fundamental to the thesis of this book is my belief that the chasm has been created, in part, by the particular metaphor that has been chosen for the activity of the Creator. We have been forcing the Creator of the universe into a box limited by human experience. The problem with the design metaphor—which comes from the world of faith—is that it implies that the evidence for design and the rules it follows will be decipherable using the tools of the other world—that of science and engineering. Most scientists, however, see no evidence for a set of design rules. Hence, the gulf grows wider.

Too many have come to believe one has to make a choice: either science is fundamentally flawed because it cannot see the design rules, or the world of faith is imaginary because it sees rules that do not exist. One cannot live, each side feels, in two worlds at once. As a result, millions of people have come to conclude that science, in essence, is so mistaken at its very core that fundamental tenets of biology, physics, geology and astrophysics are all wrong. On the other side, in the world based on a scientific view of the universe, millions of people have decided that the world of faith is so utterly out of touch with reality that its conversation is meaningless blather: two different languages, two different worlds. This book attempts to construct a bridge between those worlds.

Metaphors, by definition, are limited in their explanatory power. Perhaps, however, the best analogy for the designer is not that of an engineer but an artist, or better yet, the composer and conductor of a symphony. Can one decipher through scientific study the "rules" of great art or the "statutes" of a masterfully composed and conducted symphony? Perhaps, like the work of an artist or a symphony conductor, the action of the Creator has been so subtle and all-encompassing that it will never be possible to describe it by using the tools of science. Perhaps we in the world of faith are depending too strongly on the tools of science to point us to God, and perhaps those in the world of science are similarly failing to recognize that the tools of science, which depend upon regularity in nature, are not powerful enough to detect the work of a God who works on his own terms in his own way. Can the tools of science, for example, detect the activity of that which might well choose to remain "a secret wisdom," one hidden from the "rulers" of this age (1 Cor 2:7)? Not if that Being chooses to keep the wisdom secret, accessible only through spiritual words speaking spiritual truths (1 Cor 2:13). Perhaps if we allowed for greater mystery, such as that which impregnates creation metaphors of art or music—to say nothing of its pervasiveness in Scripture—the gulf would become a little narrower and the chasm not quite so deep.

There is another aspect to this gulf that must be addressed. Many are unable to find their way to a bridge not because of limitations constructed by a metaphor but because for them there is no metaphor. Scripture states that God did his work in six days; days are twenty-four hours in length; thus, it was all over within one week. Their fear is that the integrity of the Bible is at stake. Although ready and able to acknowledge that there is figurative language in other sections of the Bible (Psalms and Job, for example), they believe that the Genesis story is told as real history and must be treated as such.

This book rests on the assumption that Scripture is God-breathed. It is God's message to God's people. It also resides in the conviction that when Scripture is read and studied through the eyes of faith, it will lead us into God's Presence. Scripture, through the power of the Spirit, is the very bridge that will take us from the world of faith into the world of nature—the very fingerprint of God. Scripture describes the activity of God. Science, whether its practitioners realize it or not, also describes the activity of God. Hence, I am convinced that it is Scripture itself, correctly understood, through the power of the Holy Spirit, the Wisdom of the living Word, and the love of the Father for his children, that will serve as the bridge upon which we can all walk back and forth over the chasm of our own making. That is what this book is about.

ACKNOWLEDGMENTS

THIS BOOK COULD NOT HAVE BEEN WRITTEN without the support of many people. First of all, it is a product of my many years of teaching courses such as Genetics, Comparative Vertebrate Anatomy, Vertebrate Biology, Developmental Biology, Cell Biology and Molecular Biology. The questions, comments and encouragement of those students who populated these courses, many of whom became my friends, have been the impetus for my writing. I wish I could name them all, so precious is my memory of working with each of them. More recently, as the project moved from my mind to my computer, I am appreciative of the scores of students and countless others who have read and commented on the various drafts. This work has been greatly enhanced by their input. The especially thorough reviews of Karl Giberson, Al Truesdale and two anonymous reviewers are greatly appreciated.

For the past fifteen plus years, I have been on faculty at Point Loma Nazarene University, a very special place for one interested in the interaction between the disciplines of science and religion. Every Monday at noon for the past eight years, a cross-disciplinary group of faculty members have met together over lunch to discuss books at this interface. (Even prior to that we met regularly during the summers.) This book is in no small part a product of those discussions. As a biologist, I had no idea how beautiful the study of theology was until I started thinking about it alongside real theologians, biblical scholars and others. I hesitate to name all the people from the several disciplines represented in this group, but they know who they are, and I hope they know I am grateful for their impact on my life and my thinking. Most of them read an early version of the book and provided many helpful comments.

My colleagues in the biology department have provided friendship and support throughout the project. Special thanks go to Drs. Michael McConnell, Rebecca Flietstra, Michael Mooring, David Kerk, David Brown and Dawne Page. Kerry Fulcher has been my soulmate through all of this.

Emma Mooring was the artist for each of the figures. I am grateful to her for doing a masterful job.

From the beginning this book had "Coming to Peace" in its title. There proved to be a bit of irony in that title. The premature copying and distribution of an early draft brought the antithesis of peace to our campus and to me personally. I am especially grateful for the support of the president of Point Loma Nazarene University, Dr. Bob Brower, our board chair Dr. Dan Copp, and cabinet member Dr. Arthur Shingler. At one particularly low point I stayed with the project because of an encouraging word from my provost and friend Dr. Patrick Allen. It goes without saying, I hope, that the final product represents my own views, and certainly should not be taken to be the views of the university. The administration has simply been supportive of my right to express those views.

Finally, I want to thank my wife, Joyce, my daughters, Cheryl and Shelley, and my sons-in-law, Damian and Aaron, for the personal support and friendship that has kept me going.

1

SCIENCE AND RELIGION

Trying to Live in Two Worlds at Once

—

THIS IS THE STORY OF CREATION as seen through the eyes of a biologist. The Story of creation itself begins a very long time ago, but the story of my interest in it begins much more recently—about forty-five years ago—in a home near Vancouver, Canada. As a young person, I saw what seemed like the Presence of God in those around me, and I came to admire and love that Presence. Each evening I would kneel beside my bed and ask God to guide my life and fill me with the same Presence I saw in those around me. Most of the time I believed that he did. However, the evangelical Christian beliefs of my family were somewhat unusual in that part of the world at that time. Outside of my own tiny church and immediate family, I went for years knowing only a handful of people who believed in the sort of God whom we believed in. Because of that, when I was in a pensive mood, I questioned how it could be that, given all the religions in the world (including, especially, the religion of no religion), I was fortunate enough to have been born into the right one. When I was in one of those introspective periods, I had doubts and was strongly suspicious that the people who were wrong were really those of us in what seemed like a tiny circle, that of evangelical Christianity.

I still vividly recall the personal struggles that accompanied my studying the evidence for ancient humans. The images of those charts of human evolution in my seventh-grade social studies textbook are still etched on my mind. They almost cost me my Christian faith. The following summer, at a church camp, I spoke to a couple of friends, both of whom were sixth graders. I told them that they would find the seventh grade to be enormously challenging to their belief in God. "You are going to be hearing about the Cro-Magnon humans, the Neanderthals and the evolution of the human race. Be prepared for an assault on your faith," I told them. I felt fortunate to have emerged from seventh grade with mine intact.

I did make it though and proceeded into the eighth grade and beyond. But the relationship between Scripture and science continued to concern me. On one occasion, as I was reading through the New Testament, I came across a verse in Revelation that refers to an earth with four corners. "The earth does not have four corners," I said to an older member of my family. "Why would God's Word speak of four corners if the earth is really a sphere? Surely if the Bible is really the Word of God, he would not have allowed that section to appear." The family member, with a shrug of shoulders, told me that was simply what people thought in those days. I remember my sense of disappointment that others did not sense the seriousness of the inconsistency between science and God's Word, and that made me feel alone.

Usually I got around my concerns by just not thinking about them. But every now and then I would start to think again—an experience that often brought me into emotional turmoil. To me there seemed to be a deep-seated conflict between the world of science and my personal world of faith. I had one foot in each of the two incompatible, mutually exclusive worlds, and sometimes it seemed like my mind was being torn apart. Being so young, I had no idea of how to resolve the conflict. On one occasion, as I lay in bed, I looked outside my window at the nearby cherry tree. I focused my attention on a particular leaf on the tree and asked God, if he were real, to cause that leaf to quiver. It never did. On another occasion I came home from church filled with questions, fell to my knees by the green rocking chair in the living room and cried out to God, "Show me that you are real, God! Show me that you are real!" All I heard was silence.

I did, nevertheless, make it through those times with my faith intact, albeit a faith deeply rooted in hope and only superficially rooted in reason. Whenever I allowed my mind to return to the apparent conflict between science and religion, I was quickly back into turmoil. Hence, over the ensuing years, I continued to love God with my entire heart and soul, and although I did my best to love him with my mind as well, that part was not a particularly successful effort.

During those years, I was inclined toward the natural sciences and math. I found that if I restricted my intellectual energy to chemistry, physics and math, leaving aside biology, all would go much more smoothly for me. In contrast to biology, those disciplines seemed to have no direct implication for my Christian faith. Biology did, so I shied away from it in large part because studying it would entail thinking about the details of evolution, and my faith was too important to me for that.

In university, however, I took some courses that changed my life forever. At that point I was planning on becoming a physician, and that required taking some biology. So whether I liked it or not, there I was, enrolled in Biology 101. In fact, in my second university semester, I found myself enrolled in three courses, Introduction to Biology, Genetics and Developmental Biology—getting it all in one huge dose. I loved it. I had no idea how beautiful the study of life would be. Learning for the first time about what seemed to me a magical world, the world of DNA, RNA and protein synthesis, was the most exhilarating intellectual experience of my life. As a professor who today teaches a course in introductory biology, I have tried to never forget the charm and splendor that the subject held for me when I learned it the first time. I had never imagined that anything could be so elegant as the orchestrated dances that take place inside microscopic cells. The process of protein synthesis seemed to me more beautiful than the most glorious ballet. The living processes of a single cell, and the unfolding and coordination of the plan for a developing embryo, were like a magnificent symphony, and I felt that I would never be able to find greater intellectual joy than I would by spending the rest of my life studying its orchestration. I abandoned my plans for medical school and set out to become a professor of biology.

The move into studying biology was not initially accompanied by a loss of faith, in part because I saw for the first time how esthetic the living world is. It became increasingly difficult to believe that chance and natural selection, apart from God's initial design and providential oversight, could have built the wondrous processes I was studying. Hence, for the first time, I began to see that my faith and intellect might not need to be kept in separate compartments. They might someday become partners in a quest for truth.

The other important event associated with my becoming a biologist was my discovery that biologists were not much different from anyone else. They were not men and women plotting how best to overthrow Christian principles; they were simply individuals who loved doing experiments and getting answers to the laboratory questions they posed. On one occasion during this era I was asked to give devotions at the missionary meeting at my church. My topic was the Christian witness and how we as Christians are to bring Jesus into the world. Instead of stressing the terrible depravity of humanity, I found myself stressing that Christians need to be sure that their own personal lives are in order. I emphasized this by referring to one of my professors, the one who taught the course in evolution, and I remember noting that he was a warm and gentle man, the kind of person whom anyone would be glad to have for a father. My point was that evolutionists are not the conniving people they have sometimes been made out to be. They are, as I saw it, misguided people without God in their lives, just like any non-Christian friend or neighbor. I emphasized that the onus was upon us to demonstrate God's Presence in our lives. In the background as I gave this presentation was my newfound realization that scientists were *not* out to destroy Christianity; they were only interested in discovering the truth, albeit through the spectacles of unbelief.

More than thirty years have now passed since those early days when I, as a budding biologist, began to learn that the field of biology need not be alien territory for the Christian. As a teenager, I had been so impressed with the notion that science and faith are incompatible that I fully expected to someday see that there is no God and that my faith was all just wishful thinking.[1] I especially expected that studying something like biology would destroy my faith. Today I take great satisfaction in the fact that I was wrong. Science and faith are not incompatible. Although the leaves on the cherry tree never did quiver for me, and God never did come down and stand before me that day as I knelt by the green chair, the fact is that by living in his Presence for a lifetime and by studying biology and ideas about God's relationship to it, the need for quivering leaves is just a memory from my distant past. The findings of science and matters of faith do not conflict. I now realize that much of my turmoil was caused by the fact that the church was not equipped to help young people walk in both worlds.

TRYING TO LIVE IN TWO WORLDS: EVANGELICAL CHRISTIANITY TODAY

My experiences as a young person occurred in a different era, and the world of evangelical Christianity has undergone many changes since then. A whole religious subculture has sprung up to help Christian youth understand the apparent dichotomy between scientific discovery and the Christian faith. Books and seminars provide ongoing instruction at points where science and a fundamentalist view of faith seem to differ. Today, unlike forty years ago, young people can line their bookshelves with titles such as *Evolution? The Fossils Say No! The Collapse of Evolution, From Fish to Gish,* and *Creation Scientists Answer Their Critics.* There may once have been a time when the church seemed ill equipped to help a Christian young person deal with issues of faith and science, but today the church collectively spends millions of dollars every year to educate its young people and to help prepare them for an onslaught of the sort that I faced as a young person. But a question lingers: what has this huge effort accomplished?

---

[1]For me, the false impression that science and faith were incompatible was not one that I specifically got from my church. It was only a reflection of the fact that my information was coming largely from two different spheres—one Christian and the other non-Christian—and I had been unable to satisfactorily bring them together into one package. I wanted very much for the former to be true, but I could not escape the deep-seated suspicion that the love, joy and peace I found in my Christian family and church might not have had a sound intellectual base. My biggest fear was that in reality it was all too good to be true.

This brings me to the real reason behind the story I am about to tell. Most of the books about creation that evangelicals have on their shelves espouse the position that there are major scientific flaws in the view that life appeared gradually on this earth. If one reflects carefully on these books, it becomes apparent that they do not simply represent minor disagreement with science on a peripheral issue. Rather these books and the seminars and videos that accompany them advocate a view that, carried to its natural conclusion, leads to the position that the sciences of astronomy, astrophysics, nuclear physics, geology and biology are all fundamentally wrong. These sciences point toward a very old earth and universe and to the gradual appearance of new life forms on earth over billions of years. If they were wrong, it would not mean the demise of a marginal theory at the sidelines of each discipline. So central are the notions of an old earth and the gradual appearance of life to these fields of scientific endeavor that the scientists in research universities hold them with absolute certainty. Within these disciplines the earth is viewed without doubt to be billions of years old, and new species have been making appearances throughout most of that time span. So foundational is this position to all of the scientific disciplines that, were it wrong, the disciplines themselves would collapse.

To illustrate their centrality, consider an analogy from mathematics. If you were to propose that two plus two is really five and not four, you would be promoting something much broader than the incorrectness of two plus two equals four. The ramifications of your statement, if proven true, would really be the demise of all mathematical theory as we know it, so central is the "two plus two" dictum to the field of mathematics. The notion of an old earth and gradual appearance of life is that central to these scientific disciplines. This is not to say that the church, just because of the scientific centrality of the concept, should not question it, but it behooves the church to be certain that it is resting on a secure, well-reasoned foundation before it starts the dismantling process.

Although young people today are being equipped with abundant resources, these resources are primarily of one sort. The resources frequently attack the core of astronomy, astrophysics, physics, geology and biology. If science is not really as wrong as we are being told that it is, and if a sizable segment of evangelical Christianity continues to tell its children the things it has been telling them, a chasm is going to open up that will increasingly make Christianity inaccessible to individuals who believe that scientific investigation has revealed truth about the universe. People who know about astronomy, for example, will feel as though they are being asked to cast aside their understanding of this discipline if they want to follow Jesus in the context of the evangelical church. People who trust that geology is not a corrupt science will think they must make a decision between abandoning their knowledge about geology and becoming full-fledged members of Christ's body. As our young people go to college and study, they will incorrectly perceive that they need to make a decision that is focused not so much on whether to pick up their cross and follow Jesus but on whether astronomy, astrophysics, nuclear physics, geology and biology are all very wrong. Perhaps this would be justifiable if the "two plus two" in each of these sciences does not really equal four. However, what if it is actually this large segment of the evangelical church that is wrong?

The need to address the relationship between science, especially biology, and Christian faith has never been more significant than it is today. There is a real danger that a substantial number of churches in evangelical Christianity are constructing isolated islands for themselves—islands that are so separated from the world of science that any bridges that used to exist between their Christian faith and the world of academics will have been burned. The individuals in that world, however, need desperately to know about the love of God as it was lived out in the life of his Son, Jesus. The only way they will come to know Christ's love is to sense it firsthand, as it is lived out in the body of Christ, that is, the church. Is not crying out the scientific equivalent of "two plus two does not equal four" comparable to burning one of the last bridges to that world? If so, then the numerous children who venture from the island into the realm of knowledge that exists outside their island-world may drown when they find there are no bridges to carry them across. Not only that but other people's children who need so much to see God's love will be unable to make it across the bridge-less gulf to the island where the church exists in oblivious peace and tranquillity.

The existence of this antiscientific island might be appropriate if astronomy, astrophysics, physics, geology and biology really do need to be dismantled. But what if much of the work of the myriad of brilliant minds is *not* wrong? What if these minds that are exploring the intricate details of God's world are really in the process of uncovering God's mysteries unaware—mysteries about how God created? What if creation *really is* a gradual process and the problem is not a major flaw in scientific investigation but rather a flaw in the theology of the numerous Christians who do not trust scientific conclusions? What if these Christians have simply misunderstood how God desires that his Word be understood? If this were the case, the ramifications would have colossal significance.

BRIDGING THE TWO WORLDS: ALLOWING GOD'S WORD TO FAITHFULLY SPEAK

I would like to return to the question that first puzzled me as a child. Why does Scripture seem to imply that the earth has four corners if it is really a sphere? Actually that question is just one of several similar questions that I could have asked but did not because of my limited knowledge at the time. Some Scripture verses, for example, might be taken as implying that the sun moves rather the earth. One of the great battles in church history was over whether the sun or the earth exists at the center of our section of the universe. Until a few hundred years ago, the Christian church held the firm conviction that the earth is at the center. Scripture seemed to imply as much in several different places. When Galileo (1564–1642) advocated the view, earlier put forward by Copernicus (1473–1543), that the earth revolved around the sun, he met tremendous resistance.[2] In a treatise dated 1611 the Jesuit

---

[2]There was more to the resistance to Galileo's thinking than theology alone. Much was at stake, including a philosophical worldview that could not easily be toppled, unrelenting egos, career status and church politics. For a detailed analysis of the Galileo affair, see Charles J. Hummel, *The Galileo Connection* (Downers Grove, Ill.: InterVarsity Press, 1986).

Ludovico delle Colombe (1565–1616?) directly challenged Galileo on scriptural grounds. Colombe maintained that the authority on this issue must be the Bible. The biblical authors, he stated, do not err, and it is better to believe them than secular authors, who can and do err. He then proceeded to list a set of Scriptures. Here are some of the passages that he quoted:

> "You fixed the earth on its foundations" (Psalm 104:5); "God made the orb immobile" (I Chronicles 16:30); "He suspended the earth above nothingness, that is, above the center" (Job 26:7); . . . "Heaven is up, the earth is down" (Proverbs 30:3); "The sun rises, and sets, and returns to its place, from which, reborn, it revolves through the meridian, and is curved toward the North" (Ecclesiastes 1:5); "God made two lights, i.e., a greater light and a smaller light, and he made stars, to shine above the earth" (Genesis 1:17).[3]

Then, to clarify, Colombe concluded his treatise in the following way:

> Could those who are unhappy about this perhaps have recourse to an interpretation of Scripture different than the literal sense? Definitely not, because all theologians, without exception, say that when Scripture can be understood literally, it ought never be interpreted differently, realizing meanwhile that the mystical sense surpasses all philosophy and turns all science on its head.[4]

Certainly the Scripture, if taken literally, seemed clear: Is the earth set firmly on its foundations, as the psalm states, or not? Does the sun rise and set, as Ecclesiastes reveals, or not? Did the sun stand still at Joshua's command or not (Josh 10:13)? Surely, Galileo's critics felt, there can be no other legitimate manner of interpreting these verses than in the literal sense in which the church fathers had always interpreted them.

Galileo responded to the controversy in a manner that we may well take to heart even today. The following is an excerpt that illustrates how Galileo viewed the role of Scripture as it relates to science:

---

[3]Richard J. Blackwell, *Galileo, Bellarmine, and the Bible* (Notre Dame, Ind.: University of Notre Dame Press, 1991), p. 60.
[4]Edizione Nazionale, *Le Opere di Galileo Galilei* (Florence: G. Barbera, 1890–1909), 3.1.290, cited in ibid., p. 60.

I agree as you most prudently proposed, conceded, and established, that it is not possible for Sacred Scripture ever to deceive or to err; rather its decrees have absolute and inviolable truth. Only I would have added that, although Scripture itself cannot err, nevertheless some of its interpreters and expositors can sometimes err, and in various ways. The most serious and most frequent of these errors occurs when they wish to maintain always the direct meaning of the words, because from this their results lead not only to various contradictions but even to grave and blasphemous heresies. Accordingly it would be necessary to attribute to God, feet and hands and eyes and even human and bodily feelings like anger, regret, hatred, and even occasional forgetfulness of the past and ignorance of the future. Many propositions are found in the Scriptures which, in respect to the bare meaning of the words, give an impression which is different from the truth, but they are stated in this way in order to be accommodated to the incapacities of the common man.[5]

Galileo was referring to various Old Testament passages that speak, for example, of the right arm of God upholding the nation of Israel or of God seemingly needing to be reminded of things by the prophets (e.g., Is 41:10; Lam 5:20). Galileo told his critics that the Bible speaks in terms to which we humans can relate. We must not assume that God really does have a muscular right arm just because a Scripture verse speaks of it. The biblical authors used human expressions to help us visualize the power of God. So also, when the Bible speaks of the sun moving across the sky, we must understand that the sacred book is not attempting to make a scientific statement that should stand for all the ages. The Bible's purpose is to lead us to God, and it must not be used as a textbook of scientific statements about the nature of the universe.

While Galileo was dealing with critics in the Roman Catholic community, Johannes Kepler (1571–1630), a Protestant, was similarly trying to convince his segment of Christendom that the new science need not be viewed as conflicting with Scripture:

---

[5]This quotation is from a letter written by Galileo to a friend, Benedetto Castelli (1578–1643), a Benedictine priest. Interestingly the letter got into the hands of an individual named Niccolo Lorini (b. 1544), who rewrote the letter, changing certain key phrases in a misleading fashion, and sent this inaccurate copy to the Inquisitor General in Rome. The adulterated letter caused Galileo considerable difficulty many years later. The letter in its entirety may be found as appendix four in Blackwell, *Galileo*.

Let me say this about the authority of the sacred writings. To the opinions of the saints about their nature, I reply with one word. In theology the influence of authority should be present, but in philosophy [that is, science] it is the influence of reason that should be present. St. Lactantius denied that the earth is round; St. Augustine conceded its roundness but denied the antipodes [that is, the other side of the earth]; today the Holy Office concedes the smallness of the earth but denies its motion. But for me the holy truth has been demonstrated by philosophy [science], with due respect to the Doctors of the Church, that the earth is round, that its antipodes are inhabited, that it is quite despicably small, and finally that it moves through the stars.[6]

Both of these men wrote as though they were believers in the majesty of God. Kepler wrote, "Praise and celebrate with me the wisdom and magnitude of the Creator, which I lay open before you by means of a deeper explanation of the structure of the world, by the search for its causes."[7] Galileo wrote, "I have the hope that in his infinite wisdom God can direct some small ray of his grace to the purity of my mind to give me some illumination about the hidden meanings of his words."[8] Both men, one in the Protestant tradition, the other a Catholic, had the same message. God speaks to us in Scripture in a manner that will lead us to seek him. God also speaks to us through the realm of nature, and in this realm we learn about his creation.

Today practically no one holds to the view that Scripture mandates a view that the earth is flat (as I thought it implied in my early reading of Revelation) or that the earth is at the center of the universe. Instead scholars are agreed that the Bible uses poetic license and makes its point in language that could be understood by the common people at the time that it was written. No one would maintain that a reading of Job requires the view that there really are storage bins for snow and hail (Job 38:22). Few would suggest that reading about the protective right hand of God in the book of Psalms should lead to a belief that

---

[6]Johannes Kepler, *Astronomia nova*, vol. 3 of *Gesammelte Werke* (München: C. H. Beck'sche Verlagsbuchhandlung, 1937), cited in Blackwell, *Galileo*, p. 56. The bracketed sections have been added for clarification.
[7]Kepler, cited in Blackwell, *Galileo*, p. 56.
[8]Ibid., p. 216.

God the Father is a physical being with a right arm like us.

Bible scholars, even conservative ones, are agreed that the Bible uses poetic language on occasion and must not always be taken literally. Scholars are also agreed that God spoke through the culture of the day—God communicates in a manner that enables people to understand.[9] The great church reformer John Calvin (1509–1564) stated that God used the equivalent of "baby talk" so that God's people could understand what he had to say.[10] The message of Scripture has always been that God comes to us where we are—in our naiveté—and relates to us in terms that we, despite our vast ignorance, can understand. The ultimate example of this is the person of Jesus—Emmanuel, God with us. The fact that the author of the entire universe, in all of its unimaginable size and for all of its inconceivable time of existence, visited this little speck in the universe called earth and dwelt among us as a person is the foundation of our faith. But it is also the ultimate expression of God's manner of communicating with humankind. God the Creator desires to communicate in ways that all humans can understand, regardless of who they are, where on the earth's surface they are located and when in the earth's history they have existed. The Gospel of John tells us that God actively "spoke" (Worded) himself in Jesus. God does this by becoming incarnate. In Christ, God articulated himself in language we can understand. In Jesus, we have beheld God's glory (Jn 1:1-5, 14-18). Similarly, in Scripture, God communicates in a manner that has miraculously transcended all cultures, all educational levels and all time. But we must remember the purpose of both God's Word to us in the incarnation and God's Word to us in Scripture: to teach us about God and to lead people to salvation. The God who became one with us in Jesus of Nazareth, to whom the Scriptures bear faithful witness, did not choose to speak in lofty scientific

---

[9]J. I. Packer, *God Has Spoken: Revelation and the Bible*, 3rd ed. (Grand Rapids, Mich.: Baker, 1993), p. 94, has said it well: "What patience and skill He showed throughout the long history of revelation in always so adapting his message to the capacities of his chosen messengers that it never overran their powers of transmission, but within the limits set by their mind, outlook, culture, language and literary ability, could always find adequate and exact expression! But such gracious self-limitation is typical of the God of Bethlehem's stable and Calvary's cross."

[10]See St. John in the Wilderness, "The Church's Teaching and the Bible," <http://www.stjohnadulted.org/EpisH03.PDF>.

language to communicate truth about nature. If God had done this, the real message—salvation and God's love for humankind—would have been blurred. How could God have communicated with the ancient Hebrews in modern scientific terms if he expected them to understand? Could it be that John Calvin is right and that even (or perhaps especially) when it comes to science God chooses to use "baby talk" in order to communicate in a manner that transcends time and culture? If so, then it behooves us to be careful before we force the language of Scripture to become the language of science.[11]

BACK TO GENESIS: A FRESH LOOK

Although even conservative scholars agree on the notion that God communicates with humans in terms they can understand and that sometimes this involves speaking figuratively and through the culture of the day, they do not always agree as to what in the Bible is figurative and what is not. Sometimes it is clear. The earth really does move, and the statements about the immovability of the earth (Ps 93:1; 104:5, for example) are poetic. The earth does not really have four corners, and the imagery in Revelation is designed to emphasize that the angels will be coming from distant, widely separated points. Other Scriptures, however, are still open to discussion.

One of those sections where there is disagreement is the first three chapters in Genesis. Many believe that this language must be viewed as history, pure and simple. In its description of the origin of the universe and life in general, it is the equivalent of a manufacturer's construction manual; every "t" has been crossed and every "i" dotted—the ultimate engineering document.[12] Others believe that God, in desiring to communicate that he, and he alone, was the Creator, portrayed creation as occurring within a single week for reasons of significance

---

[11]Two evangelical commentaries on Genesis may be especially helpful to readers who would like to explore in depth the issues raised by figurative language: Bruce K. Waltke, *Genesis: A Commentary* (Grand Rapids, Mich.: Zondervan, 2001); and John H. Walton, *The NIV Application Commentary: Genesis* (Grand Rapids, Mich.: Zondervan, 2001).

[12]See, for example, John Whitcomb, *The Early Earth*, rev. ed. (Grand Rapids, Mich.: Baker, 1987); and Henry Morris, ed., *The Defender's Study Bible* (Chicago: World Bible League, 1999).

to the Hebrew culture.[13] According to this view, the message was never meant to be a scientific message about the moment-by-moment details of creation.[14] The account is an affirmation by the Hebrews that the God they worshiped and served is God alone. The creation and all in it depend upon him for their existence and sustenance. Unlike the surrounding nations, the Hebrews neither feared nor worshiped nature. The God who created it all had delivered them from Egyptian bondage. They knew that their God was indeed Lord over all. The significance of the creation account is that it is a grand affirmation of faith in God, not that it intends to present a detailed scientific account of how the world came to be. Indeed providing the scientific details would have obscured the real message—that of guiding people to seek God. This view also holds that the use of figurative language, with its rich symbolism and deep meaning, may have been by far the best way for God to have effectively accomplished his purpose of leading his children into his Presence.[15]

One of the great problems in speaking of the possibility of the creation account in poetic terms is that this position is viewed as being

---

[13]The highly respected evangelical scholar Henri Blocher summarizes it this way:
The use of the anthropomorphic figure of the week for the logic of creation and of its completion allows the author to outline a theology of the Sabbath. That was the theme closest to his heart. . . . Now, what is the meaning of the Sabbath that was given to Israel? It relativizes the works of mankind, the contents of the six working days. It protects mankind from total absorption by the task of subduing the earth, it anticipates the distortion which makes work the sum and purpose of human life, and it informs mankind that he will not fulfill his humanity in his relation to the world which he is transforming but only when he raises his eyes above, in the blessed, holy hour of communion with the Creator. . . . The essence of mankind is not work! (Henri Blocher, *In the Beginning: The Opening Chapters of Genesis*, trans. David G. Preston [Downers Grove, Ill.: InterVarsity Press, 1984], p. 57)

[14]J. I. Packer cautions those who treat Scripture "as if it were written in terms of the communicative techniques and conventions of the modern West rather than the ancient East, or by professing to find in it 'technical-scientific' as distinct from 'naïve-observational' statements about the natural order, when the 'technical-scientific' study of nature is less than five centuries old" (Packer, *God Has Spoken*, p. 104).

[15]Conrad Hyers summarizes this in an especially poignant manner:
A great story is like a great work of art. At a simple level, a celebrated painting may be viewed and appreciated by most anyone, and that is part of its greatness. The average untutored observer, and even the small child in hand, may enjoy the colors, shapes, and themes and be able to identify the figures and scenes in the painting. Yet, if it is truly a great work of art, behind and within these surfaces will be many subtleties of expression, style, brushwork, emotional tone, symbolic meaning, and personal

theologically liberal. Liberalism is a theological movement that began in the second half of the nineteenth century, and its proponents generally hold the view that the Bible is not the uniquely revealed Word of God. Rather, according to this tradition, it is primarily the story of one nation's ongoing encounter with God. In liberal theology there is frequently no reason to take accounts of miracles literally or to view the stories as being historically accurate descriptions of real people. The Bible is primarily a story about humankind's search for God. Furthermore, in liberal theology, transforming and transcending grace (God's reaching down to save and sanctify troubled humanity) is largely replaced by human responsibility to change society by our own efforts and love. Even the core of traditional Christianity—the resurrection of Christ—becomes, in the minds of some liberal theologians, superfluous.

Evangelical Christianity, in contrast, has continued to maintain that the Bible is much more than a story of humankind's search for God. Instead it is viewed as the inspired and faithful record of God's own self-disclosure to his people. The Bible comes to us through the people of God, the community that received and was formed by God's story. The Bible faithfully tells God's story and the story of his sojourn with us. As such, it teaches that the only way to truly live the life that God wills for us is through a lifelong personal encounter with God. Humankind still has a responsibility to change society, but that change can occur only through the power that God's Holy Spirit gives in and through lives that are miraculously changed by God's Presence. In a sense, then, it is the antithesis of liberalism, and the two have been at odds throughout the entire twentieth century and now into the twenty-first. Because of its enormous respect for the sacredness of Scripture, in contrast to liberalism's casual willingness to change Scripture to fit its

---

signature. Also registered in the painting will be hints of the various impulses arising out of the life and times of the artist which, if appreciated, would add further meaning and luster to the work. These subtler elements would not be immediately apparent to the casual, untrained observer, and they are even less visible if the observer is not part of the immediate time period and artistic circle. Yet these subtleties are the real meaning of the painting and the source of its greatness, not just its most obvious surface features. (Conrad Hyers, *The Meaning of Creation: Genesis and Modern Science* [Atlanta: John Knox Press, 1984], p. 93)

needs, evangelicalism has held rigidly to the view that the entire Bible is God's revealed Word.

Actually the view that the Bible should not be taken as a textbook about science is not a modern or a liberal idea, nor does it imply that the Bible is not God's revealed Word. Probably the most important Christian thinker after Paul in the first Christian millennium was Augustine (354–430). Augustine held the view that the Bible has a spiritual purpose that is to lead us to God. He did not view it as having a cosmological purpose—to tell us about the nature of the universe. He felt it was dangerous to insist that the Bible had scientific truths in it, because as scientific knowledge changed, so would people's trust in God's holy Word. Soon after the dawn of Christianity, Augustine wrote,

> It is a disgraceful and dangerous thing for an infidel to hear a Christian, while presumably giving the meaning of Holy Scripture, talking nonsense. We should take all means to prevent such an embarrassing situation, in which people show up vast ignorance in a Christian and laugh it to scorn. . . . If they find a Christian mistaken in a field which they themselves know well, and hear him maintain his foolish opinions about the Scriptures, how then are they going to believe those Scriptures in matters concerning the resurrection of the dead, the hope of eternal life, and the kingdom of heaven?[16]

I have already alluded to the views of John Calvin, who believed that God brought himself down to our level and spoke in terms that we can understand in much the same way that we as adults do with our own tiny children. The question of whether there was a literal creation week of seven twenty-four-hour days was not a social issue in his day, but it is important to note that Calvin did deal specifically with the issue of conflict between science and religion. He made the following statement in 1534:

The whole point of scripture is to bring us to a knowledge of Jesus

[16]Augustine *The Literal Meaning of Genesis* 1.19, cited in Francisco Ayala, "Human Nature: One Evolutionist's View," in *Whatever Happened to the Soul?* ed. Warren S. Brown, Nancey Murphy and H. Newton Malony (Minneapolis: Fortress, 1998), p. 31.

Christ—and having come to know him (and all that this implies), we should come to a halt and not expect to learn more. Scripture provides us with spectacles through which we may view the world as God's creation and self-expression; it does not, and was never intended, to provide us with an infallible repository of astronomical and medical information. The natural sciences are thus effectively emancipated for theological restrictions.[17]

Finally the great reformer John Wesley (1703–1791) had similar views about the relation between Scripture and science. On one occasion he wrote, "The inspired penman in this history [Genesis] . . . [wrote] for the Jews first and, calculating his narratives for the infant state of the church, describes things by their outward sensible appearances, and leaves us, by further discoveries of the divine light, to be led into the understanding of the mysteries couched under them."[18] On another occasion he commented on Genesis 1:3: "He made the stars also, which were spoken of only in general, for the Scriptures were written not to gratify our curiosity but to lead us to God."[19]

All down through the twentieth century, and now into the twenty-first, evangelicals have responded to the many perceived faux pas of liberal theology. Perhaps in large part because of this, many evangelicals have been hesitant about moving the line as to what is pure history and what represents other literary genres, even though a purely historical rendering of portions of Genesis seems to most scientists to be highly inconsistent with scientific fact. The fear on the evangelical side has been that if the line defining scriptural use of nonliteral genres is ever moved to a region of the Bible that includes books other than Job, Psalms, Song of Solomon and Revelation, then evangelicalism will begin to slide down the slippery slope toward liberalism, where there is little sacred about Scripture. In contrast, what may really be happening is that evangelical Christianity is missing out, not on a downhill slide,

---

[17]Cited in Alister E. McGrath, *The Foundations of Dialogue in Science and Religion* (Oxford, U.K.: Blackwell, 1998), p. 124.

[18]John Wesley, *Wesley's Notes on the Bible* (Grand Rapids, Mich.: Francis Asbury Press, 1987), p. 22.

[19]John Wesley, *A Survey of the Wisdom of God in the Creation: or, A Compendium of Natural Philosophy*, 3rd ed. (London: J. Fry, 1777), 2:463.

but rather an uphill climb—one that leads us closer to God and to his truth. Ironically the real downhill slide away from God may come from reducing the Bible to a scientific textbook, because this approach distracts from the task of searching for the Bible's deepest truths. Thus perhaps we need to see the issue as one that takes us back up the hill once more, back to where we ought to be, alongside three of the greatest church reformers since Paul—Augustine, Calvin and Wesley. The purpose of the Bible is to lead us to God and to participate by grace and faith in his plan of salvation for sinful humankind. It is possible that we have barely scratched the surface in understanding the spiritual truths that await us in our exploration of God's Word and its ramifications for a suffering society. However, such exploration may well require that we allow that God, on more occasions than we thought, uses poetic language to reveal his great truths. Let us not rule out the possibility that the account of creation may well have been one such instance.

It is several hundred years since most of the church relented in the face of an enormous amount of persuasive scientific data that the earth is not at the center of the universe. It is now almost a century and a half since data implying a gradual creation began to accumulate. What if this data is God's data—revealed to us through the medium of scientific investigation? What if scientists are not as wrong as so many evangelicals think they are?

Perhaps the only thing that is needed is for us evangelicals to put on John Calvin's spectacles of faith and then to peer carefully at the data. Maybe our young people do not have to live in two separate worlds after all. Perhaps modern science and faith can be united within one world. Consider putting on your own "spectacles of faith" and beginning the journey with me. See if you, like me, will decide that the scientific equivalent of "two plus two" really does equal four, and see if it might not be God's truth that science has unknowingly been discovering.

As we proceed to embark upon this journey, let me begin by briefly summarizing what is in store. We will start by examining the scriptural message of Genesis 1—3. We will see that that this prologue to all of Scripture, indeed all of life, reveals deep-rooted, timeless truths about the human condition and about God's solution to our situation (chapter two). From there we will do some exploration that is going to help us put this creation story into a time frame. Just when did it all begin, and how do we know? Does the apparent date of creation's beginning raise any theological problems (chapter three)? The journey moves on from the beginning of the cosmos to an exploration of the process and time frame in which God created new life. God's written Word does not provide much detail about how life was created (only about one page out of more than fifteen hundred is devoted to this topic); God's *world,* however, provides fossils stored away in rocks in a manner that is somewhat analogous to file folders arranged chronologically in a file cabinet. What can we learn about the creation of living organisms by peering into the "file cabinet" of life? And what are the theological ramifications of what we see (chapter four)?

Next we will look at what we can learn about life's history by examining the geographical distribution of living organisms. For the past fifteen years I have lived in San Diego, but prior to that I lived in a half a dozen other places. One could learn a lot about my life history by examining where I have lived and when and why I have moved. Similarly, we learn a great deal about the history of God's created life (and even God's mechanism of creation) by examining the distribution of species on the surface of the earth in both the present and the past (chapter five).

Just as one could learn a lot about my history by studying places I have lived, so also one could learn who my distant relatives are by studying my DNA. About 130 years ago one of my great-grandfathers left a German village and came to North America. Today it would be possible to go back to that region of Germany, my DNA profile in hand, and identify distant cousins who descended from brothers and sisters of my great-grandfather. Similarly, if micro (or macro) evolution has ever occurred in the history of life, it ought to be possible to test for that by examining the DNA profile of closely (and distantly) related species. Chapter six examines this question.

Finally, as the exploratory journey into the sacred realm of God's creation draws to a conclusion, we will look at the theological ramifications of what we have learned along the way. If this world is truly a product of God's creation (and, thank God, it is!), then we have much to learn about how God works by studying his workmanship. The final chapter is a celebration of this fact.

As you proceed on the journey, you will be peering through your "faith spectacles," just as I do through mine. Because the lenses through which we each peer are tinted by past experiences of our respective lives, you may not always see things in the same light as I do. Regardless of whether we see things in the same way, it is important that we, with Paul, all try to speak the following words with one voice to a world that does not wear our "faith spectacles": "What you worship as something unknown I am going to proclaim to you" (Acts 17:23). It is one thing for those scientists to understand (and in some instances worship!) the scientific equivalent of two plus two equals four, but it is another for them to understand *why* the numbers add up. In this regard all evangelicals see the same thing through their spectacles. We all see God, and in unison we cry out, "Abba, Father," as we bow humbly before the Creator of the universe. In so doing we also call earnestly in unison for others to seek him, to "perhaps reach out for him and find him, though he is not far from each one of us. 'For in him we live and move and have our being.' " Indeed, as Paul said, we are God's offspring (Acts 17:27-28). All we need to see God—this Creator in whom we have our being—is our own set of "faith spectacles." In unison we cry out to a world lost in aimless wondering, "Pick them up. Look through them. You will be amazed at the beauty of what you see."

2

THE CREATION AND FALL

Exploring the Meaning of Scripture

—

WE CHRISTIANS HAVE A TENDENCY TO discuss creation in a mechanistic fashion, paying far too little attention to the real meaning and purpose at its roots. In talking about creation, we seldom go much further than the "what happened and when did it occur" of our childhood Bible stories to explore in depth what God wants to communicate about meaning and significance—the "why" of creation. As Sergeant Friday (played by Jack Webb) used to say on the 1950s television detective show *Dragnet,* "Just give me the facts, ma'am." That is the way we are—just give us the facts!

Sometimes I wish that certain biologists would be similarly inclined. I wish that some of them would just stick to the facts. Unfortunately they are less like Sergeant Friday and more like crime witnesses who want to expound about matters beyond their purview.

Biologists spend their careers thinking, experimenting and writing about the processes of life and how they arose. The methodology biologists use, like that of scientists in general, operates on the assumption that the events being studied are subject to natural laws. That is the way science has long operated, and it has produced a tremendous success record. The scientific method works. On the other hand, just because it has worked so well does not mean that science will be able to explain everything. There is *not* good reason to extrapolate from its success so far an assumption that there is nothing besides these natural laws.

As noted author Phillip Johnson justifiably pointed out, "The literature of Darwinism is full of anti-theistic conclusions, such as that the
universe was not designed and has no purpose, and that we humans
are the product of blind natural processes that care nothing about us.
What is more, these statements are not presented as personal opinions
but as the logical implications of evolutionary science."[1] Biologists'
success at using the scientific method seems, in some cases, to cause an
unwarranted level of arrogance. That arrogance leads some to venture
beyond the realm of science into statements about reality that go significantly beyond the data in hand. Oh, that they would just "stick to
the facts"! The following statement from Richard Dawkins is just one
of many that illustrate the point:

> If the universe were just electrons and selfish genes, meaningless trage-
> dies like the crashing of this bus [a bus filled with schoolchildren] are ex-
> actly what we should expect, along with equally meaningless *good* for-
> tune. Such a universe would be neither evil nor good in its intention. It
> would manifest no intention of any kind. . . . The universe we observe
> has precisely the properties we should expect if there is at bottom, no de-
> sign, no purpose, no evil, and no good, nothing but blind, pitiless indif-
> ference. As that unhappy poet, A. E. Housman, put it
>
> "For Nature, heartless, witless Nature
> Will neither know nor care."
>
> DNA neither knows nor cares. DNA just is. And we dance to its music.[2]

Dawkins extrapolates from the data of science to conclude that life is a
blind product of DNA molecules—purposeless, with nothing behind the
scene except vast empty space. How does he know this? Has he done experiments to test this? Extrapolation may work within the natural world
of test tubes, graphs and computer modeling, but how can it be used to
move from a world governed by natural laws to make conclusions about
a world of Spirit—a world that supersedes the natural? Dawkins uses extrapolation to jump out of the realm of science and into the domain of philosophy—hardly a scientific way to use a scientific tool.

---

[1]Phillip Johnson, *Darwin on Trial* (Downers Grove, Ill.: InterVarsity Press, 1991), pp. 8-9.
[2]Richard Dawkins, *River Out of Eden* (New York: BasicBooks, 1995), pp. 132-33.

No friend of Richard Dawkins, another leading biologist, the late Steven Jay Gould, called upon scientists to recognize that science and religion occupy separate domains. (He called them nonoverlapping magisteria, or NOMA.)[3] This sounds encouraging to the theist. Gould, unlike Dawkins, was stating that religion should have a voice in the academy, that it deserves to be heard. However, as Johnson pointed out in another book, the sense of encouragement lasts only until one examines the amount of space Gould actually provided for the domain of religion.[4] It is precious little. Gould's first commandment in defining each of the two magisteria, science and religion, is "Thou shalt not mix the magisteria by claiming that God directly ordains important events in the history of nature by special interference knowable only through revelation and not accessible to science."[5] In other words, he was in favor of science not overstepping its bounds (that is, sticking to the facts), but only under the condition that the bounds for the world of science be defined as that which includes the origin and operation of the entire universe. Religion can take what is left, namely a search for meaning, morals and ethics in a vacuous world with an all-but-dead God.

Now we come to the saddest part of this story. It should not surprise us that many non-Christian scientists have failed to see the meaning of the creation story; after all, they are looking at the data without wearing a pair of faith spectacles. The saddest part to me is that many Christians use their spectacles of faith like a magnifying glass to focus only on the details of the biblical creation account (the dotted i's and the crossed t's) and fail to stand back and look at the depth and meaning of the entire story. Most academicians, because they do not own a pair of faith spectacles, see a distorted image of creation—one that does not include the Creator. Many Christians, because they choose to use their faith spectacles as a sort of magnifying glass, see only a myopic view—one that misses out on the rich

---

[3]Steven Jay Gould, *Rocks of Ages: Science and Religion in the Fullness of Life* (Westminster, Md.: Ballantine, 1999).

[4]Phillip Johnson, *The Wedge of Truth* (Downers Grove, Ill.: InterVarsity Press, 2000), pp. 95-101.

[5]Gould, *Rocks of Ages*, pp. 84-85.

spiritual significance of Genesis 1 through 3.[6]

CREATION FULFILLED: EXPERIENCING LIFE IN THE PRESENCE OF GOD

Fortunately it does not have to stay that way. As Christians, we have a responsibility to maintain a perspective that is consistent with a landscape view of Scripture.[7] When viewed in this way, it becomes clear that the focus in God's Word is on the *reason* for creation. Our Bibles have a little more than one page describing the details of what God did; the remaining fifteen hundred pages or so dwell on the reason. Hence, even though my task in this book is to explore what science, especially biology, has to tell us about God's mechanism of creation, it is important to make certain that the message in this exploration draws us to the same point to which we are drawn in Scripture. The real heart of the creation message, even when studying biology from a Christian perspective, is not to be found in the mechanical details of life and how it arose. Despite the brilliant majesty in the details of these biological processes, their elegance dims in the shadow of the person who is the subject of John's all-illuminating creation prologue: "In the beginning was the Word, and the Word was with God and the Word was God. . . . In him was life, and that life was the light of men" (Jn 1:1, 4).

---

[6]Conrad Hyers, *The Meaning of Creation: Genesis and Modern Science* (Atlanta: John Knox Press, 1984), p. 94, has put it this way:

> A great story, like a great work of art, is both simple and complex. It is simple enough in its narrative form for a small child to comprehend the essential movement of the plot, its characters and scenes, and its central themes. At the same time, to the more sophisticated hearer it is like a deep pool of meaning whose depths are not easily fathomed, perhaps never completely exhaustible, with complex undercurrents and mysterious recesses and hidden springs. Any attempt to reduce such a pool to its surface water is to mistake a pool for a puddle.

[7]Consider, for example, the thinking of the great revivalist John Wesley:

> Wesley recognized that proof texting could result in a support for virtually any position, but that when individual texts were placed in the larger context of the whole tenor of Scripture they could be more adequately understood. What Wesley meant by "the whole tenor of Scripture" is essentially what we speak of today as biblical theology. Hence, on this understanding, the basic hermeneutical discipline is biblical theology. This structure provides the context for particular segments of the Bible. (H. Ray Dunning, *Reflecting the Divine Image: Christian Ethics in Wesleyan Perspective* [Downers Grove, Ill.: InterVarsity Press, 1998], p. 21)

Christ was present at creation! Christ is God's dream for us! This person who is the hope for all humankind was there in the beginning and is still present today—a vision of what humankind can be, a vision of what you and I can be in him. The Creator longs, indeed *aches,* for us to experience the fullness of life possible only in the light of his presence.[8] The story of the creation of life does not end where we traditionally end it. It does not conclude with Adam and Eve banished from the garden and the angel's flaming sword thrashing in the darkness, blocking the way to the tree of life (Gen 3:24). Rather the creation story ends at the source from which it draws meaning—with the resurrection of Jesus. After all, the angels are not guarding the way to the tree of life anymore. Instead now they declare to each of us, just as they did to Mary Magdalene and her fellow mourners, "Why do you look for the living among the dead? He is not here; he has risen!" (Lk 24:5-6).

In reality, then, the story of creation is incomplete without the resurrection message. Creation is not fulfilled until we human beings, through the risen Christ, are filled with his Spirit—the very Presence of God—and even then it is only just beginning. Hence the story of the creation of biological life cannot be separated from the most important part, that which gives it meaning: Emmanuel, God with us; Jesus, Son of God and Son of Man. We do not know life in its fullness until the light of God's Presence illuminates our being. The creation story cannot be separated from the *new* creation story—the story of how you and I can become new creations in Christ (2 Cor 5:17). The completion of God's goal in creating humankind is not simply that we might have life but that we might have it "to the full" (Jn 10:10).

So the full story of creation cannot be found in textbooks of biology, astronomy, physics or chemistry, because they provide only a hazy glimpse of creation's elegance. Similarly, a quick read through the first three chapters of Scripture is like peering through the keyhole of a door that leads to a room full of light. To get the full story, we need to grasp

---

[8]"If indeed Christ on the Cross is the decisive revelation of God the Creator ... then *the Creator truly is love,* and divine power is not a ruling fist but an open, bleeding hand." "What a vision of God the Biblical narrative offers: a God who can grieve, a Creator who cries." Michael Lodahl, *The Story of God* (Kansas City, Mo.: Beacon Hill, 1994), pp. 60 and 82, respectively.

the key, open the door and go inside.

As we pass through the door, we find ourselves in the Garden of Eden. The early chapters of Genesis are among the most aesthetic in all of Scripture. They teach us about the human condition in a manner that may be more poignant than anything else in Scripture or indeed than anything else that has ever been written. They serve as a prologue, providing the background required to understand the rest of Scripture. Many Christians believe that although this message is rich in symbolic significance, the events described are primarily real and historically accurate in all their detail.[9] Some, on the other hand, believe that the story of the garden contains elements that are primarily figurative.[10] The latter view does not hold that the message is any less true or significant. In fact individuals who hold this view would say that the message is composed in this manner because it is so very true that it must be clearly understood, and the only way this can be done is in the form of "pictures." Regardless of one's view of whether it is pure *history* or whether it is purely *his story*, the essence is still the same: It is *in-spired* by God, offering an extremely important message, and it behooves us to understand its meaning.[11] Perhaps C. S. Lewis said it best:

> We must not be ashamed of the mythical radiance resting on our theology. . . . We must not, in false spirituality, withhold our imaginative welcome. If God chooses to be mythopoeic—and is not the sky itself a myth—shall we refuse to be *mythopathic?* For this is the marriage of heaven and earth: Perfect Myth and Perfect Fact: claiming not only our love and our obedience, but also our wonder and delight, addressed to

---

[9]See, for example, John H. Walton, *The NIV Application Commentary: Genesis* (Grand Rapids, Mich.: Zondervan, 2001). On page 212 he describes the basis of his conclusion that the story of the snake should be taken as factual, that is, the serpent really talked. (He describes this reasoning in more general terms on pages 45 to 49.) On the other hand, Henri Blocher reaches a different conclusion (*In the Beginning: The Opening Chapters of Genesis*, trans. David G. Preston [Downers Grove, Ill.: InterVarsity Press, 1984], pp. 150-54). Like Walton, Blocher believes the story must be taken at face value (that is, as the original narrator meant the story to be taken). Nonetheless, he reaches a different conclusion: there was not a literal talking snake. Both authors are highly respected evangelical scholars and both use similar reasoning to conclude that other events in the story are historical.

[10]Bernard Ramm, *Offense to Reason: A Theology of Sin* (San Francisco: Harper & Row, 1985); Dietrich Bonhoeffer, *Creation and Fall* (1937; reprint, Minneapolis: Fortress, 1997); Lodahl, *Story of God.*

[11]Lodahl, *Story of God.*

the savage, the child, and the poet in each one of us no less than to the moralist, the scholar, and the philosopher.[12]

The Garden of Eden, of course, was a paradise.[13] Humankind has always liked to think of it as a place of unimaginable beauty, but we must always remember that what made it especially appealing were not the trees, the colorful, fragrant flowers and the gurgling streams. It was the fact that Adam and Eve knew no guilt. They lived in the Presence of God with no personal experience of rebellion and not even a hint of what the words *bad* or *evil* even meant. It is not possible to understand a concept until it has been experienced or has been related to something that has been experienced, and Adam and Eve had no basis for understanding what evil meant.[14] They lived in God's Presence, clean before him, never having experienced the phenomenon of guilt. Genesis 2:25 says that they were "naked, and they felt no shame."[15] Like my innocent newborn grandson, fresh and clean from his bath, Adam and Eve knew no guilt and therefore were transparently clean before their Maker.

COMING TO KNOW ABOUT GOOD AND EVIL: GENESIS 2:15—3:6
In the center of the garden were two trees: the tree of life and the tree of the knowledge of good and evil. We are told little about the tree of life, only that it was at the center of the garden and that, after sinning, Adam and Eve were denied access to it. The implication is that the tree of life was central to all that was beautiful in the garden, perhaps even the source of that beauty. The initial focus was on the other tree, for that is the tree that bore fruit that was forbidden to Adam and Eve. God's one demand of Adam and Eve was that they allow God to be God. By obeying God's command, they were in essence acknowledging that God's wisdom was supreme: God was the Creator and they were the

---

[12]C. S. Lewis, *God in the Dock* (Grand Rapids, Mich.: Eerdmans, 1970), p. 67.

[13]Henri Blocher has said, " 'Eden' is often used in the plural for 'delight', with other related terms and the corresponding verb, to mean a life of luxury and pleasure. This must be the determinative connotation in Genesis 2. God had prepared for the man a place of pleasure, the very environment of happiness" (Blocher, *In the Beginning*, p. 113).

[14]Bonhoeffer, *Creation and Fall*, p. 87.

[15]See Dietrich Bonhoeffer, *Ethics* (New York: Macmillan, 1955), pp. 20-26, for an extensive analysis of the shame that results from the Fall.

creatures. They lived in that state of creaturely freedom for some period of time. What eventually happened, however, is of extreme significance because it is the same thing that can (and does) happen to all human beings even today. Adam and Eve were tempted to abandon their state of subservience to God; in short they were tempted to become their own masters. The way the serpent worked with Adam and Eve's psyche was sneaky. The interchange began on the most righteous of terms as a sort of religious conversation. The serpent began by asking Eve if she was certain she had understood God correctly. "Did God really say . . . ?" he asked. Eve, in the most innocent of replies, confirmed that God did say that and that she was certain he had. So far, Eve was winning and the tempter was losing.

Often we, the children of Eve, do not even make it that far. When the tempter asks us, "Did God really say?" we proceed to follow the tempter into a period of doubt, and that act of doubt may be the very thing that leads to disobedience. If you are like me, you may recall past actions that you are now certain were wrong, even though at the time you permitted yourself to be duped into believing the conduct was acceptable. We are all susceptible to the same temptation that hit Eve, in essence "Did God really mean what God seemed to say?"

So the creation story, shrouded as it is with an aura of mystery, is subtly leading us to one of its many timeless truths. This is not only about Adam and Eve; it is about us too. We, like Adam and Eve, can be lured from the garden of God's Presence. Evil can subtly work its way into our lives too, and it all starts by doubting the veracity of God's word and God's command.[16]

Intriguingly the prologue to the Old Testament is not the only introductory section of the Bible to deliver this message. The New Testament begins in a similar vein. Just as a dialogue between the tempter (in the form of a serpent) and Eve is a foundation for Genesis, so the New Testament begins in the same way when, in Matthew 4, we find Satan busily engaged in tempting Jesus. It is noteworthy that, sixty-seven verses into the New Testament and fifty-seven verses into the

---

[16]See Bonhoeffer, *Creation and Fall,* pp. 103-10.

Old Testament, the Bible shows Satan at work doing exactly the same thing. To Jesus, he said, "If you are the Son of God . . ." With the use of that "if," he was trying to get the human side of Jesus to question the Father's word. Jesus had come from the Father. Of course he was the Son of God, and of course he *knew* he was the Son of God; nonetheless Satan (just like he did to Eve and just like he does to us) was trying to get Jesus to examine whether God really meant what he seemed to say. The fact that both the Old and New Testaments start off in the same way implies a timeless truth: humankind at its core is tempted to doubt the authenticity and authority of God's leadership. We, because of the nature of the created world, will be tempted to go our own way, ignoring God's direction for our lives. Indeed the sad story of humankind repeated all down through history has, in essence, always begun with the question "Did God really say . . . ?"

The story goes on. The serpent told Eve that by partaking of the fruit she would become like God. Genesis 3:5—stage two of the temptation.

What did the serpent mean by saying that she could be like God? Since previous to this it had been God who had controlled her destiny, in essence the tempter was telling her that she, like God, could become the master of her own destiny. She could become a god unto herself.[17] Eve was tempted to exalt herself, to place herself in the position of importance reserved for God.

Consider again that confrontation between Jesus and Satan. As the New Testament begins, we are shown the picture of Satan taking Jesus to a high mountain and presenting him with all the kingdoms of the world and making the not-so-subtle promise that they could be his. Ironically, even Jesus, in his humanness, had to deal with the temptation to exalt himself. God's foundational message to us is that because of our human nature, we—like Eve, like Adam and even like Jesus—will be tempted to value prestige, power and control of our own destiny in the place of the simple call to obedient discipleship. Eve fell, and soon afterward so did Adam. Sadly, ever since, so have all their children, even you and I.

The story of created humankind is the story of individuals put-

---

[17]Bonhoeffer, *Creation and Fall,* pp. 111-14.

ting themselves on the throne that was intended to belong to God alone. God is the Creator; we are the creatures. We were created to live with the tree of life (that is, God) at the center of the garden of our lives. When we make the decision to put *our* will at the center, we displace God with ourselves. In so doing, we exalt ourselves to the point where we are attempting to become our own creators. It is *our* "infinite wisdom" that starts to rule the day instead of God's. Hungry for the control we can never attain, we snatch for symbols of affluence and prosperity that we hope will portray the pretext that we are succeeding in our grab for dominion of the "garden" of our lives. What a sad ending to this story of Adam and Eve! It is made all the more poignant in this recognition that their story is our story. Remember, however, that this is only the sixty-second verse of the Bible. There is good news coming. The room *will* fill with brightness once more.

IN THE MIDST OF OUR SINFUL STATE, GOD SEEKS US OUT: GENESIS 3:7-9

Soon after Adam and Eve sinned, God went looking for them. "Where are you?" God asked (Gen 3:9). It is significant that God sought them out, rather than the other way around.[18] It is no different for us today. We have sinned, but God comes to where we are in our self-centered world. Today, post–Adam and Eve and postresurrection, God seeks us out too. Just as the third chapter of the first book of the Bible shows us this picture of God seeking out Adam and Eve, so the third chapter of the last book of the Bible shows us a similar picture—God through his Son, Jesus, is looking for us: "Here I am! I stand at the door and knock. If anyone hears my voice and opens the door, I will come in and eat

---

[18]H. Ray Dunning puts it this way:

The Creator immediately revealed his intention to address the problem by returning to the garden as before, "as if" nothing had happened. This is one of the most beautiful pictures of God in the Bible. He is a God of grace, who does not wait for the first couple to discover their predicament but comes to them on his own initiative for the express purpose of making them aware of their self-imposed alienation from the Source of life. His question, "where are you?" was not a searching for someone he could not find. . . . The grace of God is celebrated on the very threshold of fallen human history. (Dunning, *Reflecting the Divine Image*, p. 55)

with him, and he with me" (Rev 3:19).

In our distress Jesus finds us, calls to us through the closed door and gently encourages us to open it, that closed door we have constructed for ourselves by placing our ego at the center intended for God. In Adam and Eve's case, God found them huddled behind their equivalent of a closed door—the trees of the garden. God found them in the forest with a covering of self-constructed fig leaves feeling naked and ashamed. When Adam and Eve had been in right relation to God, there had been no need for a cover. In fact we are pointedly told that even though they were naked, they knew no shame (Gen 2:25). After sinning, the scriptural account draws attention again to their nakedness; this time, however, it points to their perceived need to cover it up (Gen 3:7). Our lives, like those of Adam and Eve, are laid open before God. God can see every part of who we are. How wonderful it would be to live in the garden of God's all-seeing Presence with no guilt and no shame!

Now, post–Adam and Eve, humankind is still trying to live as master of its own fate, making itself the creator of its own existence, replacing God from its center. Consistent with our past, each of us as individuals still senses that need to make coverings for ourselves—closed doors behind which we hide in false security. The coverings may take on many forms, but they are all self-designed to hide the sense of emptiness that we can so easily feel when we are the creators of our existence. In some cases in today's society, people put all their energy into accumulating wealth so that they can purchase fancy clothes, cars and homes. This may frequently serve as a façade for the feeling of emptiness that characterizes their lives. Human beings no longer feel "naked and unashamed" as they did prior to the Fall. In contrast, they "sew fig leaves together" and make coverings for themselves. In other cases the cover is pleasure. For these people, life can seem full and exciting; the striving for "good" times becomes the essence of what it means to be alive. However, what is really taking place may be nothing more than the need to cover the emptiness that comes from not being in communication with one's Maker, the source of real life. The story of Adam and Eve's fall is the story of the human condition. We are Adam and

Eve's children, and what they experienced, we experience—that is the message of the creation narrative in Genesis 2—3.

LIVING IN THE MIDST OF GOOD AND EVIL: GENESIS 3:14-22

After the Fall, God made an intriguing observation: "The man has now become like one of us, knowing good and evil" (Gen 3:22). Clearly, humankind has inherited a world filled with both good and evil. On the side of evil, we look back over our shoulder in horror at the twentieth century. This was the century that brought us AIDS, a disease that is often spread through humankind's sinfulness but that is also destroying the lives of millions of innocent children and spouses. It was also the century that brought us the nuclear bomb, unparalleled genocide and wicked leaders who were able to whip up unthinkable evil against millions by well-turned phrases in well-timed speeches. "We stand perplexed and stupefied before the phenomena of Naziism or Bolshevism because we know nothing about man. . . . We stand face to face with the terrible questions of evil and do not even know what is before us, let alone what is against us."[19]

Clearly we have inherited a world of incomprehensible evil. However, we also have inherited a world with unrelenting hints of the good. C. S. Lewis provided a wonderful summary of these allusions in his autobiographical account of events leading to his conversion from atheism to Christianity.

> As I stood beside a flowering currant bush on a summer day there suddenly arose in me without warning, and as if not of years but of centuries, the memory of that earlier morning at the Old House when my brother had brought his toy garden into the nursery. It is difficult to find words strong enough for the sensation which came over me. Milton's enormous bliss of Eden (giving the full ancient meaning to "enormous") comes somewhere near it. . . . I call it Joy, which is here a technical term that must be distinguished from Happiness and from Pleasure. Joy (in my sense) has only one characteristic, and one only, in common with them; the fact that anyone who has experienced it will want it again. . . . I doubt whether anyone who has tasted it would ever, if both were in his

---

[19]C. Gustav Jung, cited in Ramm, *Offense to Reason*, p. 8.

power, exchange it for all the pleasures of the world. But then Joy is never in our power and pleasure often is.[20]

Beauty lies all around us, and joy is derived from this beauty, but the beauty and the joy are never *really* removed from evil and pain. We live in the middle now—partway between the Eden of humanity's past and the Glory of humanity's future. After Adam and Eve sinned, God made some observations about the sustainability of life in the world in which they and their future children were to exist. To start with, God spoke of the pain of bringing new life into existence—the agonizing joy that characterizes childbirth (Gen 3:16). Is there anything in all of life's experience that more poignantly illustrates the dialectic of joy-filled agony in which we now exist? As I write this, my daughter Shelley will give birth to her first child, Sara Joy, in a few days. Even though the experience will bring on the worst pain she has ever had to endure, she looks forward to it as being her most joyful experience as well. As I talked with her last evening, I sensed an excitement in her voice that I think runs deeper into the heart of her being than any emotion that I, as her father, have ever observed in her. God chose this experience, the agony of giving birth to a child, as God's example of what it means to live life in the world we have inherited from Adam and Eve.

God went on from there to describe a second example of what life in the "middle" is like. This time God's example was not about giving birth to new life but about sustaining old life. God addressed a topic dear to our hearts—food. We all know firsthand the sumptuous pleasure of food and drink. Indeed civilizations have long celebrated the gratification that comes from a bountiful harvest or a successful hunt. But anyone acquainted with working the land knows all too well the frustrations brought on by weeds, pestilence and drought (Gen 3:17).

---

[20]C. S. Lewis, *Surprised by Joy: The Shape of My Early Life* (New York: Harcourt Brace & World, 1955), pp. 16, 18. Lewis also made the following observation:

I do not think the resemblance between the Christian and the merely imaginative experience is accidental. I think that all things, in their way, reflect heavenly truth, the imagination not least. "Reflect" is the important word. This lower life of the imagination is not a beginning of, nor a step toward, the higher life of the spirit, merely an image. . . . But it still had, at however many removes, the shape of the reality it reflected. (Ibid., p. 167)

Among the greatest stories in American history are novels like *The Grapes of Wrath*, which so ably depict the agony of these struggles. That which sustains life comes at a cost. In the "middle," the pleasure of enjoying Thanksgiving dinner with friends and family is not far removed from the many grievous experiences that can characterize the rest of the year and the rest of the world. The universal human experience resembles a fabric woven together by differently colored strands: evil and good, pain and joy.[21]

In describing this world of "knowing good and evil," God told Adam that humankind would experience death—"dust to dust," a return to the ground from which humanity first arose (Gen 3:19). Nonetheless, on the road that led away from the garden, the road to death, there was still a glimmer of hope. Whether Adam sensed that hope, we are not told. But the eternal God envisioned a future in which the excruciating spiritual and physical death brought on by Adam's sin would die its own death. The day was coming when one particular death (that of God's Son) would lead to life—new life, eternal life—and indeed to a return to the garden.[22] It is true that humankind had sinned and was experiencing the opposite of good for the first time. However, it was still God's world they were living in, and it still had wonderful elements of God's beauty that even the sinister presence of evil could not erase. Most important of all, however, since it *was* God's world, the future would give way to the eternal, where all evil and all pain would be eradicated once and for all. The third chapter of Genesis does not declare this explicitly, but there is one allusion to it, a subtle hint, as Adam and Eve's story draws to conclusion.

A REMNANT OF HOPE: THE TREE OF LIFE IS STILL IN THE GARDEN AND STILL AT THE CENTER: GENESIS 3:22-24

The tree of life had been mentioned only in passing in the first part of the story, but as the passage comes to an end, it becomes clear that

---

[21]"Human beings are to be no superhuman heroes. Instead they are to be locked in dogged battle, knowing victory again and again but also being wounded again and again; that is how things are to be for every member of the human race" (Bonhoeffer, *Creation and Fall*, p. 133).
[22]Ibid., p. 136.

this tree did not occupy quite so peripheral a position as had at first appeared. In fact the story ends with that tree at the center, not just of the garden, but of the whole story; it becomes clear that this tree is central to what the story is really all about. The story ends with angels guarding the way to the tree with a flaming sword. Humankind is denied access.

But does the story really end there, with humankind blocked from access to the tree of life? How sad it would be if that were *really* the end of the story. In my Bible it is told on page 5 of a book that continues to page 1634. In fact the story of the tree resumes on page 1332. There, on that tree, with arms outstretched and open hands dripping blood, is the Son of God and Son of Man, Jesus. There is the ultimate in beauty and the ultimate in pain—together—in one being and in one instant. The terrible pain leads to a singular death that gives birth to singular life. Agonizing joy: Friday's death gives birth to Sunday's life.

Mark's Gospel tells us that with that physical death the temple curtain, which separated common people from that which symbolically represented the Presence of God, was ripped apart (Mk 15:38). Once again, humankind had direct access to the tree of life and to the Presence of God. The breath of God had snuffed out the flaming sword that blocked entry to the garden.[23]

What a strange paradise is this hill of Golgotha, this cross, this blood, this broken body. What a strange tree of life is this trunk on which God had to suffer and die. Yet it is the kingdom of life and of the resurrection, which by grace God grants us. It is the gate of imperishable hope now opened, the gate of waiting and patience. The tree of life, the cross of Christ, the center of God's world that is fallen but upheld and preserved—that is what the end of the story about paradise is for us.[24]

Once we recognize that the sword of the creation story has been snuffed out and that there is free access to Eden's tree of life, we see why it is hardly legitimate to write or talk about the creation story

---

[23]For an enriching exegesis of the symbolic significance of the tree of life in Scripture, see Blocher, *In the Beginning*, pp. 124-26.
[24]Bonhoeffer, *Creation and Fall*, p. 146.

without including the story's ending: the new creation possible in
Jesus. That which we mistakenly consider two stories is really one, despite the separation in space and time of its two parts. Paul made this
especially clear in Romans 5. Here he referred to Jesus as the second
Adam. If death came to the human race through the disobedience of
the first Adam, how much the more did "death to death" (that is, eternal life) come from the obedience of the second Adam, who is God's
Son? Because of that "death to death," we have access to the tree of life
again. This is the theme of the creation story. We can enter into a relationship with God that bears significant resemblance to Adam and
Eve's experience in the garden. We still live in the midst of good and
evil, but access to the fruit of the tree of life is no longer blocked by a
locked gate.

> Once more God opens the gate
> To fair Paradise today;
> No angel now bars the way.
> Glory to God, who is great,
> And praise and honor, we say.[25]

COMING BACK INTO THE PRESENCE OF THE TREE OF LIFE

After Adam and Eve sinned, God walked through the garden in the
cool of the evening. Adam and Eve, on the other hand, hid in a corner.
The message of the creation story is that as a result of Jesus coming to
the world, redeeming Adam and Eve's sin, we do not have to hide
from God's Presence anymore. If being cast from the garden meant being removed from access to the tree of life (and that is certainly the implication of the flaming sword and the closed gates that accompanied
it), then Jesus' death and resurrection make it accessible to us once
again. We can live life in God's Presence.

Another aspect of the beauty of the garden was being able to walk
alongside God without feeling guilt. Hence, not just living in his presence, but doing so with a sense that God considered Adam and Eve
clean and beautiful, is another wonderful aspect of life in the garden.

---

[25]From an old German hymn titled "Praise God, You Christians, All Alike," written by Ni-
kolaus Herman (1500–1561). Cited in Bonhoeffer, *Creation and Fall*, p. 146.

Because of God's grace and forgiveness, we can walk with God too.

A third important element of life in the garden was being able to share it with another person. The community with whom we share life in God's Presence consists of fellow believers within the church. Jesus, immediately before his arrest, prayed for the church "that all of them may be one, Father, just as you are in me and I am in you" (Jn 17:21). In a sense it is God's will that we all be "one flesh" (that is, one body; see 1 Cor 12), and that is part of the paradise of being back in God's Presence again. Just as Eve was the bride of Adam and the two of them lived in a community of love, so the church is the bride of Christ. Just as Eve and Adam lived in community as one flesh, so Christ desires that we live our lives as a "one-flesh community," one with each other in love and one with our Bridegroom—the second Adam (1 Cor 12:14-20; Eph 4:16).

It is important to make clear that the return to "the Garden of Eden" is not heaven. In its original state the garden existed on earth. To the extent that we can return to the garden now, especially to the tree of life at the center, we are still doing so on planet earth. The sense of pain, toil and struggle are still present in our lives (Rom 8:22-23). However, in the light provided by his Presence, and in the love and security offered by those with whom we live in Christian community, the pain, toil and strife become bearable. There is a peace in the midst of it all. The Creator, after all, is back at the center of our lives, and that is life in the "garden."

> We thinke that *Paradise* and *Calvarie,*
>   Christs Crosse, and *Adam's* tree, stood in one place;
> Looke, Lord, and finde both Adams met in me;
>   As the first *Adam's* sweat surrounds my face,
>   May the last *Adam's* blood my soule embrace.[26]

THE NEW CREATION: A REAL EVENT IN REAL TIME

So the story of creation is not complete without the story of the new creation that is possible in Christ. I have already mentioned that this

---

[26]John Donne, *The Poems of John Donne* (London: Oxford University Press, 1912), p. 368, cited in W. C. Placher, *Unapologetic Theology* (Louisville: Westminster John Knox, 1989), p. 127.

book is a personal story of creation told through the eyes of a Christian who happens to be a biologist. Each of us who are Christians would be able to tell our own story of how the new creation took place inside us. I am going to briefly relate my personal story of new creation. I do this not because it is particularly unique or important (it is not—there are millions of stories just like it, as many stories as there are Christians); however, as you read on and continue to understand creation through the eyes of this biologist, it is important that you know from whence this biologist has come in his views of the creation. Remember also that one cannot talk about creation in its totality unless one starts from the center, where the tree of life—the source of the new creation—is situated. Thus it is here that I begin.

I have already alluded to the frustration I sensed during those days when I had one foot in the world of Christianity and the other in a world of secular knowledge. At that early stage of my life I thought that if I ever immersed myself in biological knowledge I would quickly slide down the slippery slope to agnosticism. It is largely because of this (I hesitate to admit) that my original plan was to immerse myself in what I naively considered to be the more innocuous subjects of chemistry and physics. I did not want to live life in confusion, and it seemed to me that those sciences would not confound my spiritual instincts.

All of that came to naught, however, after I took some required biology. I was no longer able to hold myself back from the study of life. Yet, to my surprise, the early years of immersion in biology had no negative impact on my faith. I became increasingly impressed by the apparent design of life, although I became convinced that God's design had been realized gradually and not suddenly.

My faith did weaken, but not for the reason I had expected. My faith weakened because my developing career as a geneticist came to take first place in my life. My personal relationship with God was relegated to the back seat, and in fact, for a period, God was probably out of the car altogether. It was not that I had stopped believing in God; rather, I had stopped caring.

I suspect that is where I would have spent my life, if it had not been for two events. The first happened in the lab in which I was doing research, and it happened soon after I had completed my doctorate in genetics. At that time the musical *Jesus Christ Superstar* was a hit on Broadway, and a group of scientists in the lab were discussing the musical and trying to recall the names of Jesus' disciples. One person in particular had heard about my Christian background and turned to me, expecting that I would be able to fill him in on some missing details. I had the strangest sensation when he turned to me, because I recognized that although there was a time when Jesus was my best friend, now he was not only *not* my best friend but he was even on the verge of becoming a distant memory. I had not opened my Bible in months and had not engaged in serious devotional study for a couple of years. Furthermore it had been what seemed like a very long time since my last one-on-one conversation with God. I had no right to be consulted as a person who knew anything more about Jesus than anyone else. Whether God planted the question that initiated this mode of thought, or whether God just used the question to speak to me, I do not know. One thing is clear, though, and that is that God, through his persistent grace, was purposely calling me back.[27]

The second event was equally important. Within several days of the above-related experience, a Christian professor at the university where I was working invited me to lunch. That visit over lunch led to an invitation to come to his church, and with that I was on the road back to God.

Without those two nudges, closely and appropriately timed, I suspect my life would have been vastly different. Even at that, however, the road back was not as straightforward as I had expected it would be. I found that by my having stopped caring about the existence of God, I carried some heavy baggage that could not easily be dropped. I was genuinely not sure whether God was real. The first step back involved

---

[27]"Where are you?" (Gen 3:9). Quoting from Franz Delitzsch, and speaking of Adam, H. Ray Dunning has written, " 'God seeks him not because he is lost from his knowledge but from his communion.' The quest was intended to arouse in Adam a realization that he was now lost, and no remedy for this predicament could occur without this realization taking place. Hence the grace of God is celebrated on the very threshold of fallen human history" (Dunning, *Reflecting the Divine Image*, p. 55). And so it was with me—the beat goes on.

falling to my knees at the side of my bed and emotionally exclaiming to God that, although I was not sure whether he was there, I would live as though he was for a while, because I knew of no other way of finding my way back to him. The new creation had begun. It was a gradual process for me, although it is not for everyone. God became increasingly real to me over the next couple of years, so much so that what started out as faith in the unknown turned into knowledge that carried a high degree of confidence, bordering on certainty. Paul spoke about such an experience as mine in 1 Corinthians 2:14: "The man without the Spirit does not accept the things that come from the Spirit of God, for they are foolishness to him, and he cannot understand them, because they are spiritually discerned." With the new creation, our spiritual senses are awakened and we begin the lifelong process of seeing God increasingly clearly as we live in his Presence—in the garden.

Just as creation takes place at God's initiative and continues in response to God's ongoing Presence and command, so the new creation depends upon God's initiative. It is true what Paul states in Romans 1:20: "God's invisible qualities—his eternal power and divine nature—have been clearly seen, being understood from what has been made." Nonetheless this is not the whole story, as the rest of Romans makes clear. The great twentieth-century theologian Karl Barth said that with our own eyes and minds we are led up the edge of this world's existence, and at that edge we find strong hints that there is something more.[28] To proceed beyond this, we need revelation. It is extremely important to stress this. It is not our minds that lead us to God; we come to know God because God chooses to reveal himself and his nature to us. We cannot find God, Barth said, by reasoning our way to him. God is too great to be fathomed by our puny human minds alone. Were it not for God choosing to reveal himself to us, we would be like the Athenians in Acts 17 who constructed an altar to "the Unknown God." But God, through the life, death and resurrection of Christ, has revealed himself to us, and through his Word and his precious Holy Spirit, God continues to reveal himself anew.

---

[28]Karl Barth, *The Epistle to the Romans*, 6th ed., trans. Edwyn C. Hopkins (London: Oxford University Press, 1968), p. 46.

Because of this dependence on God's revelation, we must not give undue attention to the aspect of Christian apologetics that tries to prove by scientific arguments that there is a Designer. Even if we were successful at doing this, getting someone to accept that there is a Designer has little to do with the heart of the creation story. Paul stated clearly that the great truths about God come through revelation, not through human wisdom:

> In the same way no one knows the thoughts of God except the Spirit of God. We have not received the spirit of the world but the Spirit who is from God, that we may understand what God has freely given us. This is what we speak, not in words taught us by human wisdom but in words taught by the Spirit, expressing spiritual truths in spiritual words. (1 Cor 2:11-13)

We must not expect that minds that have not been newly created in Christ will be able to express accurate truths about creation. And as that is the case, perhaps the real challenge for Christianity in the twenty-first century (as it relates to creation) is not to get the creation story into science classrooms. The task, after all, is not so much for us to change minds; rather it is for God to change hearts. It is only with changed hearts that the creation story becomes complete. The story of a changed heart cannot be told with placards and demonstrations demanding that the Christian story get equal time in the classroom. It cannot even be told by a nonregenerated science teacher who knows nothing of God's love attempting to lay out the creation story. This is a story that is best told while kneeling humbly at the foot of a cross: God created all of life in its exquisite beauty, and that same Creator-God suffered and died for me, unworthy though I be, so that I might experience life as it was really meant to be lived. That is the biblical story of creation, in its fullness, taking all 1,662 pages of my Bible into account.

Sometimes, by insisting that a truncated, "one page" version of the creation story be inserted into the science classroom, we are forgetting that the heart of the message is a revelation from God himself, a message "taught by the Spirit, expressing spiritual truths in spiritual words." Furthermore, as discussed in chapter one, there is reason to be concerned that even the truncated and "despiritualized" version of the creation story that many Christians want inserted into the science classroom is based upon a scriptural interpretation that may be flawed, inconsistent with the thinking of some of history's leading Christian activists—Wesley, Calvin and Augustine. And finally, not only may this version be based upon a faulty view of Scripture, but its understanding of science may be especially flawed. It is this, the scientific question, with which we will be engaged throughout the remainder of this book.

There is no message on earth more important than the creation story (when told in its completeness). Hence we had better be certain that we have it right or, at the very least, that we are not significantly distorting it. At the same time, however, Christianity calls for a balance that is heavier on the side of love than it is on the side of knowing all the details correctly. Paul wrote, "Knowledge puffs up, but love builds up. The man who thinks he knows something does not yet know as he ought to know. But the man who loves is known by God" (1 Cor 8:1-3). But Paul also wrote, "This is my prayer: that your love may abound more and more in knowledge and depth of insight" (Phil 1:9).

Hence, as a scientist who is writing about "knowledge and depth of insight," my task in writing this book is to do all I can to maintain a balance and to be sure that the equilibrium point I find is the edifying Christian one.

3

PUTTING CREATION
INTO A TIME FRAME

—

IN THE TWO PREVIOUS CHAPTERS I EMPHASIZED that the purpose of the Bible is to lead us to God. The Bible tells us about our lost spiritual state and about God's plan for spiritual restoration. Certainly this is the major thrust of God's Word, from Genesis to Revelation. Although leading us to God is the Bible's primary purpose, the foundational premise is that God's people need to know that the universe exists because it was commanded to do so by God. The God of Revelation 21:5, who said, "I am making everything new!" is also the God of Genesis 1:1, who "in the beginning . . . created the heavens and the earth." The God who makes us new creatures in Christ (2 Cor 5:17) is also the God who created us to begin with (Gen 2:7). This is a crucial scriptural message. The universe is not here by accident, nor do humans live on this earth by mere happenstance. All of this happened because God commanded (Worded) it into existence: "He [Christ] is the image of the invisible God, the firstborn over all creation. For by him all things were created: things in heaven and on earth, visible and invisible, whether thrones or powers or rulers or authorities; all things were created by him and for him. He is before all things, and in him all things hold together" (Col 1:15-17).

It is unfortunate that a great deal of energy has been expended to debate the question of how long it has been since God delivered this command. One interpretation of Genesis 1 is that it happened about six thousand years ago. Another interpretation, held by individuals who respect the Scriptures every bit as much, is that it is not possible to say on theological grounds alone just how long it has been since creation was initiated. For a long time, Christians had no way of knowing which of the two methods of interpreting Genesis 1 was the most likely to lead to the truth. We are told in 2 Peter 3:8, "With the Lord a day is like a thousand years, and a thousand years are like a day." Peter was telling us that our time frame is not God's, and he was reminding us not to try to fit God into our tiny boxes.

As mentioned earlier, today's situation is similar to that which confronted Christians four hundred years ago. Before Galileo collected his scientific data, Christians could not decide which of two interpretations of the passage "the earth is fixed" (Ps 104:5) was correct. Some said the passage should be read figuratively; others, literally. Both interpretations had the same theological content ("God is faithful"), but they had different scientific content (earth at the center versus sun at the center). Before Galileo, Christians could not know which interpretation was the best. In addition to studying God's Word, however, Galileo also studied God's creation, and from that he concluded that the figurative interpretation was correct. Similarly, we now face two possible interpretations of the question, "How long has it been since God created?" It is logical to expect that studying God's world may help us understand the two possible interpretations of God's Word.

USING RADIOACTIVE DECAY TO MEASURE THE AGE OF ROCKS

To determine how long it has been since God created the earth, we need to discuss some of the elementary properties of matter. There are ninety-two elements, of which eighty-four can be found on earth. Examples include carbon, oxygen, hydrogen and phosphorus. Many of these elements come in different forms, called *isotopes*. The element carbon, for example, comes in three forms: ^{12}C, ^{13}C and ^{14}C. Although they differ slightly in mass, each of carbon's three forms behaves the same way as the others in chemical reactions.

Each atom of an isotope has a defined number of neutrons and protons housed centrally in a structure called the *nucleus*. The isotope ^{12}C, for example, has six protons and six neutrons in its nucleus, whereas

^{14}C has eight neutrons and six protons. The excess of neutrons in a ^{14}C atom confers instability to the nucleus. Because of this, occasionally the nucleus decays into a form that is more stable. This can occur if one of the eight neutrons splits into two parts: a proton and an energetic electron. When this happens, the electron (termed a *beta particle*) goes flying out of the nucleus, leaving the proton behind. The result is an atom with one less neutron (seven) and one additional proton (seven). The extra proton results in a change in the chemical properties of the atom, since atoms with seven protons correspond to a different element—nitrogen. To summarize, carbon-14 is unstable and decays with time into nitrogen. The release of energy associated with that decay can be measured and is referred to as *radioactivity*.

Not all isotopes are unstable. For example ^{13}C, with its seven neutrons and six protons, is a stable element, not subject to decay. Of the 84 elements found in nature, there are 339 isotopes, and the majority of them are stable. It is the unstable ones that are useful in determining the age of the oldest rocks on earth.

The rate of decay of different types of elements has been carefully analyzed over the past one hundred years and is extremely well characterized for different isotopes. Consider uranium-235 (^{235}U), for example. It decays, through a series of events, to the element lead-207. Scientists have considered the rate of this decay and have found it to be astoundingly slow. It would take 713 million years for half a sample of uranium-235 to decay into lead-207. Frequently, when I talk to my students about this, they are incredulous that such a long time could be measured. "How would scientists ever know this?" they ask. The answer is straightforward.

When a uranium atom decays, it emits a pulse of radiation measurable with a Geiger counter. Each decay event sets off one click in the Geiger counter. If you have an ounce of uranium, a Geiger counter can determine that approximately 4 billion decay events occur per second. This sounds like a lot and seems to imply that uranium is highly unstable, but it is not when we realize how many atoms did not decay in that second. Even in an hour, only one in every trillion uranium atoms will decay. Given this information, one can easily determine how long it would take before one of every two uranium atoms have decayed into lead, namely 713 million years.

If the earth were infinitely old, there would be no uranium-235 on this planet. It all would have decayed into lead. The presence of uranium-235 is proof of the earth's finite age. So how old is the earth? In order to get an estimate for this we need to measure how much of the uranium has decayed. How could we do this? To illustrate the method, we will make a simplifying assumption. As we examine the age of a particular very old rock, let's assume that there was no lead in the rock when it was first formed.[1] If this were true, then if we found that a particular mineral in a rock contained equal amounts of uranium and lead, the rock would be 713 million years old. All the lead would have come from decayed uranium. If the elements were now equal in amount, that would mean half the uranium had decayed, giving a half-and-half mixture. If, on the other hand, the sample contained about three times as much lead as it did uranium, we would say that only one-quarter of the original uranium is still present and that the rock is now 1.426 billion years old.

Now that you are familiar with the concept, we need to examine the simplification. One cannot, of course, assume that there was no lead in the rock to begin with. Thus there needs to be a way of estimating how much lead was there in the beginning when the rock was first formed. There is a simple way of doing this. The lead formed from uranium is known as lead-207. But there is another form of lead known as lead-204, and extensive data show that, chemically speaking, lead-204 and lead-207 behave identically. Thus when a mineral is first made (that is, when a rock is forming), the chemical process of mineral formation cannot distinguish between the two lead isotopes. When the rock is forming, each of the two lead isotopes would be chosen in a nondistinguishing manner; they would be in the same relative amounts as they are in the earth's crust in general. Now we come to the important point. If uranium-235 were incorporated into the rock when it was first formed, it would slowly decay to produce extra lead-207 but not lead-204.[2] If the rock

---

[1]Do not be alarmed by the simplifying assumption. It is made only to be sure that the reader understands the concept. We will go on to desimplify it once the concept is clear.

[2]Since the initial amount of lead-207 can be readily calculated, given that we know (1) the

were only a few thousand years old, there would be almost no measurable extra lead. However, if it was hundreds of millions of years old, there would be much more of it. The amount of extra lead is precisely equal to the amount of uranium-235 that has decayed.

Just to be sure that the rationale behind the dating mechanism is clear, I will introduce a simple analogy. Imagine that in visiting a foreign country you are taken hostage by guerrillas. You are kept in solitary confinement with access to no one—it is just you and the duffel bag in your possession when you were taken captive. Wanting to have some way of keeping track of the date while you are locked up, you rummage through your bag and find two boxes of facial tissues. You take them out of the boxes and count them—three hundred altogether. Here is your plan for keeping track of time: every day you will take one of the tissues from the pile of three hundred and use it to wipe your face and hands. Each used tissue corresponds to one day. On day one there are 299 new tissues and one used one. As time progresses, the pile of used tissues increases, so that by the time 150 days have passed (about five months), half the tissues are in the clean pile and half in the used.

In the world of rocks, uranium is the equivalent of the clean tissues and lead-207 is the equivalent of the used ones. Uranium turns into lead, just like new tissues turn into used ones. The molecular clock, like the daily use of a tissue, is ticking. One click, one day—time moves on. The difference, however, is that the molecular clock ticks, not for three hundred days, but for millions of days, indeed for millions of years. All down through the eons of time, the clock in the rocks has been ticking. In a sense, then, the uranium-containing mineral has also been "held hostage." In this case it has been "captured" in a rock, and its decay product, lead-207 atoms, like the used tissues, has remained locked up inside of that rock since the moment it was first formed—hundreds of millions, perhaps billions, of years ago.[3]

The analogy with tissues rests on the assumption that on your day

amount of lead-204 in the rock and (2) the relative amount of lead-204 to lead-207 in the earth's crust, it is a simple matter to calculate the extra lead-207 in the rock.
[3]No analogy is perfect. In contrast to this tissue paper analogy, the absolute number of decaying atoms is not a constant as time goes by. What is constant is the *rate* of decay for a given number of parental molecules. However, as time goes by, and as the absolute number of the

of capture you had no used tissues. If you had any tissues from your pockets at the start of this experience, your "calendar" would be inaccurate unless you could determine the number of initial used tissues. Indeed this is exactly the situation that one must deal with in measuring dates through determining the amount of uranium-235 that has decayed into lead-207. It is necessary to determine how much preexisting lead-207 would have been present at the time of rock formation so that one can calculate the amount of extra lead-207 that is formed as a decay product. Fortunately, just as you can determine the number of preexisting used tissues by counting them, so the method of determining preexisting lead-207 (see note 2, pp. 64-65) is equally reliable.

As good as your mechanism of keeping track of time in captivity seems to be, it may not be foolproof. What if, for example, some of your used tissues were discarded by mistake? If that were to be the case, then as time went by, the ratio of new to used tissues would not be an accurate indicator of elapsed time. Similarly, in dating rocks, scientists recognize that this sort of problem could have occurred in the history of a rock. Consider the following, for example. Lead is quite vaporous. Thus if a 1-billion-year-old rock had ever been heated to a very high temperature because of volcanic activity, then some of the lead-207 might have evaporated from the molten rock. Like the mistakenly discarded used tissues, some of the lead could have been "lost." There are ways of detecting such events and correcting for them, most of which are too technical for a general book of this sort.[4] However, we can consider a few of the rather straightforward mechanisms by which scientists can check for problems of this type in the dating of the rocks. One is to use an alternative, "back-up" dating system.

One example of a second system, considered even more reliable than the uranium-lead scenario, involves potassium-40, another unsta-

---

parental atoms becomes smaller, so also there is a concomitant decrease in the number of decay products produced.

[4]For a detailed discussion of dating mechanisms, see G. Brent Dalrymple, *The Age of the Earth* (Stanford, Calif.: Stanford University Press, 1991). Another source, which is more condensed than the the the book by Dalrymple, is Kenneth R. Miller, "Scientific Creationism vs. Evolution," in *Science and Creationism*, ed. Ashley Montagu (New York: Oxford University Press, 1984), pp. 28-35.

ble isotope. Over time potassium-40 decays into argon-40. It takes about 1.25 billion years for half a sample of potassium-40 to decay into its product. (Again, it is important to remember that the method of determining this "life span" is straightforward; see above.) The potassium-argon mechanism is especially reliable because in the formation of many minerals, potassium atoms have a fixed position in an atomic pattern. As an example of such a pattern, picture the red and black squares on a checkerboard. Each square, red and black, has a fixed and defined position on the board. So it is with the position of potassium atoms in the mineral of a rock. When first formed, a mineral has a defined number of potassium atoms, just like the checkerboard has a defined number of red squares. All the atoms fit together just like the squares. Since potassium-40 is unstable, it will decay with time. Any deficiency in the expected amount of potassium should be present in the form of its decay product, argon, a gas that gets trapped in the rock. The dating mechanism is wonderfully self-correcting: if the number of missing potassium atoms (just like "missing red squares" on a checkerboard) does not equal the number of extra argon atoms, then scientists know there must have been a "meltdown" or some other catastrophic event in the rock's history that makes the mechanism unreliable for that particular rock.[5] On the other hand, if the missing potassium atoms and the extra argon atoms are equal in number, then scientists can determine the age of the rock by determining the ratio of potassium-40 atoms to argon-40 atoms.

Let us return to the analogy of your being held in captivity. Let's say that you really are a little skeptical about the reliability of the tissue-counting method by which you determine the date. You worry, for example, that some of the used tissues were discarded by mistake. When one is held captive, little things become big, and this becomes a source of frustration for you, especially since you were promised release on day 300. Just what date is it, anyway? What is a captive to do? Let's say that on day 150 you are allowed a short visit with the person who had

---

[5]In the analogy with the tissues, we would be able to say that the number of missing clean tissues must always equal the number of used tissues. If it did not, then we would know that our system of dating the time was unreliable.

been your traveling companion. He, like you, was taken into captivity, and like you, he had been held in solitary confinement ever since. After exchanging the normal pleasantries of two people briefly reunited after being held captive for 150 days, the two of you turn to the subject of the number of days in captivity. You explain your system to him and indicate that you think it is day 150 but that, because of the possibility of losing some of the tissues, you lack confidence about this. Much to your delight, you learn that your companion has had a similar system for measuring the passing of the days. In his bag there had been a package of pistachio nuts—203 of them. Once every other day he had eaten one of his nuts, keeping the old shells. Since he currently had 75 empty shells and 128 full ones, the two of you, each with your own dating systems, were in complete agreement. It is day 150 and your lingering doubts disappear. Two independent confirmations make you convinced—only 150 days to go.

Like two captives double-checking the date since their capture, scientists frequently double-check the date of rocks, and just to be sure of its correctness, the double-checking is done by using different mechanisms (for example, uranium/lead and potassium/argon). If the two methods do not agree, then there has been some irregularity in the history of the rock and further analysis is necessary. When dating methods do agree, then just like the two captives, one with his tissue, the other with his pistachio nuts, there is a high level of scientific confidence that the age of the rock is accurate.

Let's look briefly at a third dating method, one that involves analyzing the decay of rubidium-87 to strontium-87. In the example of the new and used tissues, recall that any used tissues in the pockets prior to the start of captivity would have caused a significant problem in determining the date unless you knew how many there were. Similarly, recall that in the uranium-lead system it is necessary to determine the extra lead-207 (that is, that which is produced through the decay process) formed over time. One advantage of the rubidium-strontium technique is that it totally removes the need for knowledge about the amount of decay product at the start. A second advantage is adaptation for exploring the age of several different minerals in the same rock.

If all minerals do not give the same age, then it becomes clear that this rock has been subject to volcanic heating or some other disruption over the preceding millions of years and thereby is not suitable for dating. The beauty of the rubidium-strontium technique is that it is inherently self-checking (by analyzing multiple minerals in the same rock) and is not subject to the concerns about preexisting decay product. Using only one mechanism makes one subject to the same problems you would have in your captivity scenario were you to remain isolated from another confirming source. Confidence builds when there are several independent ways of measuring time. Actually there are forty independent isotope systems used by geologists for dating minerals. Each year, close to a thousand research papers are published using these systems—all of which are in virtual agreement with one another. Hundreds of thousands of rock samples have been dated by hundreds of different lab groups. So, returning to the analogy, it is not quite the same as a double-check between just two timekeeping methods. It is many, many different methods, all putting the earth's time frame into the same context.

OBJECTIONS BY PROPONENTS OF A YOUNG EARTH

Inconsistencies in the dating of rocks. Proponents of a young earth point out that results among dating techniques are not in perfect agreement. They also point out that some rocks cannot be measured using these techniques for any of various reasons. The geologists themselves are in perfect agreement with them on these points. However, even if we allow that the techniques may have an error margin of from 5 to 10 percent, we would still be left with an earth that was over 4 billion years old instead of current estimates of 4.6 billion. In order for the earth to be six thousand years old, the techniques would have to create errors many orders of magnitude beyond that. To write about errors that throw off readings by small percentages and to hint that these invalidate the technique may be unfair to readers who are unfamiliar with the details. Anyone who has spent extensive time working in science labs knows that techniques rarely work perfectly. The fact that different and independent radiometric techniques are in *relative* agreement with one another, given that they are measuring clocks that have been ticking for hundreds of millions of years or more, is a confirmation of their validity. The fact that they are not always in perfect agreement points to the limit of these scientific techniques, but it does not invalidate them. Remember that as we consider which of the two interpretations of Genesis 1 is correct, the question is not whether the earth is 4.3 billion years old or 4.6 billion years old. We can leave questions like that to the scientists as they work through any details that minor inconsistencies in their data invoke. To us the important question is whether the earth is six thousand years old or 4.6 billion years old. We must not be fooled into thinking that minor fluctuations in the data that is accepted as valid by virtually all geologists is relevant to this question.

Could the decay rates have changed? In our analogy of the clean and used tissues, we said that we could measure elapsed time by counting the number of used tissues and cross-checking with the decline in the number of clean ones. As long as one obeys the rule of one tissue per day, then we would be able to tell exactly how many days had transpired since the beginning of confinement. Of course any alteration in the frequency of tissue use would disturb the whole chronological system.

Proponents of a young earth have long argued that the decay rates of today need not have been the same as the decay rates of the past. Obviously, if there were a time when the various changes (potassium to argon, uranium to lead, rubidium to strontium, for example) did occur more rapidly, then the "clock" would be useless. Thus, in fairness to advocates of a young earth, we need to consider this idea carefully. Radioactive decay from one element to another involves a change in the nucleus of the atom, thus we need to briefly digress to discuss the structure of an atom.

An atom consists of a nucleus, at its center, surrounded by a cloud that contains a distinctive number of electrons. The electrons are in constant motion at unimaginably high speeds. An atom is tiny, but the nucleus in its center occupies an especially minuscule area. To illustrate, let's pretend it is possible to magnify an atom so that the nucleus is the size of a soccer ball. At this magnification, the area occupied by the whole atom would have a diameter larger than the height of Mount Everest. The electrons, still extremely tiny even at this magnification, would be zooming through this huge space with nothing else present, only that solitary, dense ball in the center. In summary, an atom, tiny as it is, consists almost exclusively of open space. The minuscule, dense nucleus at the atom's center has totally distinctive properties from the huge space that surrounds it.

The forces that hold things together within that single nucleus are different from the type of forces holding together different atoms in a molecule. A water molecule, for example, consists of two hydrogen atoms held to a single oxygen atom (H_2O). The interaction between different atoms is a property of the electron cloud in the open space, and it is not difficult to disturb these interactions by various physical and chemical means. By comparison, however, the properties of the "glue" holding the parts of the nucleus together are about 1 million times stronger.[6] The parts of a nucleus cannot be altered easily and are almost immune to outside interference.

Radioactive decay is a property of changes in the nucleus, not the electron cloud in the open space. When an element decays (for example, uranium into lead), the properties causing this to happen are nuclear events, which are highly resistant to outside interference. Scientists have tried hard to alter decay rates. They have attempted, for example, to alter rates by heating to temperatures as high as 2500°C or cooling to as low as –253°C and found virtually no alteration of the decay rate. Measurements have been done under pressures of several thousand atmospheres as well as differing gravitational and magnetic fields, virtually without effect.[7] All types of decay that are used

---

[6]To appreciate how great 1 million times is, consider the following analogy. As I write this, I have a one-pound cup of coffee in front of me. The force that holds the cup to the table is easy for me to counteract—I just reach for the cup and lift it. On the other hand, if it were possible to pack 1 million times as much weight into that cup, it would be like packing a weight equivalent to about three hundred SUVs into the space now occupied by my coffee. Even the most powerful crane in existence would not be able to budge the cup if the force holding it down were that strong.

[7]For a more detailed discussion of attempts to modify the decay rate, see Dalrymple, *Age of the Earth*, pp. 88-89.

in radiometric dating are essentially immune to physical and chemical influences. Any decay mechanisms that could conceivably respond slightly to chemical influences (for example, potassium/argon) have never been observed to do so. Christian and non-Christian nuclear physicists are virtually in 100 percent agreement that the decay rates could not have been significantly influenced by anything throughout earth's history.[8] However, even if it *were* to be discovered that *all* the different mechanisms of decay could have been influenced by some force that would alter *each* of their rates in parallel, it is even more unthinkable to Christian and non-Christian physicists alike that they would *all* be altered in such a way that it would produce the massive percent error that would be required to incorrectly estimate the age of the earth as 4.6 billion years when it was really six thousand years.

Some readers will remain unconvinced that the earth is billions of years old. *I don't trust those physicists,* they may think. *How would they know whether or not something yet to be discovered may be shown to have influenced decay rates?* The reason for this distrust is simple. Unchanging decay rates and an old earth imply the use of figurative language in the creation account. Although many acknowledge figurative language in Psalms and other poetic books of the Bible, they experience much discomfort about the notion of poetic license in the creation account. I understand the basis for this discomfort and the reasons for being hesitant. It really *is* important to be certain. With that in mind, please read on.

Radiometric dating depends upon a key assumption (unchanged decay rates), and even though probably every single nuclear physicist on earth (Christian and non-Christian) is in agreement that decay rates could not have not been altered in the history of time, the issue is so important that we must ask whether there is corroborative information. Are there other ways of dating the earth? Are there reliable methods that do not depend on the constant decay rates that concern some Christians—those in the family who hesitate to trust the opin-

---

[8]"Nuclear physicist" is defined as someone who has a Ph.D. in the field of nuclear physics.

ion of nuclear physicists, unanimous or not?[9]

Many of us have had the experience of estimating the age of a tree by counting its rings. In elementary school we learned that trees grow faster in the summer than in the winter. Hence the seasonal growth pattern—each ring corresponds to one year. The oldest known trees in existence are the bristlecone pines inhabiting the eastern slopes of the Sierra Nevada mountain range near the California-Nevada border. By counting the rings, we know these ancients are about six thousand years old. Since many of us have seen and counted rings, and since six thousand years is consistent with a literal interpretation of Genesis, few would be uncomfortable with this. However, the data takes on an intriguing twist when one analyzes some of the dead trees found in the vicinity. By analyzing their rings, it becomes apparent that the oldest were first formed 11,800 years ago.[10] That alone places the earth's origin out of the range of a strictly literal account.

Going back twelve thousand years in time takes us to the last ice age, so the technique of counting the rings of bristlecone pine trees cannot be applied to dates earlier than this. However, there are analogous techniques that allow investigators to count the years well beyond twelve thousand. One is to count the seasonal ice rings extending deep into the glaciers of Antarctica and Greenland. The ice, of course, was made from falling snow. Just like the rings in a tree, the ice betrays seasonal fluctuations associated with the compressed layers of snow. Layers of dust, for example, are more pronounced in the summer than at other seasons. Furthermore, bubbles and ice crystals are larger in the summer than winter. These are just two of several oscillating parameters that allow investigators to tick off the years, one at a time, as they

---

[9]See Dalrymple, *Age of the Earth*, pp. 364-392, for examples not discussed here. In addition, the inquisitive reader is strongly encouraged to refer to Roger C. Wiens, "Radiometric Dating: A Christian Perspective," revised version (2002), American Scientific Affiliation, *On-Line Resources on Faith/Science Issues*, <http://www.asa3.org/ASA/resources/Wiens.html#page.%2016>. The discussion of tree rings, ice cores and lake sediments that follows is based upon information in this paper.

[10]The method of determining when these dead trees were alive is to calibrate the pattern of their outer rings with the pattern of living trees. This provides a time frame for the year of formation of the outer wood of a particular dead tree. By counting rings backward (that is, internally) from this known date, it is possible to show that the internal wood of the oldest dead trees was made 11,800 years ago.

determine the date of formation of each layer. Using specialized drilling rigs, they have extracted sections of continuous cylinders up to nine thousand feet long. Hundreds of thousands of measurements have been done on samples from single cylinders, and the oldest go back 180,000 years!

Another related, but totally independent, way of "counting rings" comes from the analysis of sediments in lakebeds. Like trees and packed snow, the sediment that falls to the bottom of a lake produces an annual, season-specific pattern. In the spring the sediment is rich in minerals from swollen streams, whereas in the summer and fall it is rich in organic material from decaying plant fibers, algae and pollen grains. Hundreds of lakes have been analyzed in this manner, and the oldest dated sediment layers are thirty-five thousand years of age. Because the layers become compressed, the technique becomes unreliable for sediment older than that, but the rings can clearly be counted back much further than six thousand years.

Tree rings show that the earth is at least 12,000 years of age. Lake sediments show that it is at least 35,000 years old. Ice cores up to 180,000 years old have been extracted. And radioactive dating of ancient rocks takes us ever deeper into the ancient history of God's creation.

THE AGE OF THE UNIVERSE: ESTIMATES FROM THE SCIENCE OF ASTROPHYSICS

The next independent confirmation of the ancient age of the earth comes from a totally different type of investigation—the study of stars, or the science of astronomy. As we begin this discussion, it is important to note that astronomers and astrophysicists believe there was an origin to our universe—a time when it began. Not only that, but one of the most reasonable hypotheses for the earth's beginning is that it came from "nothing" (again this hypothesis is not a religious one—it is based purely on knowledge from a subdiscipline of modern physics known as quantum mechanics).[11] In addition, data related to the origin

---

[11]There is considerable discussion of what "nothing" actually means. See Timothy Ferris, *The Whole Shebang* (New York: Simon & Schuster, 1997).

of the universe strongly implies initial conditions seemingly fine-tuned for the possibility of life.[12]

The nearly indisputable finding that the universe really did have a beginning, and that quite possibly it started with a "quantum fluctuation" from nothing, may well be one of the most theologically satisfying conclusions to ever come from science. Liberal theologians at the end of the nineteenth century had concluded that the earth and universe were timeless and therefore had decided that the Genesis account should be taken as nothing more than a human myth or legend. The noted theologian Karl Barth, writing primarily in the first half of the twentieth century, reacted to the liberalism of his teachers and founded a theological movement known as neo-orthodoxy. One of the founding principles of his theological view was that the Bible is God's revelation to humans and therefore needs to be taken seriously. Barth, based on faith in Scripture alone, and against the tide of his liberal colleagues, argued that the universe had to have had a beginning. Further, he argued, it began from nothing.[13] His conclusion was not based upon science; it was purely a theological conclusion.

Now, half a century later, scientists almost unanimously accept the notion of a beginning for the universe. Some Christians are still hesitant to accept their position, since it is grounded firmly in the view that the beginning occurred a very long time ago. Nonetheless it does agree wonderfully with the scriptural account: "In the beginning God created the heaven and the earth." There may be some figurative language in Genesis 1, but the message is clear: there was a beginning and it came about as a result of God's activity.

The big bang theory hypothesizes a universe with a beginning at a single point in time and space where a submicroscopic singularity was the entire mass of the whole universe. An "explosion" of unimaginable proportion occurred that sent everything outward at speeds comparable to the speed of light. Ever since that singular moment (the begin-

---

[12]For a detailed discussion of this from a Christian perspective, see Hugh Ross, *The Creator and the Cosmos* (Colorado Springs, Colo.: NavPress, 1993), chap. 14.

[13]Karl Barth, *The Doctrine of Creation*, vol. 3 of *Church Dogmatics* (Edinburgh: T & T Clark, 1958), pp. 84-90.

ning of time as we know it), the universe has been expanding outward, and astronomical calculations suggest it will probably continue to do so for as far as astronomers can see into the future.

If the universe is flying apart, then astrophysicists should be able to determine the speed at which it has been moving. From this calculated speed, it should be possible to determine how long it has been since all the parts of the universe began their journey. Here is the rationale using an analogy with which we can all identify.

Let's say that you are young and deeply in love with someone in another town. After a dream weekend together, the time comes for the inevitable good-bye kiss and your departure. Your final words are that you will call her (or him) in exactly three hours. "Be at the phone," you say as you get in your car. You get on the freeway, set the cruise control and spend the next couple of hours thinking about you-know-who. Suddenly it occurs to you that in the haze of departure you paid no attention to what time you left. It will not be possible to call her at precisely three hours as you promised. If you call now, she will not be at the phone yet, and you cannot leave a message since the answering machine is broken. If you are late in calling, she is going to be in a frenzy, thinking that you are lying dead at the side of some roadway. Fortunately, however, you had set your cruise control for sixty-five and punched the trip odometer as you started the car. Being astute at calculations, you determine that when you have gone 195 miles, it will be exactly three hours since your departure. Your odometer clicks in—195 miles. You pick up your cell phone—together again.

As long as you understand that calculation, you will understand the principle by which scientists calculate the age of the universe. If scientists can determine the distance from earth to a distant galaxy, and if they can determine how fast it is moving away from us, then they can determine the time interval since earth and that galaxy were together at the moment of the big bang.

Determining your speed in the car was easy because you had set the cruise control. What about the speed of movement of a galaxy—how would one ever determine that? In order to show how this is done, I offer another illustration. Let's assume that someone is driving down the highway in a pickup truck. In the back is a drummer banging on a bass drum. As the truck passes by, you would notice a seeming change in the sound. As the truck moves away, the drum would seem to take on a lower pitch as the truck recedes, compared to the sound perceived while it was approaching. You will probably never see anyone in a pickup truck banging on a drum, but you would observe a similar phenomenon if you were standing beside a freeway while a passing car was continuously sounding its horn or if you were beside a railroad track as a moving train sped past you blowing its whistle.[14] In each case the sound would become deeper as the vehicle moved away from you.

Why would the sound of the drum seem deeper after the pickup truck passed by? The reason is simple if you understand that sound travels as pressure waves. The closer the pressure waves are to each other, the higher the pitch of the sound. If the air pressure waves are closer together, your ear registers that as a high-pitched sound. At each beat of the drum, the pressure waves (set up by the vibrating membrane of the drum) would travel toward you. The pressure waves would naturally travel toward your ear, but if the source of those waves were moving toward you as well, then the waves would be closer together and you would hear a higher-pitched sound than that which would actually be generated. After the truck had passed by, the pressure waves from the vibrating membrane of the drum would still reach your ear, but now each wave of pressure would be a little further apart, because the source of the waves would be moving away from you. Hence it would sound as though it had a deeper pitch. This phenomenon is known as the *Doppler effect* and it could, in theory, be used to measure how fast the truck was moving toward you or away from you. Indeed this principle enables police officers to use a radar gun to measure the speed of oncoming vehicles, and it allows baseball scouts to determine the speed of a prospective pitcher's fastball.

---

[14]The analogy of a drummer in the back of a pickup truck, awkward though it is, has been chosen because it nicely illustrates the nature of sound. Each pulsation of the vibrating drum membrane sets up a traveling pressure wave. The faster the membrane vibrates, the closer together are the pressure waves and the higher is the pitch of the sound. The more commonly used illustrations of a car horn or train whistle do not, in my opinion, provide as adequate a picture of the basis for the mechanical nature of sound.

Using this principle, it is possible to estimate the speed at which galaxies are moving away from us. Light travels in waves, just like sound.
And just as sound waves have a deep pitch if they arrive at our ear
spaced far apart, so light appears red when the light waves striking our
eye are spaced far apart. (Light waves that are close together appear
purple, and intermediately spaced waves may appear green or yellow,
depending upon their spacing.) Just as a truck that is moving away
from us results in the drum sound being deeper, so a star moving away
from us emits light shifted toward the red end of the light spectrum. By
measuring the shift toward red, it is possible to measure the speed of a
receding galaxy.

Thus, just as you were able to determine the speed at which you
were traveling away from the love of your life, so it is possible to measure the speed at which a galaxy is moving away from us. Remember,
however, that in order to determine when the three hours had passed,
you had to know not only your constant speed but also your distance
of travel. So simply calculating the speed of a receding galaxy provides
insufficient data for a calculation of time; we must also know its distance. The principle behind the measure of distance is even simpler
than that behind the measurement of speed. Imagine a flashlight shining in the night. The closer you are to the light, the brighter it is. If the
flashlight is shining from three hundred yards away, little of its light
reaches your eyes, whereas if it is one foot in front of your face, almost
all of its light is directed at you alone. If you knew the brightness of
your particular flashlight at its source, you would be able to tell how
far the flashlight was away from you by measuring how bright it seems
to you. If you had an appropriate measuring device, you could use a
physics formula that would allow you to calculate distance based upon
the amount of light that strikes your measuring device. Thus, for any
given brightness, you would be able to tell the flashlight distance. This
is precisely the principle that is used to determine the distance to a star
in a remote galaxy.[15]

---

[15]It is necessary, of course, to know the actual brightness of the star at its source, and this can
be done in several ways. For a detailed discussion of this, see W. L. Freedman, "The Expan-
sion Rate of the Universe," *Scientific American* 267, no. 5 (1992): 54.

When speed and distance are determined for a variety of galaxies, scientists calculate a time period of from 12 to 16 billion years since the material in our section of the universe parted company from the material in distant portions of the universe. Geologists, you will remember, have calculated the age of the earth (determined by a totally different mechanism, not in any way related to the red-shift measurements of astronomy) to be about 4.6 billion years. The material under our feet, in other words, did not get organized into what we call earth at the beginning of the universe. Remarkably, these two totally independent mechanisms, one measuring the age of rocks by geology and the other the age of the universe by astrophysics, give us a similar age. One extremely sophisticated measurement comes up with a universe billions of years old, and another totally independent way of doing measurement comes up with an earth that has been in existence for billions of years. Thus we have discussed two ways of arriving at the age of parts of the universe, and both point to an age that is far older than six thousand years. I cannot overemphasize the significance of the fact that this conclusion is based upon two sets of independent corroborating evidence. Nuclear physicists, Christian and non-Christian, agree the decay rate of atoms has remained unchanged throughout earth's history, and consequently physicists accept radiometric dating as a reliable method of estimating the earth's age. Christian and non-Christian astronomers—a completely different group of experts using a totally different set of measurements—calculate an age for the universe congruent with radiometric dating.

In discussing the age of the earth, we went on to show that there are several other independent ways of measuring the age of certain components of the earth—trees, ice and lake sediments. What about the universe? Are there other methods of measuring its components? The method just described examined the universe's age by measuring the time since components of the universe had separated from each other in the big bang. This was made possible by measuring the "red shift" of receding stars and galaxies. But are there other ways?

Indeed there are. Consider the following, for example. Light travels at the speed of 186,300 miles per second. Since the nearest star to earth is the sun, and since the sun is 93 million miles from earth, this means that a photon of light takes 8.3 minutes to complete the journey from its solar source to the atmosphere of earth. That calculation is easy, and probably none of us would doubt its veracity. It is just as easy, moreover, to calculate the time of "light en route" for stars and galaxies that are further away—much further. The most distant galaxies that can be detected are at least 12 billion light-years from earth (about 7,000,000,000,000,000,000,000,000 miles). This means that the light now arriving at earth left its source 12 billion years ago. If it has been that long since the light left, then it must be at least that long since that galaxy was first formed. Twelve billion years is amazingly close to what we have just discussed as the age of the universe as measured by red shift. This calculation is viewed as extremely reliable as long as the speed of light has not changed drastically since the initiation of creation. And physicists are certain that it has not.[16] We are left with only one conclusion: the universe is not young. These two methods of estimating the universe's age are only two examples. There are other independent methods as well. Based upon a great deal of rich, internally coherent data well beyond the scope of this book, there is no doubt in the minds of virtually all professional astronomers that the universe is ancient indeed.[17]

Not only do the experts agree, but the conclusions we have been discussing, both for dating components of the universe through astrophysics and for dating components of the earth through geology, come from deep within the framework of their disciplines. The conclusion that creation is ancient does not come from interpretations at the periphery of these disciplines; it is at the core of all that nuclear physi-

---

[16]The speed of light is a property of the fundamental laws of electromagnetism (Maxwell's equations). If the fundamental laws had changed, those alterations would have impacted the lines of light spectra (that is, patterns of emitted light) that emanated from the atoms of individual elements. Since the spectral lines are identical in the ancient light compared to light generated today, the laws operating at the time of the emission of the ancient light must have, in effect, been the same as those in operation today. No change in the laws, no change in the speed of light.

[17]For details of other methods, see Howard J. van Till, *Portraits of Creation* (Grand Rapids, Mich.: Eerdmans, 1990); and "Hubble Uncovers Oldest 'Clocks' in Space to Read Age of Universe," news release (April 24, 2002), HubbleSite <http://hubblesite.org/newscenter/archive/2002/10/>.

cists, geologists and astronomers do every day. For you or I to say that they are wrong is to say that these entire disciplines—geology, nuclear physics and astronomy—have got almost everything wrong. The disciplines are founded on the sorts of principles that lead them to trust their measurement about the age of the earth and universe.

If any one of the independent techniques is correct, that is enough to tell us that the Genesis account must be read with some degree of interpretation. The tree ring data alone is inconsistent with a strictly literal reading of Genesis. The genealogies of Genesis are the key to dating the earth at six thousand years. If the earth is at least 11,800 years old, one has to assume that there are ancestors missing from the genealogies. As soon as one does that, he or she is entering the realm of interpretation and is no longer taking Genesis in a strictly literal manner. If either the lake sediment or the ice core data is even close to being correct, the study of Genesis as science would require some interpretative reading. Thus, to remain true to a strictly literal reading of the first chapter of Genesis, one has to take the position that all the scientific disciplines named above are wrong. Not one of them can be correct.

Given the overwhelming amount of evidence, it is appropriate for Christians to accept that science is revealing details of God's activity. By closing our minds to this form of revelation, we are missing the opportunity to peer into the workings of the God we love so much. Sometimes we, as humans, become so bound up by technicalities of our own making that we are not free to sense the majesty and beauty of God's activity. Similarly, many astronomers, geologists and physicists, with their noses buried in books and eyes glued to computer screens, do not see the majesty of a timeless God in a mechanistic world of calculations and myopic observations. At the same time many Christians, with minds firmly attached to a single interpretation of the meaning of the word "day" in Genesis 1, deprive themselves from understanding the way in which God really created. Hence we have a discovery that has tremendous ramifications for pointing us toward the hand of God in creation, and too many of us are missing it.

In the 28th chapter of Genesis we are told of Jacob's dream. The dream was about God and his activity in the future nation of Israel.

Genesis 28:16-17 describes Jacob's reaction upon awakening: "Surely the LORD is in this place, and I was not aware of it." He was afraid and said, "How awesome is this place! This is none other than the house of God."

What will it take for many Christians to realize that they are missing an opportunity to feel and sense the Presence of God in creation? Science studies that creation. Since it is God's creation, "surely the LORD is in this place." Like Jacob, too many of us are missing out on nature's majesty. Oh, that we would see the activity of God and then, with our knees, hearts and minds bowed in worship, that we would echo the words of Jacob in a unified chorus: "How awesome is this place! This is none other than the house of God."

4

THE FOSSIL RECORD

NOT ONLY DO ROCKS GIVE US IMPORTANT information about the age
of the earth, but certain rocks, due to the process of fossilization, also
provide information about the sorts of organisms that were present at
the time of rock formation. The primary way fossilization is initiated is
through the rapid burial of organisms in sediment. As time goes by, the
sediment gets packed more and more firmly as new sedimentary layers are added above. With time the water is squeezed out, and eventually the sediment becomes mineralized (that is, converted into rock),
leaving an impression of the preserved parts of the trapped organism.
Usually, but not always, the fossil consists only of the hard parts,
namely the skeleton or shell.

GRADUAL CHANGE IN FOSSILS: CORRELATION WITH AGE OF
THE ROCKS

In rocks over 1 billion years old (see chapter three for a discussion of
dating mechanisms), the only signs of preexisting life are the micro-
scopically small fossils of single-celled organisms. In fact, generally, it is
only as scientists explore sedimentary rock younger than 550 million
years that fossils of multicellular organisms are found. Significantly,
however, rocks of that age contain only *simple* multicelled organisms.
Animals without a backbone (that is, invertebrates) are found in rocks
of this age, but fossils of more sophisticated animals are never found. If
they examine rocks that are a little more recent—say, 500 million years
of age—they find fossils of fish, but these fish are very different from

ours of today; the bodies of these fish were apparently surrounded by bony armor, and they contained no jawbones in their skull. Rocks that are 350 to 500 million years old have fossils of fish that have jaws, but they never have the remains of amphibians (such as frogs and salamanders) or reptiles. Beginning in rocks that are about 350 million years of age, scientists find the remains of the first land animals, amphibians and insects, followed in about 50 million years by reptiles and, beginning at about 230 million years, by mammals. Finally, in rocks that are about 150 million years of age, fossilized birds have been found.

The assortment of birds, mammals and other vertebrates present in these early years is much different from the sorts of animals that exist today. Throughout that time, from 230 million years ago until 65 million years ago, dinosaurs dominated the reptile world. The initial birds, as shown by the oldest rocks, had teeth and had real tails (quite different from the little nubbins that birds have at their hind end today). The mammalian fossils that are found in those oldest rocks are all tiny—about the size of a mouse. All of that changes, however, as younger rocks are examined. Gradually, as the rocks examined are younger and younger, we see fossils that increasingly resemble the fauna present on our earth today. Plant fossils also undergo changes that are correlated with the age of the rocks. Examine figure 4.1 and keep in mind that there is a very good correlation between the age of the rocks and the sorts of organisms that are present. The diagram shows only a single type of organism for each date. Keep in mind that there are many of these extremely unusual species present in rocks of the early years. Our more "modern" species of mammals are only found in rocks that are younger than 65 million years.

It is as though the rocks are a great file cabinet of some of the organisms that have lived on the surface of the earth. We can date the "file cabinet drawer," then look inside. What we see is a near-perfect correlation between age of the drawer and the sorts of organisms that are found in it. It is difficult to reach any conclusion other than that there has been a gradual change in the types of organisms that have existed on earth. Those of us who accept this record and believe in a Creator think that what has been discovered is the great file cabinet of God's

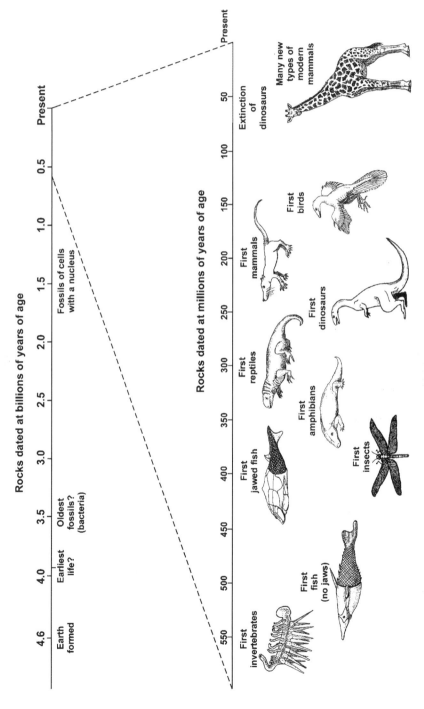

Figure 4.1. The first appearance of various life forms in the fossil record.

creation—250,000 species preserved for us to examine in wondrous detail. There is nothing unbiblical about this. Remember, we are trying to distinguish between two possible views of Genesis 1. The first asserts that God created and that there is no figurative language associated with the Genesis 1 description of creation. The second view asserts that God created but that the account of God's work is recorded in the form of a great hymn celebrating God's work without trying to present a scientific record of precisely what happened. We see hymns of that sort throughout the Scripture, especially in the Psalms. Psalm 18 speaks of God having nostrils that breathe out smoke and a mouth that spews fire. Just as for Genesis 1, we can consider two views of this psalm. The first asserts that God really does have nostrils and a mouth and that God really does breathe out smoke and fire when he is angry. The second asserts that the psalmist, David, was describing the anger of God in a manner to which we can all relate, using figurative language that leads us to a better understanding of the nature of God. We might never have known for sure which view of Genesis 1 was correct were it not for God's allowing humans to examine the fossil record and discover the nature of God's creative work in all of its majesty—gradual, not sudden.[1]

It is important to note, at this point, that the record of the rocks does not in any way imply that God was absent from creation or that God merely established the rules and then sat back and watched it all unfold. It simply says that initially the creation consisted of simple organisms and that in later times they were joined by newly created, increasingly sophisticated organisms.

THREE VIEWS OF THE MEANING OF THE FOSSIL RECORD

For the Christian, given the immense age of the earth, and given the fossil record as I have described it thus far, there are three reasonable possibili-

---

[1]Although it is true that we might never have known *for sure* which view is correct without data gathered from God's world rather than God's Word, nonetheless many theologians believe that one can frequently tell whether a given text should be taken figuratively or literally by using exegetical tools. This involves a careful analysis of the language, setting and overall biblical context. The widely respected evangelical theologian Henri Blocher explains these tools in an especially articulate analysis of the early chapters of Genesis. Henri Blocher, *In the Beginning* (Downers Grove, Ill.: InterVarsity Press, 1984).

ties that might (at least initially) appear to be consistent with that record.

Possibility 1. God created each individual species from scratch (that is, from nothing), one species at a time. In the early days of God's activity, God chose to create the simplest organisms, but as time went by, God eventually got to the more sophisticated ones. In each case, though, God created each species new—from nothing.[2]

Possibility 2. God created specific types of organisms in bursts of creative activity and then, by what some people refer to as microevolution, organisms underwent changes to produce a series of related species. For example, perhaps God created a prototype dog organism. As time went by, foxes, wolves, hyenas and even our modern domestic dog arose from the prototype by natural processes. According to this view, the various dog-related species that exist can all trace their lineage back to a single dog prototype created by God. Dogs and cats, on the other hand, being very different animals, do not share the same common ancestor. They come from different prototypes.

Possibility 3. God creates by guiding and influencing a process that involves gradual change. Animals, plants and other organisms really do share common ancestors, but through a process continually under the control of God's Presence, the history of life has taken the course that it has. According to this view, God is not necessarily more active at one time than another. Rather "the Spirit of God [is] hovering" over creation (Gen 1:2), always present and always in control as creation unfolds according to God's will and God's command.[3]

We cannot, in the opinion of many Christians, distinguish among

---

[2]Some readers will hold to a variant of possibility 1. Remaining skeptical of dating mechanisms (despite the information provided in chapter three), they believe that God created each species from scratch but that God did it only six thousand years ago and in six twenty-four-hour days. We will call this variant possibility 1a. There is much more to be said about this possibility throughout the remainder of the book. Its correctness or incorrectness does not hinge upon dating mechanisms alone.

[3]Some individuals hold to a variant of possibility 3. According to this view, God established a set of rules and, following that, let things run with minimal interference. Many, including myself, are uncomfortable with this view largely on theological grounds. The God of the Old and New Testament is not an absentee landlord. The biblical view of God is that his Presence is immanent and accessible. If that is true for the God of the Bible in its entirety, I would hold that it also the case for the God of creation. The biblical account gives no hint of a Creator who starts the process and then steps aside.

these three possibilities on the basis of Scripture alone. The biblical account tells us that God created, and science makes it clear that God did it over a long period of time (see chapter three). Scripture does tell us a little about the nature of God's action. For example, Genesis 1:20 states, "Let the water teem with living creatures, and let birds fly above the earth," and Genesis 1:24 states, "Let the land produce living creatures according to their kinds." Clearly it happened at God's command, but how? All three possibilities emphasize God's creative activity, and all are equally consistent with Genesis 1.

Given the contention that each of the three possibilities is "scripturally equal," we will now begin the process of determining which is most consistent with what we know from sources other than Scripture. In so doing, it is important that one not make the assumption that the gathering of information from the created world is somehow stepping away from God's Word to us. John 1:1 says, "In the beginning was the Word, and the Word was with God, and the Word was God." And John 1:3 states, "Through him all things were made; without him nothing was made that has been made." This world that science studies is God's created world. When we leave our Bibles and set out to study the world around us, we do not somehow leave God behind, back in our Bibles. God *was* present in his creation, and God *is* still present in his creation. Hence, as we look at that creation, we are exploring the things of God in a manner that has some similarities to what we do when we study Scripture. The Bible is a sacred book, but there is also a sense in which the earth and its constituents—as God's handiwork—are sacred too. As we study God's universe, we do not leave God's Presence. As long as we are Christians, peering into creation through the lens of faith, we abide in that Presence.

THE SUDDEN APPEARANCE OF CELLS ON EARTH?
One of the most amazing facts arising from the study of rocks is that evidence of life has been found in rocks as old as from 3.5 to 3.8 billion years in age—fairly close to the age of the earth itself.[4] When the earth

---

[4]E. G. Nisbet and N. H. Sleep, "The Habitat and Nature of Early Life," *Nature* 409 (2001): 1083-91; S. Simpson, "Questioning the Oldest Signs of Life," *Scientific American* 288, no. 4 (2003): 70-77.

was first formed, it was continually bombarded by gigantic meteors and its surface was very hot. Most scientists estimate that it would not have cooled down sufficiently for life to become established until very close to the time when evidence for life actually appears in the fossil record. Life, of course, is extremely complex, and although we may not know what processes were taking place in the oldest of the cells seen in the fossil record, it is truly amazing to see evidence for cells at all in rocks from the earth's cradle period.

When scientists look at this data without the lens of faith, they propose, given the atmospheric conditions and the composition of the earth, that the origin of life is a highly probable natural event. As Christians, we believe that although it was indeed a highly probable event, its high probability relates to the fact that it was responding to God's command and God's Presence.

Two fundamental questions related to the origin of cells present themselves. One relates to the chemistry of the molecules found in cells. Much research is going on pertaining to the origin of these molecules. Unfortunately it is not known for certain what the atmospheric conditions at the time of life's birth were like. If, as many scientists believe, the atmospheric conditions were such that electrons could easily be removed from newly formed molecules (this is termed a *reducing atmosphere*), then molecules like amino acids, purines, pyrimidines and sugars, all of which are fundamental to life as we know it, would readily have been produced. The hesitation about whether the early conditions were "reducing" was alleviated somewhat by the discovery of a 4.6-billion-year-old meteorite that broke off from an asteroid and landed on the earth's surface. It had most of these substances within it.[5] If the molecules were readily produced in a meteorite, within our own solar system, it seems likely to many scientists that they would also have been readily produced on the surface of the earth. Nonetheless there is debate over the issue, and the fact is that scientists do not know for sure whether the atmosphere

---

[5]E. T. Peltzer, J. L. Bada, G. Schlesinger and S. L. Miller, "The Chemical Conditions on the Parent Body of the Murchison Meteorite: Some Conclusions Based on Amino-, Hydroxy-, and Dicarboxylic Acids," *Advances in Space Research* 4 (1984): 69-74.

here was conducive to the removal of electrons.[6]

Putatively describing the origin of molecules that serve as the building blocks of life is quite different from describing the origin of the intricate "machinery" that makes up a functioning cell. Herein lies the second question: the origin of cells themselves. Living cells are like a miniaturized factory, a hub of assembly and disassembly, complete with their own set of intricate instructions that are followed to a T. The world of science has hardly begun to explore how the cell, in all of its complexity, might have arisen. In fact so amazed are some scientists with the rapidity of the appearance of cells on earth (almost immediately after the earth cooled enough to allow its existence) that they have proposed that life did not originate here. With that in mind, it has been suggested that life might well have got its start elsewhere in the universe, someplace where more time might have been available for it to get started. In that case, according to the proposal, it would have been carried here on a meteorite or some other extraterrestrial body.[7]

As Christians, we view the appearance of those cells through our lens of faith. The first cells, we believe, appeared when they did in response to God's command and through the continuous presence of God's Spirit. Whether cells originated 3.8 billion years ago, 3.8 million years ago or even 3,800 years ago is of no particular consequence to us. Once life is viewed through the lens of faith, once we believe that it happened at God's command and because of God's Presence, theologically it becomes somewhat irrelevant as to when it happened. We can simply "sit back" and let the data of God's created world tell us when. Consider once more possibilities 1 through 3 described above. When it comes to the origin of cells, the three do not differ; they only relate to the origin of species. Each of them proposes that cells appeared because of God's command. How long it took for God's command to be fulfilled is immaterial. God may have performed a miracle such that, out of nowhere, in an instant, the first cell appeared. I wish you and I were able to get into a time machine that would take us back in time to

[6]For a review of this work, see A. Lazcano and S. L. Miller, "The Origin and Early Evolution of Life: Prebiotic Chemistry, the Pre-RNA World, and Time," *Cell* 85 (1996): 793-98.
[7]See Francis Crick, *Life Itself: Its Origin and Nature* (New York: Simon & Schuster, 1981).

be present for the event. Probably we would want to bring along a microscope so we could observe it, along with some test tubes so we could analyze the nature of the molecules inside the cells. If we were able to do this, it is possible that our observations would show that the first cells appeared in an instant. That would be fine. It would be consistent with Scripture, and we could then return to the twenty-first century to report our exciting adventure.

However, is there not an alternative observation that would also be consistent with Scripture and with each of those three possibilities related to the origin of species? Is it not possible that God's Presence and God's command might have subtly influenced natural processes, causing the otherwise very unlikely to become likely? According to this line of thinking, God might have worked in such subliminal ways that you and I, with our microscopes and test tubes, would never be able to point to a specific miracle—not, that is, until we stood back, looked at the completed product and calculated the probability of that set of events occurring *without* God's Presence and *without* God's command.[8] In fact, is it not possible, by this view, that it might have taken millions of years from start to finish for the molecules to assemble into the completed factory that is the cell? (Remember, the difference between 4 billion years when the earth may have been starting to cool and 3.8 billion years when cells may have appeared is 200 million years.)

Consider the following analogy. Let's pretend we could go on a different journey in time and space back to the studio of Leonardo da Vinci to observe him painting the *Mona Lisa*. If you and I were able to go back in time to watch and analyze da Vinci's individual brush strokes with our handy microscope and test tubes, we would never know a masterpiece was being painted. As we used our twenty-first-century sophistication to examine the chemical composition of the paint laid on the canvas, we might be able to explain all the details of why some chemicals have one color and others a different color. We

---

[8]Because it is not possible to go back in time with our microscopes and test tubes, we will never be able to do this formal calculation. However, living in the present, especially if we look at the product through faith spectacles, we can become certain that what we observe has been produced by the master painter—our Creator, God.

might be able to explain the principle of how the paint sticks to the canvas and why some canvases are better than others. We might even analyze the brush stroke and explain perfectly all the maneuvers of the painter's hand and brush. "Looks like an ordinary painting to us," I am sure we would conclude. Little would we know, by those techniques alone, that the mind of a genius was guiding the paint as it appeared on the canvas. Analyzing only the brush strokes cannot demonstrate the artistic majesty of da Vinci's work. Only as we stand back and view the completed painting in all of its beauty can we recognize that a master has been at work guiding the brush to the artist's desired end.

If this is how God created life—gradually, using strokes that to scientists almost appear to be ordinary chemistry when analyzed through the myopic lens of their scientific tools—would it be any less of a miracle? Even if scientists were able to explain the detailed, natural-appearing steps in the history of life's origins, does that in any way imply that the work they describe was not guided by the hand of the Master? The majestic living picture of the interior of the cell is a masterpiece like no other. Created by the Word of God's command and the Spirit of God's presence, and nurtured by the vision of God the Father for his offspring, the cell is God's painting come to life. When one examines this whole living picture in all of its moving majesty, is the question of whether it took 200 million years or 200 microseconds even relevant? Gradual or sudden, is one somehow less the work of God than the other?

The three possibilities for the origin of species are all consistent with New and Old Testament Scripture. Each recognizes that "in the beginning was the Word. . . . Through him all things were made; without him nothing was made that has been made" (Jn 1:1, 3). Further, each recognizes that species originated because "God's Spirit was hovering over the waters" (Gen 1:2). Possibility 1 states that each new species arose from nothing. Possibility 2 states that each new prototype arose fresh, perhaps from nothing, and that new, related species arose from the prototype by "microevolution." Possibility 3 states that each new species arose from previously existing species. With respect to each of these three possibilities, the question of whether cells arose gradually (over hundreds of millions of years) or suddenly (in an instant) is irrelevant. The important thing is that it happened at God's command and because of God's Presence.

THE SUDDEN APPEARANCE OF MULTICELLULAR LIFE?

The "rapid" and unexplained appearance of cells is just one intriguing piece of information to come from the fossil record.[9] I have emphasized that the rapidity and inexplicability may or may not have theological significance. As Creator, God may or may not choose to work in sudden, dramatic fashion. It is entirely possible that God may choose to work so subtly in influencing natural-*appearing* processes that the mechanistic-reductionist approach that scientists use would fail to detect contingency on God's command and Presence. God is free to work in whatever way God chooses, be it subtle or explosive.

From the appearance of the first cells, we move on to explore other intriguing stories that emerge from analysis of fossil data. Much has been written about the "sudden" appearance of animal life about 545 million years ago. Having occurred at the beginning of what is known as the Cambrian geological era, this apparently seminal event in the history of life has been termed the Cambrian explosion. Although scientists are still debating the evidence, one view of the fossil record is that many of the major animal body plans (they are called phyla) appeared within 15 to 20 million years of each other. A body plan is simply the basic design features of an organism. Arthropods (crabs, insects and spiders, for example), with their jointed legs and external body skeleton, represent one body plan. Annelids (like the earthworm), with their repeated body segments, are built according to a different body plan. Nematodes are unsegmented worms, and they represent a third body plan. Our own group, known as the phylum Chordata, has a body plan that consists of a nerve cord running down the back side and several distinctive embryonic features (gill pouches and a support rod, known as the *notochord*). All members of our group have these features—frogs, mice and fish, to name just a few. Almost all of the basic

---

[9]It is termed "rapid" in the geological sense, that is, relative to the time of earth's formation and in light of the appearance of cells "soon" afterward. Depending on one's perspective, upward of 200 million years is no short period of time.

body plans that exist in the animal world (including our own) appear to have made their grand entrance on earth about the time of the Cambrian explosion. This does not mean insects appeared at that time (indeed they did not), but organisms with key design features similar to those that characterize insects and crabs *are* found in rocks of this age and are not found in rocks older than this. Also, it certainly does not mean that frogs and mice were present then, but fossils with some of their basic features, such as a spinal cord running along the back, are found in rocks of this age and have not been observed in rocks older than 550 million years.

Because of the "explosion" in fossil diversity in rocks of this age, some Christians take this to be an indication of a burst of creative activity of God. The notion of an "explosion of new species" in a geological "instant" is especially noteworthy in the light of possibility 2—the creation of prototypes in a flurry of creative activity.[10]

The idea of a Cambrian explosion became especially well known as the result of a highly popular book called *Wonderful Life*, by the late Harvard scholar Steven Jay Gould.[11] It is important to note, however, that the existence of this explosion is highly controversial in the halls of science. Gould was an outstanding writer who produced books and articles intended for the nonscientific public. Because of that, ideas he supported are especially well known by nonscholars, while the ideas of competing scientific views are not as well known. The fact is that many biologists doubt that the Cambrian explosion ever really occurred. Some think it is an artifact. What really happened, they believe, is that about 550 million years ago a change resulted in a much greater likelihood of fossilization. Because of that, they reason, the "sudden" appearance of multicellular animals in the fossil record is not so much the reflection of a dramatic change in *which* animals were here; rather it is a reflection of the preservability of those animals that did exist and thereby their likelihood to make an appearance in the fossil record.[12]

---

[10]Keep in mind that this "geological instant" is 10 to 20 million years, or about 250,000 to 500,000 human generations.

[11]Steven J. Gould, *Wonderful Life* (New York: W. W. Norton, 1989).

[12]See, for example, G. A. Wray, J. S. Levinton and L. H. Shapiro, "Molecular Evidence for Deep Pre-Cambrian Divergencies Among Metazoan Phyla," *Science* 274 (1996): 568-73.

Other biologists stress that the organisms discovered in fossils of the Cambrian era did not represent truly distinct body plans—not yet. According to this view, they were, in many cases, intermediates with some of the attributes of a particular phylum, but not all of them.[13]

Regardless of whether the Cambrian explosion turns out to be real, caution is advisable before we latch onto possibility 2. Even if there was a flurry of new prototypes created at that time, its result is not nearly as dramatic as many in the public seem to think. There were no insects, sea stars, crabs, snails, spiders, fish, frogs, lizards, crocodiles, birds, mice, dogs, cats, monkeys, elephants, whales, land plants and countless other "prototypes"—these all occurred much, much later. Figure 4.2 depicts several of the sorts of animals that were present about 545 million years ago based upon the fossil record. Note that theirs were very different from the body forms to which we are accustomed. The "prototypes" of today's organisms make their appearance gradually in the fossil record and at successive times (examine figure 4.1 again). In short there is little evidence to support the notion of a small number of distinct bursts of creative activity (possibility 2), and this is further substantiated below.

Before we go on to explore what the fossil record has to say about the appearance of other multicellular organisms, it is important to pause and think about what we personally experience, as Christians, with regard to the nature of God's activity. Most of us believe God does not *only* work in our lives through sudden and spectacular means; God's Spirit works in our lives in subtle ways as well. In fact most of us would agree that God's Holy Spirit is always at work in our lives and that his Presence is frequently manifest in a manner so subtle that if we were to analyze many of the individual events, the manifestation of God's Presence might even be open to other interpretations. Often it is only as we stand back and look at God's work through our lens of faith that we are able to perceive that it was the Holy Spirit who made the difference—God's gentle, subtle but all-powerful Holy Spirit.

---

[13]For a good review of this idea, see S. C. Morris, "Nipping the Cambrian 'Explosion' in the Bud?" *Bioessays* 22 (2000): 1053-56.

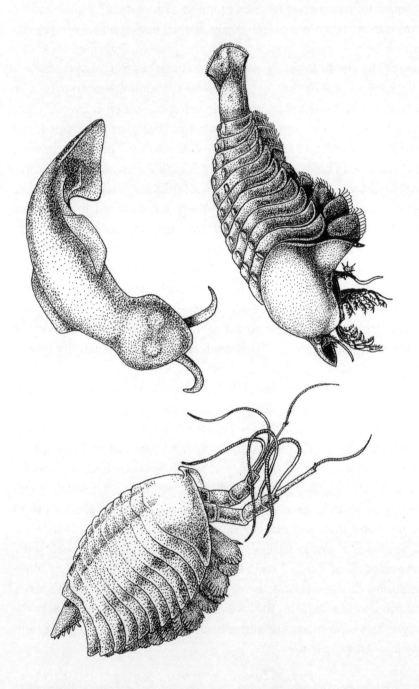

Figure 4.2. Examples of fossilized animals present in rocks dated at about 545 million years

One of my favorite passages of Scripture is the story of Elijah when he was at the lowest point in his life. So depressed was he that he said, "I have had enough, LORD. Take my life" (1 Kings 19:4). After some time, God led him up a great mountain, where Elijah was told that the Presence of the Lord was about to pass by. This is what happened:

> A great and powerful wind tore the mountains apart and shattered the rocks before the LORD, but the LORD was not in the wind. After the wind there was an earthquake, but the LORD was not in the earthquake. After the earthquake came a fire, but the LORD was not in the fire. And after the fire came a gentle whisper. When Elijah heard it, he pulled his cloak over his face and went out and stood at the mouth of the cave. (1 Kings 19:11-13)

The reason Elijah put his cloak over his face as he emerged from the cave is that in the soft, almost silent whisper was to be found the Presence of God. God works in different ways, and if God's work in creation was primarily in the form of a whisper, then we need to be prepared to come out of our cave and, like Elijah, stand in awe, because we are emerging onto the holy ground of God's creation. Follow along through the rest of the chapter as we explore whether possibility 3 is the correct one, but do so in a spirit of worship—"cloak over your face"—listening for the whisper of God.

THE SUDDEN APPEARANCE OF SOME MODERN PROTOTYPES?

Elephants? Few mammals are more recognizable for their distinctive body form than the elephant. Its massive trunk is used in breathing, smell, touch, manipulation of objects and generation of sound. So sensitive are its muscles and nerves that with the end of its trunk an elephant can pick up a peanut, crack it open with the little tip on the trunk's back side, blow away the shell and gently place the two kernels into its mouth. In contrast to this delicate procedure, an elephant can use its trunk to lift and move logs weighing nearly half a ton.[14] To counter this massive weight (plus the five-hundred-pound mass of the

---

[14]J. Shoshani, "Understanding Proboscidean Evolution: A Formidable Task," *Trends in Ecology and Evolution* 13 (1998): 480-87.

head itself), the elephant has a short neck for mechanical advantage and a tendon as thick as the human arm stretching back to anchor the head to bony projections jutting upward from individual vertebrae.[15]

In addition to its many distinctive outward features, the elephant has many unusual skeletal features of the sort that are preserved in fossils. The massive amount of muscle in the trunk must be anchored to the skull, so the elephant possesses a large and distinctively placed opening through which the ends of these many muscle groups pass on the way to their internal attachment site. Other mammals have the same opening, but it is not nearly as large and is placed lower on the skull. Further, the elephant has another opening, known as the *infraorbital canal*, through which a large mass of blood vessels and nerves pass. Other mammals have this same opening, but it is proportionally much smaller in them. Elephants are also distinctive for the formation of tusks, which are really just overgrown 2 incisor teeth (that is, the second tooth in from the middle).

In short, the shape, bone structure and features of the skull, the structure of the neck and limbs, and other skeletal features set the elephant apart from all other animals. We might think of the elephant as a sort of prototype. Since it is large, with thick bones, it is easily fossilized and readily recovered by paleontologists. What does the fossil record have to say about the origin of this prototype—was it sudden (possibility 2) or gradual (possibility 3)? What about the possibility that each member of the prototype was created one at a time from scratch (possibility 1)? Let's examine what the fossil data has to tell us.

Fossils provide a record of 164 different elephant-related species, all considered to be within the group known as Proboscidea. Only two remain in existence today: the African elephant *(Loxodonta africana)* and the Asian elephant *(Elephas maximus)*. The wooly mammoth *(Mammuthus primigenius)*, a third species that went extinct four thousand years ago, has been preserved in ice, and there is at least a slight possibility that it may someday be brought back into existence through cloning technology. Another species of mammoth, *Mammuthus columbi*,

---

[15]J. Shoshani, "It's a Nose! It's a Hand! It's an Elephant's Trunk," *Natural History* 11 (1997): 37-44.

with its fourteen-foot-long tusks, and the slightly smaller and distantly related mastodon, *Mammut americanum,* probably thrived in my own San Diego neighborhood until about twenty thousand years ago. We know this because within 120 miles of my home is the site of the La Brea tar pits in downtown Los Angeles. For centuries, animals would visit this site, thinking that it was a pond, only to get trapped in a gooey mess of partially liquid tar where they would then become preserved in perpetuity as fossils. If you happen to visit southern California, drop by for a visit at the Page Museum, where you will be able to see a couple of these individuals in all of their bony wonder.

Because elephants and their cousins have such distinctive skeletal features, and because they fossilized particularly well through history, it is possible to trace the history of these magnificent beasts. Fossils formed about 50 million years ago preserve the representation of animals that had many of the skeletal features of the elephant group. In those days they were the size of a small pig and did not have a trunk (as judged by the skull features mentioned above). However, in rocks that are younger (30 to 40 million years old), it becomes apparent that members of the elephant family were becoming much bigger and that they had the appropriate openings to accommodate a small trunk. As they increased in size, the head was concomitantly lifted a greater distance from the ground—the taller the body, the further the mouth is from a ground food supply. The elephant-related families have had two ways of handling this problem of increased distance to the ground: one was to increase the length of the lower jaw; the other was to have a long trunk. Figure 4.3 has a drawing of *Platybelodon,* which had a very long lower jaw with two long, flat teeth protruding from it, creating a jaw that was almost like a shovel. The figure also shows a cousin species, alive at the same time, without the long jaw but with a very long trunk. By 7 to 10 million years ago, the species that were present all had full-length trunks and those with the long lower jaw had gone extinct.

Let's return to the first of the three possibilities for the mechanism of creation, namely the idea that each species was created from scratch, one at a time. If this was indeed the mechanism used by God, it is intriguing that God made no elephantlike organisms for the first 98.7

Rocks dated at:

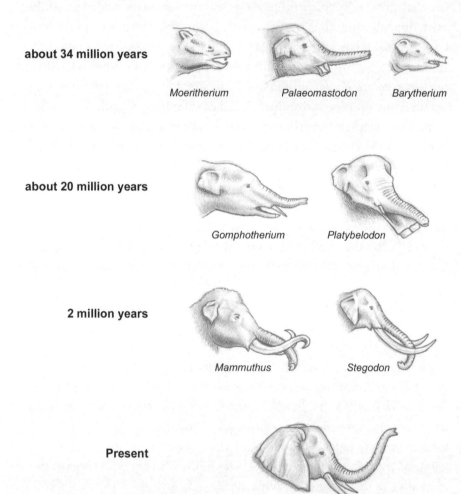

about 34 million years

Moeritherium   *Palaeomastodon*   *Barytherium*

about 20 million years

Gomphotherium   *Platybelodon*

2 million years

Mammuthus   *Stegodon*

Present

Loxodonta

Figure 4.3. Changes in the elephant line over the past 34 million years

percent of the earth's history. (The last 55 million years corresponds to just 1.3 percent of the history of the earth.) It is also interesting that when God started to create elephantlike species, none of them had a trunk. All of these animals went extinct. He then proceeded to create new species with trunks, initially short, but as time went by, he made new, taller species and gave them much longer trunks. They also went extinct. Finally, over the past 5 million years or so, God created species that increasingly resemble the species of today. If God did create each of the scores of elephantlike species from scratch, it is clear that there is a pattern to that construction. The closer we get to the present, the more the new species came to resemble our current species.

This notion that God suddenly started to make elephantlike species from scratch in the last 1 percent (or so) of earth's history is intriguing, especially if one also considers the gradual change in God's products as the millennia wore on. However, there is nothing in Scripture that mandates this "creation from scratch" view, or even insinuates it, and because of that we can be hesitant to accept it. The Bible says that the creation of life's varieties happened at God's command, but it says nothing at all about whether it occurred from scratch, nor does it say with certainty that it happened by one unique command for each unique species. If a person wants to believe this, he or she is free to do so, but it is inappropriate to insist that this is *the* biblical view.

An alternative way of thinking is that all creation happened at God's command and under the influence of his Presence but *not* in a manner that is analogous to Geppetto building Pinocchio in his woodworking shop or a group of architects and engineers designing and building a magnificent bridge (possibility 1). The Bible tells us that God created, but it does not tell us how, and we need to be careful that we do not force the God of the universe into one of our human molds. We must not limit God's activity to our conceptions of how we think we would work if we were God.

What do we learn about the nature of God's activity from studying the Bible? One thing that we learn is that God builds freedom into his creation. Consider, for example, John 3:16: "God so loved the world that he gave his one and only Son, that whoever believes in him shall not perish but have eternal life." The key phrase in this passage is "whoever believes." In other words, God is not coercive. He gives us the freedom to believe or not to believe. Those who choose to believe will have eternal life; those who do not so choose will not have eternal life. This emphasis on freedom in God's creation is seen throughout the Bible. God's Presence affects outcomes, often in miraculous ways, but always in the context of human freedom. King Saul let God down and failed the nation of Israel terribly; King David, on the other hand, was a man after God's own heart (1 Sam 19:14). They were both free men, not pawns of a puppet master in the sky nor robots responding to a celestial button pusher. Their choices were made in God-granted liberty. When Ananias and Sapphira sold their property (Acts 5:1-11), they could have given all of the proceeds to God. They made the choice not to do so, and they made that choice in freedom. When the dying Stephen prayed, "Lord do not hold this sin against them" (Acts 7:60), he was not coerced into uttering those heart-wrenching words. They came from the depths of who he was. It was a cry of love for his executioners, and there was no marionette master pulling the strings of his vocal cords.

The Bible states that God gave the creation command and that this resulted in each of the various "kinds" being produced. It is clear that, as a result of God's command and in his Presence, scores of elephantlike species were created, but the Bible does not specify that God uttered a unique command, one at a time, for each new species. Just as God built freedom into the nation of Israel, and just as God builds freedom into our lives today, so freedom may well be a central component of God's biological world as well. This is not to say that God is not playing a supervisory role in creation in a manner resembling the role God plays in my life and yours. But there is no a priori scriptural reason to assume that the biological world was created one species at a time by the God of the universe "pushing creation buttons" each time he wanted a new species. He does not do that in the daily affairs of my life (for which I am grateful), and there is no reason, scriptural or otherwise, to assume that he does that in the biological world either. God's Spirit guides the progression of life. His Presence is never far from creation, just as it is never far from the events of my life. Nonetheless God respects my freedom and (I suspect) values freedom in the rest of creation as well.

Turtles? One of the big objections that certain people have to the notion of creation by gradual change is a perceived (in their minds) absence of transitional forms in the fossil record. In the remainder of this chapter, I will explore whether this perception is correct. We will do that by examining the fossil record of several different groups of animals to see if transitional species exist in the record and, if not, why not?

Just as elephants are highly distinctive in the mammalian world, so too are turtles in the world of reptiles. Few body forms are more distinctive and recognizable. Although approximately 260 species of turtles still exist in the world today, many of these are environmentally sensitive and in danger of losing out to the onslaught of human activity.

The turtle body plan is one of the oldest and most conservative (unchanging) among all vertebrates. Turtles first appear in the fossil record in rocks dated at 210 million years of age, making them four times more ancient than the elephant-related group we talked about in the previous section. Now for the important question: do they appear all at once, or is it possible to detect some turtlelike species that resided on earth "shortly" before turtles themselves appeared? Figure 4.4 shows the existence of a group of reptiles that have a number of skeletal features characteristic of the turtles. At 255 million years ago, organisms existed that had small, bony plates in the center of their backs. These plates were not complete enough to have served the current function of the turtle shell: protection and insulation. It is believed that they existed to provide additional structural support for the backbone. In rocks that are not quite so old (248 million years) fossils are found in which the bony plates cover most of the upper surface but are not fused. Another species present at about the same time had fused bony plates that did indeed cover the entire body. It was not a characteristic turtle shell, but it certainly resembled it, and these organisms had other skeletal features as well that resembled the turtle body plan.[16] Most significant of all is that these organisms exist in the fossil record at just the right time—just before the appearance of full-fledged turtles.

---

[16]Michael Lee, "The Turtle's Long-Lost Relatives," *Natural History* 103 (June 1994): 63-65.

Age of Rocks

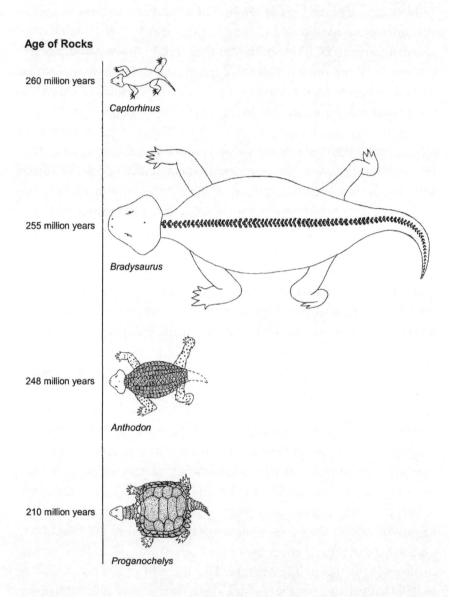

260 million years — *Captorhinus*

255 million years — *Bradysaurus*

248 million years — *Anthodon*

210 million years — *Proganochelys*

Figure 4.4. Changes in turtle-like fossils over time

Elephants and turtles give the same message. They do not appear fully formed all at once in the fossil record. Just before they make their debut, other animals with similar but more primitive features make an entry, only to leave when the "real thing" comes along. Perhaps the whisper at the mouth of our cave is trying to tell us something—something about God's subtlety and something about how God's creation command was really carried out.

Whales? Few groups of animals fascinate us more than dolphins and whales. Together the seventy-five species are known as *cetaceans.* One member of the group, the blue whale, at up to one hundred feet and 160 tons, is the largest animal ever to inhabit the earth, eclipsing even the largest of the dinosaurs. My office in San Diego is located on a bluff overlooking the Pacific Ocean. In the winter months one can sometimes see tour boats congregating at a certain spot out in the ocean. If one looks closely, a spout of shooting air and water will soon be apparent from the vicinity of the boats—a sign that the search for a migrating gray whale has been successful.

We humans love whales. Be it the awe-inspiring song of a courting male humpback, or the majestic beauty of the Orca whale Shamu springing out of the water to the applause of its fans at Sea World, a majesty about the whale grips our spirit. There has long been a mystery associated with whales. The book of Job refers to a massive sea monster, Leviathan. We do not know for sure what is being described (some think it was a huge crocodile, but it could just as well have been a whale) when the Lord says:

> Can you pull in the leviathan with a fishhook
>   or tie down his tongue with a rope?
> Can you put a cord through his nose
>   or pierce his jaw with a hook? . . .
> Any hope of subduing him is false;
>   the mere sight of him is overpowering.
> No one is fierce enough to rouse him. (Job 41:1-2, 8-9)

The mystery associated with whales may be best represented in the novel *Moby-Dick,* a masterpiece written by Herman Melville almost one and a half centuries ago. Melville used the whale to personify the mysterious force of evil, lingering in the background mysteriously and haunting the human spirit. In one section Melville had the narrator of his story wrestling with the question of how to classify this mystifying beast. Is it a whale or a fish? He begins by citing the great biologist Linnaeus and then moves on to his own diagnosis:

> "On account of their warm bilocular heart, their lungs, their movable eyelids, their hollow ears, penem intrantem feminam mammis lactantem," and finally, "ex lege naturae jure meritoque." I submitted all this to my friends Simeon Macey and Charley Coffin, of Nantucket, both messmates of mine in a certain voyage, and they united in the opinion that the reasons set forth were altogether insufficient. Charley profanely hinted they were humbug.
>
> Be it known that, waiving all argument, I take the good old fashioned ground that the whale is a fish, and call upon holy Jonah to back me. This fundamental thing settled, the next point is, in what internal respect does the whale differ from other fish. Above, Linnaeus has given you those items. But in brief, they are these: lungs and warm blood; whereas, all other fish are lungless and cold blooded.
>
> Next: how shall we define the whale, by his obvious externals, so as conspicuously to label him for all time to come? To be short, then, a whale is a spouting fish with a horizontal tail. There you have him. However contracted, that definition is the result of expanded meditation. A walrus spouts much like a whale, but the walrus is not a fish, because he is amphibious, but the last term of the definition is still more cogent, as coupled with the first. Almost any one must have noticed that all the fish familiar to landsmen have not a flat, but a vertical, or up-and-down tail. Whereas, among spouting fish the tail, though it may be similarly shaped, invariably assumes a horizontal position.[17]

Even today, 150 years later, whales have seemed like a biological enigma to many. Herman Melville's narrator aside, they clearly are mammals. Nonetheless, judging from the fossil record, until recently they appeared suddenly—fully and uniquely formed—with no sign of the missing links between them and the rest of the mammalian world. Although biologists have long expected that the missing links may

---

[17]Herman Melville, *Moby-Dick* (New York: Barnes & Noble Books, 1994), p. 132.

someday be found, there was no sign of them—not, at least, until paleontologists diligently set out to search for them in just the right places.
All has changed. Several key links have now been found and the degree of resemblance of these transitional fossils to modern-day whales
is correlated with the age of the rocks in which they are found.

Modern whales have a special sound detection system that is geared
to detecting the directionality of sound in water. It is extremely efficient. Indeed echolocation (the use of sound) is an important naviga-
tional tool in toothed whales and dolphins. Most of the sound is detected, not through external ears like we have, but as a result of
vibrations of the jaw, which are then transmitted to the middle ear
through a "fat pad," which sits in an enlarged hole near the jaw and adjacent to the middle ear. From there, the sound vibrations are deci-
phered in much the same way as they are in other mammals. The jaw
hole, site of the fat pad, is a skeletal feature that is a diagnostic characteristic of whales and dolphins. They all have it. Recently, however, the
fossilized skeleton of a 52-million-year-old whale, *Pakicetus*, was found
in Pakistan at the edge of what is believed to have been a great sea. It
had various diagnostic features that clearly identify it as a small (wolf-
sized) whale. The teeth in this specimen were not whalelike, however;
instead they closely resemble those of certain terrestrial animals
thought previously to be related to whales. Further, the animal had a
terrestrial hearing mechanism—no sign of a housing for the fat pad ap-
paratus that is diagnostic of other whales and dolphins.

Shortly after *Pakicetus* was discovered, another important find occurred, this time in the Egyptian Sahara—many fossils of a whale species, *Basilosaurus*. The rocks in which these fossils were found were considerably younger—about 40 million years of age—and this species is
large (fifty feet). Most noteworthy about these fossils is the wonderful
preservation of an almost complete hind limb. At eighteen inches, the
limb was tiny compared to the fifty-foot length of the whale, but it is a
near-perfect mammalian limb, with exactly the same bone structure as
in other mammals (see figure 4.5). Nearest the body is the standard
thighbone (the femur). Heading out to the tip is a good knee bone (the
patella) and the two calf bones that all of us mammals have (the tibia

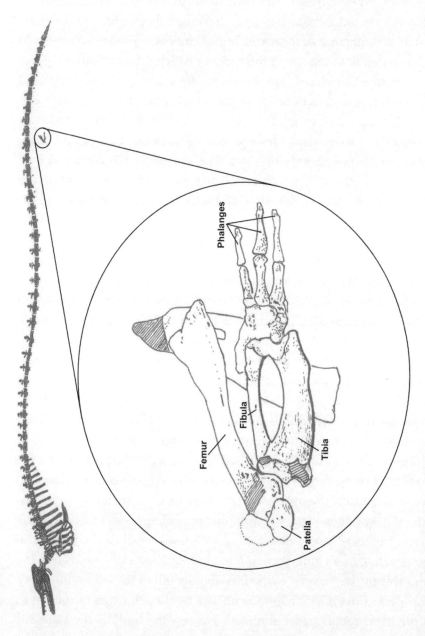

Figure 4.5. *Basilosaurus*, with hind limb (40-million-year-old fossil)

and the fibula). Finally the whale had a foot, with the appropriate ankle, foot and toe bones. Tiny when compared to the rest of the body, this foot probably served no function; rather it was almost certainly a residual structure that was no longer useful but had not yet been eliminated.

To bring the story to completion, we would like a fossil intermediate in age between the almost "modern" *Basilosaurus*, with its 40-million-year-old limbs, and *Pakicetus* at about 52 million years of age. About four hundred feet above the formation that yielded *Pakicetus* was another bed of sedimentary rock that was found to have an almost complete specimen of a whale called *Ambulocetus*. This animal had a variety of skeletal features that clearly earmarked it as a whale, but it had two features at its rear end that were diagnostic of transitional species: full-length hind limbs and a tail (see figure 4.6). The structure of its vertebral column convinces paleontologists that it moved through an up-and-down motion of its spine, much like the vertical motion associated with the cheetah and other members of the cat family. The large feet on this organism were believed to take the place of the fluke of later whales; they would generate the thrust when moved vertically just like the massive, powerful fluke that we see today whenever Shamu surfaces for us at Sea World. As the years have gone by, more intermediates have been found and the story of intermediate fossils from organisms closely related to predecessors of the hippopotamus to whales has become one of the greatest "transitional species" stories in all of biology.[18]

There is an important lesson in this for us. Whales were long cited by some individuals as a clear example of a body plan that must have been built from scratch (possibility 1), since they seemed to appear suddenly in the fossil record. We must be careful about inserting God's activity only where human knowledge appears to be deficient.

---

[18]Three recent articles demonstrate the remarkable advances in understanding of the ancestral history of whales. For a general summary, see K. Wong, "The Mammals That Conquered the Seas," *Scientific American* 286, no. 5 (2002): 70-79. For a more technical discussion, see J. G. M. Thewissen, E. M. Williams, L. J. Roe and S. T. Hussain, "Skeletons of Terrestrial Cetaceans and the Relationship of Whales to Artiodactyls," *Nature* 413 (2001): 277-81; and P. D. Gingerich, M. ul Haq, I. S. Zalmout, I. H. Khan and M. S. Malkani, "Origin of Whales from Early Artiodactyls: Hands and Feet of Eocene Protocetidae from Pakistan," *Science* 293 (2001): 2239-42. Further totally independent genetic evidence for the historical relatedness of whales and hippopotamuses is discussed in chapter six.

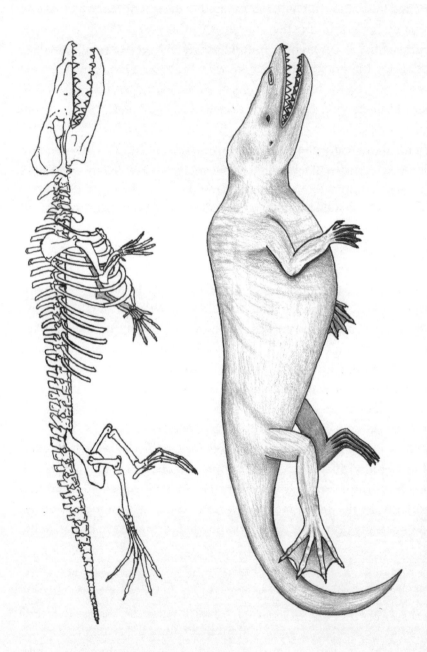

Figure 4.6. *Ambulocetus,* an animal with many whalelike skeletal features present at the time of transition to whales

The gaps in the fossil record are not the places where we should search for God. Rather *all* that happened occurred because of God's Presence, God's command and God's consent. No search is needed! "Though him all things were made; without him nothing was made that has been made" (John 1:3).

The initial transition to land: tetrapods? Rocks of an age older than about 400 million years reveal that the terrestrial, or dry land, portion of the earth was barren for the first 90 percent of its existence: no plants and no animals. All of that changes dramatically, however, beginning in rocks that are younger than 400 million years of age. Those rocks tell us that the earth took on a whole new appearance as land plants were created and the land became green for the first time. Initially the plant species were all small (about twelve inches in height at the most), but it did not stay that way for long. Once plants found these new niches, they thrived. By about 380 million years ago, plant species the size of shrubs were present and the first green revolution was well under way.

Initially animals remained in the oceans; the fossil record of land animals is silent for the first 30 million years after the plant invasion began. Just as rocks of the first 4.2 billion years are silent with respect to land plants, so rocks of the first 4.23 billion years (or so) are silent with respect to land animals. Not surprisingly, however, given all the potential food out there on the land, a new group of animals appears in the fossil record beginning about 370 million years ago. These organisms had several innovative structures that came in handy for life on land among the plants. The most noteworthy structure was legs in the spot where fins reside for seafaring animals. As time went on, there were many additional changes, such as alterations in the structure of the vertebral column. In fish the vertebral column is important for the attachment of muscles that guide the undulatory movement of motility in the water. On land the vertebral column takes on a whole new function; now it is needed as a support rod to hold the body up against the force of gravity as its new limbs lift it up and move it forward. Lungs were not a particularly novel requirement since many fish species already had lungs to supplement their gill respiration. (Indeed even today there are hundreds of air-breathing species of fish.)

Until the past ten years or so, biologists and paleontologists were intrigued by the fact that fossils of this period were either fish or tetrapods (organisms with limbs), with little sign of clear-cut intermediates. That has changed dramatically over the past ten years as a result of several key fossil discoveries. The fish equivalent of limbs are fins. Many of the fish of that era, like today, had spines in their fins with none of the bone structure that characterizes the limbs of land animals. There were, however, a group of fish that did not have spines but rather had distinct bones similar in some ways to those in the limbs of tetrapods. Until recently, recognition of this similarity required a little imagination; it was not particularly convincing. As of 1998, though, that changed. A fossilized fish fin of a new species was discovered in a rock of exactly the right age (370 million years)—just when we might expect transitional organisms to be present. It has a distinct humerus, radius and ulna and a set of eight digits articulating with the fin/hand in much the same way as they do in one of the earliest tetrapods (figure 4.7). Yet the organism with this bone structure in its fin was clearly a fish, as indicated by several skeletal features of the bones that attach the fin to the main part of the body axis.

What about the earliest tetrapods? Unlike fish, all living land vertebrates have a maximum of five digits in the fore and hind limbs. Indeed, in the whole history of life, there have been only a handful of exceptions to this maximum-of-five rule. Remarkably, those exceptions are found only in fossils within a narrow age range—about 370 million years ago. Figure 4.8 shows two of them and compares them to a typical five-digit tetrapod present a little later (320 million years ago).[19] Note that one of these transitional tetrapods had eight digits just like the fish shown in figure 4.7; the other had seven. Note also that both had only a small number of wrist/ankle bones (another transitional feature), which contrasts the more abundant bones in the ankle of the 320-million-year-old fossil tetrapod.

The finding with respect to limbs points out only one of the traits

---

[19]Figure 4.8 is redrawn from F. H. Pough, J. B. Heiser and W. N. McFarland, *Vertebrate Life*, 4th ed. (Upper Saddle River, N.J.: Prentice-Hall, 1996), pp. 288, 302. The species represented are (from left to right) *Acanthostega*, *Ichthyostega* and *Diadectes*.

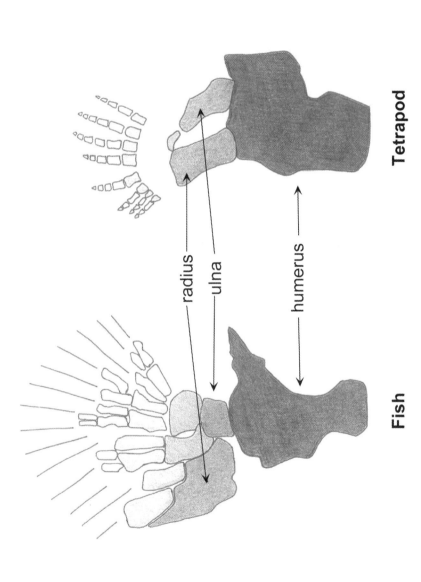

Figure 4.7. Comparison of bones in a specific fish fin to those in the forelimb of a specific tetrapod. (For details see E. B. Daeschler and Neil Shubin, "Fish with Fingers?" *Nature* 391 [1998]: 133.)

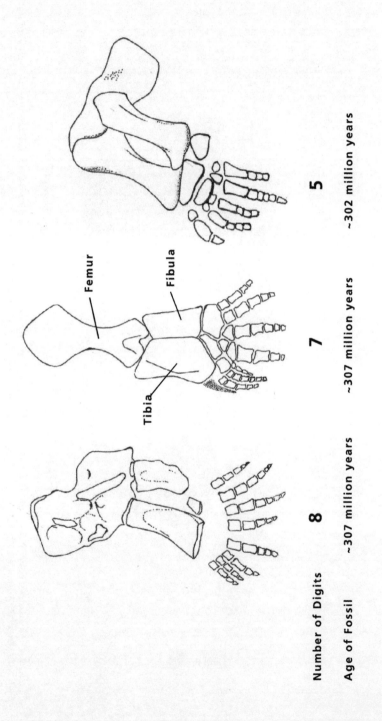

Figure 4.8. Early tetrapod forelimbs

that significantly blur the line between fish and tetrapods in organisms found in rocks dated at about 370 million years of age. *Acanthostega* was much more like a tetrapod than it was like a fish; nonetheless it had several features indicating the presence of internal fishlike gills. Here is another example of transitional features present at just the right time.[20]

The finding of species with transitional features in exactly the time frame in which land animals first begin to appear in the fossil record is too big a coincidence not to mean something. Transitional fish/tetrapod species are found only in rocks of an extremely narrow window of time (about 0.2 percent of the earth's history), and immediately after this, fossils of land animals are found. It seems to me and to almost all other biologists that the data are telling us something about that transition to land. The first land animals were so fishlike that it is virtually certain they were derived from fish.[21]

Should this be a concern to us as Christians? Not at all. Remember the three possibilities that we have been discussing throughout this chapter. Possibility 2 states that God stepped in at those times when a new body plan was needed. Possibility 3 states that God never steps out—all that happens, little and big, takes place because of God's Presence. God, according to possibility 3, is influencing creation events to ensure that what happens proceeds according to God's will and plan. All of the three possibilities are equally compatible with Scripture since God's written Word is silent on the details of the mechanism. To learn about the mechanism, we turn to the data from God's creation. The fossil record is one piece of that data.

Reptiles to mammals? Mammals have been around for a very long time. They first make their appearance in the fossil record in rocks dated at about 225 million years of age. This was well into the age of reptiles. For example, ichthyosaurs (magnificent reptiles that bore a remarkable resemblance to our modern-day dolphins) were frolicking in the sea. At

---

[20]M. I. Coates and J. A. Clack, "Fish-like Gills and Breathing in the Earliest Known Tetrapod," *Nature* 352 (1991): 234-36.
[21]M. I. Coates, J. E. Jeffrey and M. Ruta, "Fins to Limbs: What the Fossils Say," *Evolution and Development* 4 (2002): 390-401.

the same time, the less streamlined plesiosaurs, which used their long, broad and flat limbs as oars to row through the water, were present as well. Dinosaurs were just starting to come into existence, along with the turtles we talked about above. There were no birds in the sky, but the new pterosaurs were just about to make their debut. Magnificent creatures, these ranged from the size of a sparrow to one species that had a wingspan of almost fifty feet. Imagine a creature like this on the top of your home with the wings stretched out well beyond the rooflines on each side. All organisms that fly, be they birds, bats or insects, need to have a flat airfoil surface (that is, wings) to provide lift against the air. In the pterosaurs the lift was provided by way of a membranous flap of skin that stretched from between the body and its attachment to an unimaginably long "ring" finger that grew to become as long as the entire body. (All the other fingers were of normal length.) The stretched-out skin, anchored to the body at one edge and to the enormous finger on the other, served as a massive "Superman's cape" for gliding.

This is the world into which mammals came and in which they lived during those early years. Unlike some of their reptile cousins, and unlike the situation many years later, the early mammals did not dominate the animal landscape. They were tiny animals, usually not much bigger than a mouse. Various skeletal features imply that they had a highly developed sense of smell and much more sensitive hearing than their reptile counterparts. Because of this and other considerations, many scholars think they scampered around for food at night when their warm-bloodedness and improved perception abilities might have provided an advantage against larger reptile predators.

The fossil record indicates a subgroup of the reptiles, known as the *cynodonts*, appeared for the first time about 260 million years ago. As scientists examine fossils that are younger (245 million years old), they begin to see a number of changes in the cynodonts. Specifically, they become increasingly mammal-like. We will focus on just one of these changes—one that is particularly diagnostic of the difference between a reptile and a mammal. Mammals have a much more sensitive system of hearing than do reptiles. Perhaps, if you had a good high school biology course, you will remember that there are three tiny bones in the middle ear—the malleus, the incus and the stapes (also known as the hammer, anvil and stirrup). You might even recall a little about how the system works. When sound waves arrive at the ear, they cause these three bones, each attached to the other, to vibrate. The vibration of the stapes, the last in the three-bone series, behaves like a miniature drumstick, tapping on a tiny opening (the oval window). All mammals employ these bones to perceive sound (see figure 4.9).

Reptiles like the cynodonts have only one bone in the middle ear, the stapes. However, they have two interesting bones located close to this. Termed the *articular* and the *quadrate* bones, they serve as the hinge between the upper and lower jaw. In mammals a different set of bones, the *dentary* and *squamosal*, make up that hinge. Now we come to the amazing part of our story. The cynodonts alive right before the time of the first mammals contained a subgroup of species with a double hinge. The first hinge was a dentary-squamosal junction (just like that found in mammals), and a little further back in the mouth was the second hinge, the "old-fashioned" articular-quadrate junction. Remarkably the old junction is now abutted right up against the eardrum, and it seems highly likely that it was serving a double purpose: that of a hinge and, because of its abutment to the ear drum, that of a transmitter of sound vibrations. Figure 4.10 illustrates this in detail.

The point of all this is that cynodont fossils only slightly older than the origin of mammals have a transitional middle ear. Two bones that had been previously used as the junction point for the jaw are reduced in size and joined by a new set of bones serving as a second junction point. The two reduced bones are positioned adjacent to the "drumstick" (the stapes) in a manner that strongly resembles the incus and malleus in mammals. Virtually all biologists believe that with time, over hundreds of millennia, the other junction point for the jaw became primary and exclusive, while the quadrate-articular bones were freed up to become the famous incus/malleus of the middle ear.

All down through history there had never been organisms like these cynodonts. Indeed, soon after the appearance of mammals, they all went extinct, never to appear again. They were present on the surface of the earth for at most 1 percent of the earth's history, and it just so

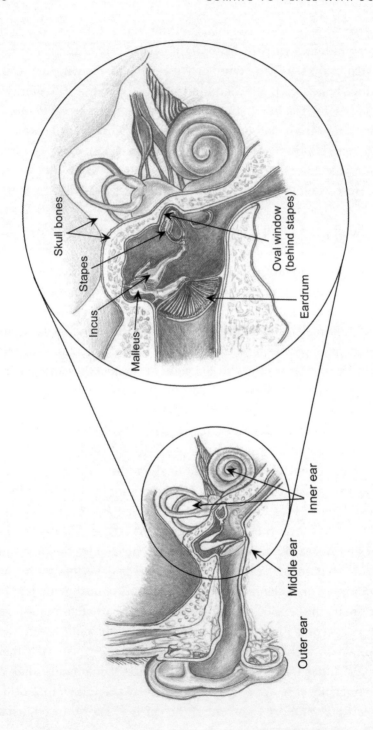

Figure 4.9. The bones of the middle ear

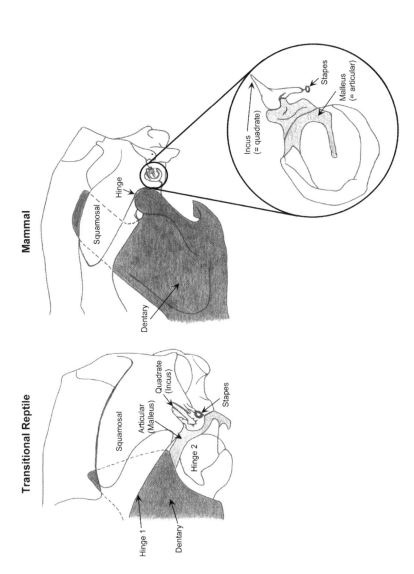

Figure 4.10. Bones of the jaw hinge and the middle ear in a transitional reptile and mammal (See Pough, Heiser and McFarland, *Vertebrate Life*, p. 607)

happens that this corresponds to the time when mammals appear in the fossil record for the first time. Not only that, but also they bear a number of other mammalian trademarks, especially as they relate to tooth structure and other features of the skull. It is hard to be aware of this information without concluding that there really is a set of excellent candidate species for transition between reptiles and mammals. It is simply not true that mammals appear suddenly in the fossil record, fully formed, with no sign of transitional species. In fact the exact reverse is true.

Reptiles to birds? In 1861 a fossil was found with a set of interesting features. That fossil is now known to be about 150 million years old, and six others have been found (figure 4.11). This organism, known as *Archaeopteryx*, had wings, feathers and other features that characterize birds. However, there were some significant differences between it and modern birds. First, you will remember from Thanksgiving dinners that modern birds have something we sometimes refer to as the "parson's nose" at their tail end (officially the structure is called a *pygostyle*). The pygostyle is the equivalent of a bird's tail. It is always a short, fat little structure to which the tail feathers are attached, and birds are able to turn it in flight for maintaining balance. It consists of a set of tiny fused vertebrae. *Archaeopteryx*, like reptiles, did not have a pygostyle. It had a long tail that was almost as long as its body, with feathers coming out from either side (figure 4.12).[22]

Other differences are interesting as well. Those of us who enjoy eating chicken wings will know a little about the anatomy of the wing. Consider this as we start at the inside and work our way out toward the tip. First (and closest to the breast) there is one bone, the humerus. You will remember this bone; it is the one with the most meat on it. (We humans have the same bone. It underlies our biceps.) Then proceeding toward the tip, there are two bones, just like our forearm has two bones in it. But beyond that, instead of fingers, a bird has a single stub. Feathers are attached to this thick fingerlike projection, and the bird can twist and turn it in flight at slow speeds for better navigation.

---

[22]Redrawn from Pat Shipman, *Taking Wing* (New York: Simon & Schuster, 1998), p. 126.

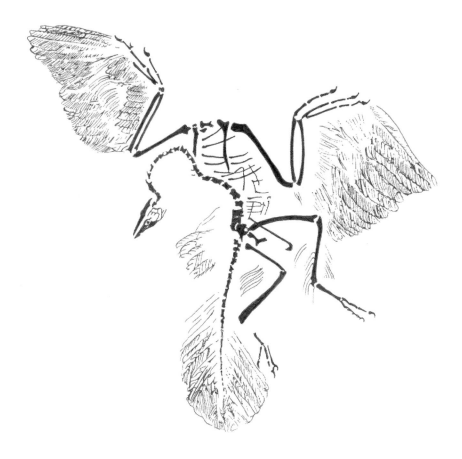

Figure 4.11. *Archaeopteryx* **fossil**

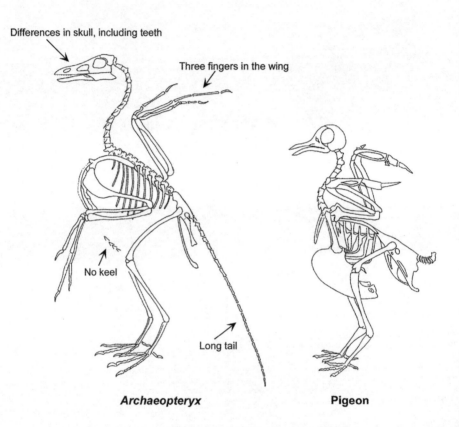

Figure 4.12. *Archaeopteryx* contrasted with a pigeon

Archaeopteryx did not have this little nubbin; instead, like its dinosaur cousins, it had three fingers in the forelimb—three fingers sticking out of its wing. Another thing you may have noticed if you like breast meat is that birds have a large sternum that is almost like the keel of a sailboat. This device serves for attachment of the massive breast muscles that are needed to manipulate the wings. In contrast *Archaeopteryx* did not have a keel at all; it had a regular flat sternum in its chest, just like reptiles (or for that matter, just like us mammals).

Birds and dinosaurs both have three toes facing forward and one toe facing backward. In dinosaurs the backward-facing toe is quite high up and extremely reduced in size. In modern birds that fourth toe is curved toward the three front toes. In fact its curvature is so pronounced that it can oppose the front toes and serve as a grasping device that enables birds to lock their toes around tree branches. Anyone who has watched a canary on its perch has observed how the rear toe curves in under the perch, while the three forward toes curve over it. In *Archaeopteryx* the rear toe was intermediate in position between that of certain dinosaurs and birds. Instead of pointing backward, it was curved inward, but it was certainly not opposable, as it is in modern birds. Finally, like reptiles, *Archaeopteryx* had teeth.

Archaeopteryx is not the only transitional bird species that has been found in fossils, although it is particularly interesting since it has so many reptilian features. Fossils of a number of other species of birds that existed 100 million years ago have been found as well. It is apparent that some of the birds that existed at that time still had teeth, the tails were longer and a number had fingers with claws sticking slightly out of the wings.

Almost unanimously, paleontologists now believe they can explain the lineage of birds. There were a group of dinosaurs, referred to as theropods, with three toes, hollow bones and bipedal limbs (that is, capable of supporting two-legged walking). These are all birdlike traits. Not all theropods had three fingers like the early birds did (some had four), but there was a subgroup that did, and it was this group (known as the Tetanurae) that is believed to have given rise to the predecessors of birds. There is another subgroup of these Tetanurae that had other shared features with *Archaeopteryx* (which I will not go into here), and thus the progression continues. It is especially interesting that fossils of this last subgroup (the Maniraptora) have been found with an adult sitting on a cluster of eggs. Apparently this dinosaur was buried and subsequently fossilized while clutching its eggs like a bird would. The structure of these theropod eggs has been analyzed, and it has certain features found otherwise only in birds.

Thus the lineage to birds is becoming increasingly understood.[23] Since 1990, three times as many bird fossils have been found from the period of 150 million years ago up to 70 million years ago as had been found in all the rest of recorded history. Analysis of these fossils and others that will soon be discovered will continue to provide details about the bird lineage.[24]

Much has been written by nonexperts about the notion that *Archaeopteryx* is not a true transitional organism. It is true that *Archaeopteryx* is almost certainly a side branch in the lineage that leads to birds, but this is irrelevant to the point under discussion. Here is why. As will become apparent in the next section, fossils that scientists actually find represent only a tiny fraction of the species that actually existed on earth. The chance of finding one of the species that is actually on the lineage to living birds (or any other group of organisms for that matter) is exceedingly small. What paleontologists find are fossils of species that are related to those that are on the lineage. *Archaeopteryx* had features that were birdlike and reptilelike. Biologists believe that there were hundreds (perhaps thousands) of similar species that existed between 100 million and 200 million years ago, and most would have been

---

[23]See S. Chatterjee, *The Rise of Birds* (Baltimore: Johns Hopkins University Press, 1997); and Shipman, *Taking Wing*.

[24]So many transitional species of birds and dinosaurs have been discovered in the past decade that it is now difficult to define the difference between what has classically been defined as a bird from that which has been classified as a dinosaur. Various dinosaur species have been found in the past several years that remarkably demonstrate all the major transitional stages in feather creation. See R. O. Prun and A. H. Bursh, "Which Came First, the Feather or the Bird?" *Scientific American* 288, no. 3 (2003): 84-93. A four-winged dinosaur that shares many features with *Archaeopteryx* has just been discovered. It used its four feathered wings as an airfoil for gliding, in much the same way as flying squirrels use their extended skin flap to glide from tree to tree today. See X. Xu, X. Wang, X. Kuang, F. Zhang and X. Du, "Four Winged Dinosaurs from China," *Nature* 421 (2003): 335-41.

members of little side branches. It just so happens that *Archaeopteryx* is the one that existed in an area of the world that was ideally suited for making fossils, and as a result, a tiny fraction of its population was preserved as fossils for us to see today. Maybe someday other "cousin species" will be discovered. Perhaps even one day somebody will discover a fossil of a species that really was in the direct lineage to birds. However, there would be no way of knowing if it was, and even if it was, it would not be significant—all we need are the cousins. Let's see why.

WHY CAN'T SCIENTISTS FIND MORE TRANSITIONAL FORMS?

Over the past decade or two there has been a tremendous increase in the number of transitional species that have been found. Possibility 1 (sudden creation of each new species from scratch) and possibility 2 (sudden creation of each new prototype from scratch) are inconsistent with the existence of these transitional species that we have been discussing. Much has been made (primarily by nonbiologists) about the relative scarcity of transition forms compared to the preponderance of species fitting clearly into one group or another. I would maintain that the existence of transitional organisms *at all* in the fossil record is sufficient evidence to show that possibility 3 (gradual creation of all life forms) is a much better fit for the data than the other two. Ironically, possibility 2 grew tremendously in popularity among nonbiologists during the 1990s despite the fact that this was the greatest decade in history for the discovery of transitions. Undoubtedly part of the reason for this is that it takes a while for findings published in the scientific literature to trickle down to nonbiologists. Nonetheless the question remains: why are there not more transitional species? We certainly do not have an abundance of them in the fossil record, and none of them are alive today. Why? The answer is straightforward.

The rarity of fossilization. Although 250,000 species are filed away on paleontologists' shelves, this represents just a tiny fraction of the total number of species that have existed on the surface of the earth. It is estimated that on earth today there are upward of 10 million species, and it is likely that this represents less than 1 percent of the species that have ever existed on earth. As wonderful as fossils are for exploring the history of life, fossilization is an exceedingly unlikely event. Only a minuscule fraction of the organisms happened to be at the right place at the right time to be preserved in perpetuity. Usually when an organism dies, it decays, leaving hard parts that are eventually subject to microbial decomposition, scavenging or chemical destruction. In order for it to be converted into fossil form, most often the body has to be suddenly buried in a rapid accumulation of sediment. The overwhelming majority of organisms, especially land organisms, would never be in the right time and the right place to be preserved forever in this manner. In order for the hard parts to be converted into rock, they usually need to be buried rapidly in sediment in a manner that does not result in major disruption of the body.

Yet despite the unlikelihood of fossilization, we do have a tremendous number of fossils. Given this, should not that massive collection of fossils be a random sample of all the organisms that ever lived, including a huge number of transitional forms? The answer is no, and there is an important reason for this. I will attempt to illustrate it as follows.

Transitional species are expected to occur primarily in tiny populations. Consider an island population of a nonmigrating species of birds with a short beak.[25] Let's say there are one hundred birds on the island. Pretend that a genetic change occurs in one bird. As a result, its beak is a little longer than those of the other birds on the island. Perhaps that genetic change enables that bird to be more effective at digging little worms out of decaying logs. Hence it lives a longer and healthier life and produces more offspring than any of the other ninety-nine birds on the island. The result would be that in the next generation a higher percentage of birds would have long beaks. Let's say that the genetic change doubles the efficiency of reproduction and thus, unlike all the other birds that leave just one offspring surviving to adulthood, it leaves two. Those two continue to be more successful than their short-beaked cousins. So maybe one generation later, birds with long beaks constitute 4 percent of those on the island. In this hypothetical exam-

---

[25]Although the example given here is hypothetical, for a wonderfully written examination of real-world changes in beak structure over time in small, isolated populations of finches, see Jonathan Weiner, *The Beak of the Finch* (New York: Alfred A. Knopf, 1995).

ple, within a reasonable time, the bird population consists largely of the long-beaked variety. Now let's say that as time goes by there are some other genetic changes that take place—changes that alter the reproductive habits of the birds. Maybe, for example, a genetically based change occurs so that females prefer males with long beaks. As time goes on, that trait also gets incorporated into the birds on the island as well. Now not only do they all have long beaks but also, because of the second genetic change, they actually have a strong preference for other birds that have long beaks.

Now let's move over to the mainland, where there is a population of one hundred thousand of the same hypothetical species of bird. Let's say that the first genetic change occurs there also—one bird has a long beak. Assume that this bird also has a slight advantage, just like the bird on the island. In the next generation maybe it leaves two offspring, whereas the average for all of the others is only one. That means that now two out of one hundred thousand birds have long beaks. A year later, maybe it would be four, then eight out of the hundred thousand. However, it would take a much, much longer time for the birds with long beaks to take over the population. Not only that, but there are other technicalities that reduce the probability of such a large population changing to become long-beaked. Most genetic changes are "recessive," meaning there have to be two copies of the new variety of the gene for it to be expressed. Each bird has two copies of each gene. It is unlikely that an individual bird will have a single copy of a rare gene; just imagine how unlikely it is for both its copies to be of the rare variety. However, because of inbreeding (readers who are dog fanciers know all about this), it is *much, much* more likely for our small population of one hundred birds to have two copies of the same rare form of a gene. In this small population, where all the birds are related to one another, it is not particularly uncommon for individuals to have two copies of the same abnormal gene. Thus, without going into all the technical details, it is clear that a small population can change its genetic makeup *much* more rapidly than a large population.

One other aspect of the two bird populations needs to be explored. Recall that a second genetic change occurred on the island. As a result of that second change, the birds on the island underwent a change, so that they would only mate with birds that have long beaks. In essence, then, the birds on the island became a separate species. The usual distinguishing factor that determines whether two populations are members of the same or different species is whether they will mate with one another. Consider the mainland population. In this large population, if a genetic change occurred that resulted in birds preferring longer beaks in their mating partners, such birds would not do well there, where almost all the beaks are small. Thus in a large population there is a strong stabilizing effect that tends to prevent major changes in mating. However, in a small population, especially one that is under environmental stress or that has new and unused forms of food or habitat available to it, there is a strong tendency for species to change rapidly.

The bottom line behind all of this is that populations that are subject to change are small populations isolated in some manner from the large population. (An island existence is only one way of a population's becoming isolated from its larger "parental" population.) But how does that relate to the scarcity of transitional forms in the fossil record? The main point is that where species change their characteristics, they do so in small, isolated populations. And remember that fossilization is an exceedingly unlikely event. Thus, when fossilization does happen, there is a much higher probability that it will happen somewhere in the larger landmass. If the population that is changing occupies a landmass that represents (for example) only 1/100th of a percent of the area occupied by the large population, then that means the probability of fossilization is extremely low. Similarly, if the transitional forms are present for only a relatively brief period of time as compared to the larger stable populations, then this further lowers the probability of being able to "catch" a transitional form in the fossil record. The fact is that some transitional forms *have* been "caught" (and we have discussed some of these), but most have not. This is not surprising; it is exactly what geneticists would predict.

This may well be the most misunderstood fact by individuals who believe the earth is young. Recently I had dinner with a noted individual who has traveled the world as a proponent of a young earth and sudden creation. "The absence of transitional organisms in the fossil record clinches the argument," he said. First of all, he is wrong about the absence of transitional organisms. A number of transitional forms *have* been found. However, the real issue is that he, along with countless others who believe in a young earth, do not understand the reasons for the scarcity of such fossils. Since it is so important to clarify this misunderstanding, I want to finish this part of the discussion with a simple illustration.

Let's say that you were asked to travel around the country with a high-powered camera taking random zoom shots from a plane. There is only one requirement for your journey: your flight path must be totally random. Let's also say that when you were done, you had 250,000 photographs, each showing a piece of land one thousand square feet in area (a little larger than the yard of a typical home). Now for the assignment. From this set of photographs, your task is to develop a picture of life in America. The fact is that if you had 250,000 photographs, and if they were truly random, then there is only a 25 percent chance that even one of your photos would have a person in it. In fact, even if you had sufficient pictures so that you could actually begin to construct a scenario of life in America, you almost certainly would have no pictures of the places that especially influence what happens in America—the Capitol and the White House, for example. Furthermore, important locations like these are generally larger than the thousand-square-foot plots of land that fit your pictures. The chances of your having even one of those key pictures in your random collection (even if you had 250 billion photographs instead of 250,000) would be slim to none.

I am afraid that my dinner companion had an inadequate understanding of statistics and genetics. (His expertise was in another discipline.) The fossils we have are like random snapshots, and the complete collection, as it exists today, is a highly incomplete picture of the history of life on earth. Just as a random set of snapshots would give us at best only a fragmented, incomplete picture of life in America, so the fossil data is expected to provide only a tiny glimpse of the life forms that actually have existed here. Further, the species that will be represented are expected to be from the large, nonchanging populations and seldom from the tiny populations, where much of the really interesting action is taking place.

IF CREATION OCCURS BY GRADUAL MODIFICATION (POSSIBILITY 3), WHY DON'T WE SEE IT HAPPENING TODAY?

The fossil record clearly shows that the spectrum of organisms that existed on earth in the distant past was very different than it is today. The life forms have changed dramatically from those present in earlier years. Further, it should be apparent from the just-completed brief synopsis of the fossil record that the change has been a gradual one. Transitional forms do exist in the fossil record, and although the record is incomplete, there are some good reasons for that incompleteness. As a professor of biology, I am frequently asked the question as to why, if gradual change is the mechanism God has used in creation, we do not see those gradual changes taking place today.

The fact is that we do see gradual changes taking place today. Although one well-known example of this, the peppered moth, has been partially discredited,[26] there are lots of examples in the biological literature of organisms changing their characteristics with time in response to environmental changes.[27] Critics, however, point out that these minor changes are meaningless since they are only that— minor changes.

So, have scientists ever observed anything big, like a new structure? There *are* examples of new structures. For example, fruit flies with an extra pair of wings can be readily bred. Even here, however, where the changes are big ones, critics correctly point out that the extra pair of

---

[26]Jonathan Wells, *Icons of Evolution* (Washington, D.C.: Regnery, 2000) can be consulted for one view of this story. However, in so doing, it is important to also refer to the original scientific critique, which states, "Differential bird predation . . . is the primary influence on the evolution of melanism in the peppered moth" (Michael Majerus, *Melanism* [Oxford: Oxford University Press, 1998], p. 116).

[27]See M. Orr and T. B. Smith, "Ecology and Speciation," *Trends in Ecology and Evolution* 13 (1998): 502-6. Also see Weiner, *Beak of the Finch*; and D. E. Soltis and P. S. Soltis, "Polyploidy: Recurrent Formation and Genome Evolution," *Trends in Ecology and Evolution* 14 (1999): 348-52.

wings are totally nonfunctional and it would take many more changes for them to be made functional.

Has science ever observed anything really big, like a bona fide new species? Here, too, science can point to some changes that reproductively isolate two groups of organisms. By most definitions of a species, we now have two where previously there had been one.[28] However, even at this, the newly created species do not differ in any major fashion from each other.

Humans have been able to produce all sorts of different dogs, but hundreds of years later, they are all still dogs, members of a single species. Despite the wondrous diversity produced by pigeon breeders, we are still left with pigeons, not a single new bird species. If the Word of God's spoken command and the ongoing Presence of God's Spirit has resulted in creation through gradual modification, then why are humans unable to duplicate the process? Why can't we guide it in a manner that will produce major changes in body form?

There is a simple answer to that question. Simple as it is, however, our limited perspective of time makes it extremely difficult to comprehend. Before addressing that limited perspective in detail, there is one sideline that must be noted. Dogs are still dogs and pigeons are still pigeons because breeders have merely been rearranging the pre-existing instructions (genes) for making dogs and pigeons. The time frame over which they have been working, long as it may seem to us, has been too short to obtain many new versions of genes. For the most part, all that the breeders have been doing is rearranging the old genes, putting them into new combinations to produce new varieties. Plans can be rearranged over the span of human history—hundreds of years. The production of *new* plans takes much, much longer because it requires many little genetic changes, each of which is exceedingly rare.

We humans find it difficult to appreciate that things we cannot do in our lifetime could easily be accomplished, if guided by God's command and God's Spirit working through an influence on natural pro-

[28]Orr and Smith, "Ecology and Speciation."

cesses down through the eons of time.[29] We need to work on gaining an appreciation for just how long is the time that has been available to God. If we do that, perhaps we will see that the human inability to observe or duplicate the work of creation is irrelevant to the question of whether it may actually have taken place that way.

GAINING AN APPRECIATION FOR TIME

The second thing I hear from my students (besides the question about why humans have not been good at duplicating or observing the process) is that it is one thing to explain how birds could get longer beaks but it is quite another to explain how a reptile could change into a bird. After all, skin would have to change into feathers, forelimbs would have to turn into wings, and the lungs of a reptile would have to undergo major changes from the "dead end" lungs that reptiles have to the "flow through" lungs that birds have. There are two important responses to this question. The first is that anything is possible in response to the command of God's Word and the Presence of God's Spirit. The second is that we must continue to work on gaining some appreciation for the tremendous amount of time over which it has been taking place.

If the earth is really as old as it appears to be, it is important for us to try to visualize just how much time this is. That is not an easy task, because we are used to thinking in terms of decades and centuries. For us, one hundred years is a very long time. Most of us have seen the film *Back to the Future*. Picture yourself going back in time one hundred years and trying to communicate with people about all that has transpired in the past one hundred years. They would barely be able to understand what a car is, let alone all that a modern car contains, such as electric windows, air bags and keyless entry. They would marvel as

---

[29]Perhaps, as mentioned above, God even allows a fair amount of freedom in the creative process. The Old Testament, after all, says that it happened at God's command. It does not fill in many details for us. The New Testament says that "through him all things were made." This statement also is silent with regard to mechanism, even after adding the proviso "without him nothing was made that has been made" (Jn 1:3). Scripture is telling us that it all happened under God's authority and in God's Presence. The immanence of that Presence no more rules out creative freedom in life's history than it rules out creative freedom in the life of the Spirit-filled believer. In sovereignty, God wills freedom for all creation.

you told them about refrigerators, electric ranges, television and movies, to say nothing of microwave ovens that produce hot rolls in fifteen seconds. Imagine their bewilderment as you tried to explain to them what a computer is and how the Internet allows you to order a product from the other side of the Atlantic at the click of button. Picture their faces as you tell them that every day thousands of people fly from London to Los Angeles in twelve hours and how engineers were able to construct rockets that would carry men to the moon and back! To us, one hundred years is a very long time and a great deal can happen in that period.

What about 4 billion years in the history of life—just how long is that? Let's condense 4 billion years into one year. If we could do that, then 2 billion years ago would correspond to June of that year and 500 million years ago would correspond to November 16. In fact each million years would equate to only two hours. Thus 1 million years ago would correspond to ten o'clock on New Year's Eve. At fifteen seconds before midnight, Julius Caesar would be born. At about five seconds before midnight, Columbus would set foot on the shores of the Western Hemisphere. Finally, at 0.8 seconds before midnight, you would be born, only to die (assuming you live to be one hundred) at the stroke of midnight. The one hundred years I spoke of above, with all its potential for change, would be over in the blink of an eye.

If the earth is really as old as it appears to be, then the amount of time for the fulfillment of God's command in the Presence of God's Spirit is almost unfathomable. Pretend that you are making a time line of the history of the earth. In your time line you decide that each year will correspond to 1/1000th of an inch. If you were try to do this starting with the creation of the earth at the left edge of your paper, and marking off 1/1000th of an inch for each year, then your paper would need to stretch about sixty-seven miles. The most recent one hundred years, with all its changes, would represent a speck the thickness of a pencil line at the right-hand edge of the sixty-seven-mile-long sheet of paper. It is hard for us to think of such a vast time interval, since we do not yet have God's perspective of eternity. For our eternal God, those 4.6 billion years are not even the blink of his eternal eye. In fact it is likely that for an eternal God there is, in essence, no such thing as time as we know it. It is even conceivable that God might be able to go back and forth in time, just as you and I go back and forth in space. Thus, even though we find it difficult to think in terms of long periods of time, we must be willing to try if we want to understand God as Creator.

No other species that God has created is able to do that, and it is not easy even for us. God, however, has given us that privilege—the joy of being able to peer back into time to see the masterpiece unfolding. Let's not close the eyes of our mind to God's work in the past, if only because it may reveal important facets of God's work in the present.

5

BEYOND THE FOSSIL RECORD

Looking at the Geographical Distribution
of Life's Diversity

———

IN THE PREVIOUS CHAPTER WE SAW that the fossil record suggests there has been a continuous and ongoing change in the sorts of organisms that have inhabited the earth throughout its history. The spectrum of plants and animals that inhabit the earth today seems very different from that of 50 million years ago, which in turn seem very different from the organisms present 500 million years ago, which in turn . . . and so on back to the beginning. Far from being inconsistent with Scripture, this data informs us a little about what it means for creation to have occurred in response to God's command and in the ongoing Presence of his Spirit. The changing distribution of organisms through time makes it clear that God's act of creation has been a gradual one, taking much longer than some had imagined.

What a privilege it is to peer back through the eons of time using our lens of faith! Through that lens we learn something about the nature of God's activity that no one, until recently, has been fortunate enough to see. Having done that, I would like to turn that same lens and use it to peer into a different set of dimensions—those of space. Instead of looking backward through the dimension of time, let's focus our lens outward on today's creation and examine its distribution geographically as it is spread over the surface of the earth. By studying the distribution of creation in the here and now, and coupling that to our study of its distribution through time, the nature of God's activity comes into even clearer focus.

GEOGRAPHICAL ISOLATION: ITS SHORT-TERM CONSEQUENCES

Race differences in humans. Several years ago I spent an afternoon at Heathrow International Airport in London. I suspect that no place on earth provides a more illustrative example of the results of human geographical diversity. As I walked through the airport, I heard vast differences in how people spoke and saw equally distinctive habits of dress. I noted cultural differences in the roles of adult males and females and the way in which children were treated. I walked from one area of the airport where many people had extremely dark skin to another area where skin was fair and hair was blond. The people who were congregated around the Japan Airlines gates looked very different from most of those waiting to board Malaysian Air. The experience was a testimony to the diverse heritage of the human race.

The basis for all this diversity, of course, is that until recently the human gene pool (our complete collection of genes) was segregated into separate world areas. People in Finland look different from people in Africa because the two gene pools have been geographically separated from one another for a long time. After geographical separation for thousands of years, distinctive traits have accumulated in each world region. The overall form of the body is determined by the genes we all share from our common ancestors, but as time in isolation has passed, geographically unique forms of certain genes accumulate, and this in turn results in distinctive physical characteristics.

Although the people who inhabit Japan look different from those in Sweden, they are all certainly still members of the same species. Both groups share a common set of ancestors, and although thousands of years have since transpired, the differences among groups are really somewhat superficial. Humans do bear the imprint of geographical isolation, but because the isolation has been only thousands of years, the imprint is a minor one. What about animals and plants? Do they exhibit the trademarks of geographical isolation that humans do? Actually they do, but studies of these organisms take us much deeper into the ramifications of geographical isolation. If new varieties of life forms occur because of accumulating genetic differences with time, then large-scale studies of animals and plants allow us to explore the effect of geographical separation that spanned not thousands of years, as has been the case for humans, but hundreds of thousands or even millions of years. It is this important subject that will occupy our attention throughout this chapter.

The effect of geographical isolation in the Hawaiian Islands. Consider the Hawaiian Islands, for example. All these islands came into existence in the same way—they emerged from the ocean, the result of a rising thrust of volcanic activity. The island of Kauai is the oldest at about 5 million years. The Big Island of Hawaii, still volcanically active, is the youngest at about 700,000 years. With the nearest continent or island group over two thousand miles away, the Hawaiian Islands represent geographical isolation at its extreme, and that isolation has existed from the beginning. Just as Japan was populated by humans whose ancestors originated elsewhere, so the ancestors of the animals and plants of Hawaii colonized each newly appearing landform as it reared its head above the surrounding ocean waters.

It is easy to see how human migration can occur—the travelers themselves are able to construct the means of transportation. But how could animals and plants colonize isolated specks of land? The hardiness of plant seeds is legendary, and the dispersal of seeds in air currents and drifting logs almost certainly initiated the colonization of this distant land soon after its formation. Initially, upon their arrival, there would be nothing but barren rocks, sand and the occasional piece of decaying driftwood. Indeed even today a visit to portions of the Big Island, with its vast stretches of black volcanic rock, gives us a good picture of how Kauai, the first island, would have appeared initially. Now, 5 million years later, it is known as the Garden Isle and has been the setting for movies such as *Jurassic Park* and *South Pacific*, noted for their botanical richness, among other things. With time, the presence of plants has modified the barren landscape, producing fertile soil that has allowed new, less hardy plants, which also arrived as seeds, to establish themselves.

Visualizing animal colonization is more of a challenge. Undoubtedly some species of insects were carried across the ocean in the crevices of drifting logs. Others, because of their small size and wings,
probably arrived by air, carried across the miles by air currents. Although a journey of this sort might seem unlikely to you, remember the
limitations of your perspective. A million years is ten thousand centuries, and events that seem quite unlikely are not so unlikely, given
enough time. So air currents and logs carrying insects and other land
invertebrates could well result in colonization on occasion. On the
other hand, even in ten thousand centuries, it is difficult to imagine a
scenario that would bring larger organisms across a thousand miles of
ocean—unless they had wings. Interestingly there is only one mammalian species that is classified as being native to Hawaii. It does not take
a rocket scientist or even a biologist to successfully hazard a guess as
to what sort of species it is. There is only one mammal that has wings:
the bat. Hence we need not be surprised that when humans set foot on
Hawaii a little more than a millennium ago, there was only one mammal present—a type of bat found only in Hawaii. The only other
"large" animals found upon human arrival were many species of
birds. The fact that the only "large" animals present had wings indicates strongly that their ancestors got to Hawaii by air travel.

The previous chapter discussed the notion that the offspring of organisms that are isolated in some fashion (such as being marooned on
an island) can accumulate character differences over time. Indeed, if
the time is prolonged, they may become so different that they will not
even be capable of breeding with the parental stock at the site of origin
any longer. In Hawaii it is now hundreds of thousands of years since
that species of bat and those various species of birds arrived on the island. The large animal species native to Hawaii are unique, found nowhere else in the world. They all have wings, indicating their ancestors
made the journey from elsewhere, but intriguingly there are no members of these species elsewhere on earth. Why would that be? There is
one simple conclusion. Just as humans in Japan have become increasingly different from humans in Africa, so the bat and bird species that
took up residence in Hawaii changed significantly over time. In this

case, however, with the much greater time period (hundreds of thousands or millions of years rather than thousands of years), it resulted in such significant changes that they really have become their own unique species.

Just as Hawaii has its own unique species of birds and bats, so also it has a unique array of insects. There is, for example, a small fly, known as *Drosophila*, that has received a great deal of attention from geneticists over the years. About three thousand different species of this fly are distributed over the world, eight hundred of which are found in Hawaii.[1] Significantly the Hawaiian species have certain trademark characteristics that set them apart from other species in the world. To biologists, it is clear from these characteristics that they arose from a small number of colonizing species, but as time has gone by, they have diverged, becoming adapted to particular environments. Some species, for example, are well adapted for feeding upon the microorganisms found in a certain type of decaying plant that exists only in the dry areas of an island. Others are adapted for life in association with the sorts of plants that live in the rain forest. Despite the vast array of species, each adapted to a particular food source, it is clear that these different species are related to one another, because they all share some characteristics found nowhere else in the world.

Thus, unlike the bat, which changed gradually to become a single distinctive species, the *Drosophila* flies changed more dramatically to become many new species. They became highly adapted to specific microclimates and food sources, and as a result, multiple species were formed, each adapted to its own specific niche. Nevertheless, in both cases (bats as well as *Drosophila*), and indeed for the entire flora and fauna of the Hawaiian Islands, there is one dominant theme: all is determined by which organisms served as founders. The variety of insects in Hawaii is distinct from the variety of insects in other parts of the world because it is limited by which organisms happened to have landed there. Moreover, the reason there are almost as many different species of *Drosophila* in Hawaii as

---

[1]See H. L. Carson and K. Y. Kaneshiro. "*Drosophila* of Hawaii," *Annual Review of Ecology and Systematics* 7 (1976): 311-45; W. B. Heed, "Host Plant Specificity in Hawaiian *Drosophila*," *Taxon* 20 (1971): 115-21.

there are in all other parts of the world combined is that many species of insects present on the mainland were *not* present in Hawaii. Thus the reason why a new species of *Drosophila* flower feeders could so readily be formed was the absence of any other species of insect specialized for feeding on that type of flower. None had made the journey to Hawaii. Thus the niche, or specialized lifestyle, for a particular type of flower-feeding insect might have been open, thereby allowing one group of the little flies to become ideally adapted to that specific niche. Hawaii bears trademarks of its history—it has tens of thousands of unique native species. The particular assortment of native species clearly was determined by which organisms made the journey.

Does this imply that God is not Creator of all of the majestic plant and animal life of Hawaii? Not at all. It only implies that creation was gradual and that it occurred by modification of the preexisting life forms that settled in Hawaii. But on the other hand, it *does* imply this. That is, it *really does imply* that, in response to the Word of God's creation command and in the Spirit of God's Presence, species that had arisen elsewhere were changed gradually into their Hawaiian counterparts. Just as black skin in humans is generally a trademark for the ancestry of an individual, so the Hawaiian trademarks of all the species of fruit flies, birds and the bat point clearly to the idea that gradual modification has been the creation theme in Hawaii. This theme of gradual change is starting to become familiar. When we were using our lens to look back in time, we saw exactly the same phenomenon. Let's turn the lens to look at other areas of the world.

LAKES AS THE EQUIVALENT OF ISOLATED ISLANDS
One might wonder if the animal and plant life of Hawaii is an anomaly. What if the God of sudden creation (possibility 1) just chose to put a unique set of animals on Hawaii? Who are we to question God's motives for putting such organisms there? Maybe it is just coincidence that God chose to only put organisms in Hawaii that are capable of becoming airborne or that could survive the long journey embedded in a drifting log. With that possibility in mind, let's explore a different example of the effects of geographical isolation.

For organisms that live on land, isolation may come from colonizing a distant island. On the other hand, in the world of water, lakes can become isolated from one another also. If there is no system of interconnecting streams and rivers, one lake can be isolated from another for thousands or perhaps millions of years. Hence, for organisms that live in water, the aquatic equivalent of an island is an isolated lake. Lakes come and go with time in the history of the earth; therefore studying lakes can teach us important lessons about creation.

In Africa three lakes have received extensive study: Lake Victoria, Lake Malawi and Lake Tanganyika. The latter is the oldest, with an estimated age of about 10 million years. Lake Malawi was formed about 4 million years ago, and Lake Victoria is about 500,000 years old. Note that the time of formation of each of these lakes is similar to the time frame for the formation of the Hawaiian Islands. Thus one can ask the question whether each lake has its own unique species of fish. The hypothesis of creation through gradual modification would predict that since the fish of Lake Tanganyika have been isolated from those in lakes Victoria and Malawi, over time they would have become distinct species.

Species are adapted to particular lifestyles. Leopards, for example, are ideally adapted for the life of a predator. They are fast, have sharp teeth, can stalk their prey and have coloration enabling them to hide from prey for as long as possible before striking. Other animals are adapted for a much different style of life. Cows, for example, have multiple stomach compartments and flat teeth for grinding, suiting them for the life of a grass eater. You and I would not do well on a diet of grass, nor would we do well as stalkers of deer and antelope, were it not for our weapons. Just as there is a variety of lifestyles for which organisms on land are adapted, so also there is a variety of food sources in the water. Algae grow on rocks, and they are a source of nutrients to some fish. Insect larvae are especially abundant in and around the crevices between rocks. Mollusks (organisms like clams and snails) exist in shells, and they provide an ideal food source for fish that are able to crush those shells. Even the bodies of other fish could potentially become a source of nutrients. Thus, just as there are a variety of ecological

niches on land, so also there are many sorts of opportunity for specialization in a lake. Fish might be expected to become specifically adapted
for a lifestyle suited to eating a particular type of food, just as occurs
on land. Indeed one might even expect that the same sorts of special-
izations would exist in each of the three lakes mentioned above.

When a lake is first formed, it does not contain a rich variety of life.
Its initial fish population depends upon whatever happens to arrive
there by way of the streams that empty into it. However, if the theory
of gradual change in organisms is correct, then those fish that do arrive
may gradually become adapted to the various food sources that become available. As the lake matures, an increasing number of ecological niches become available and, increasingly, specialization becomes
an advantage.

A group of fish known as cichlids are found in all three of the African
lakes referred to above.[2] These fish have certain structural features that
set them apart, making it clear that they are all related to one another.
They also have certain behavioral features. Cichlid species, for example,
care for their young after they are born. Frequently the way this occurs
is that the female scoops her fertilized eggs into her mouth and then in-
cubates them there until well after they have hatched. Once they reach
a large enough stage to fend for themselves, she allows them to leave,
entering the real world—that found outside her own mouth. Lake Tanganyika contains about two hundred species of cichlids, each adapted
to a particular style of feeding and behavior. Certain species, for example, are adapted to scraping the scales from other fish and nourishing
themselves on the protein in the scales. Others specialize in eating larvae; still others, eggs. Some species are adapted to the life of scraping
algae from the surfaces of rocks and other material. They have chisel-
like teeth that are ideally shaped and structured for scraping. Other species have narrow, pointed heads, sharp snouts and long, fine teeth.
These species are specialized for removing insect larvae from tiny crevices. There are some species adapted to crushing mollusks and others
that specialize in nipping the tail fins off other fish.

---

[2]See L. J. Stassny and A. Meyer, "Cichlids of the Rift Lakes," *Scientific American* 280 (1999): 64-
69.

The species in Lake Malawi that are adapted to feeding upon insect larvae in crevices are extremely similar in coloration, shape of the snout and tooth structure to the species that do the same thing in Lake Tanganyika and Lake Victoria. The same is true for other species adapted for scraping algae from the surface of rocks or for scraping the scales off other fish. In fact so closely alike are the similarly adapted species in the different lakes that you and I would hardly be able to tell them apart (figure 5.1). Nevertheless the species in different lakes are truly distinctive: they cannot interbreed.

The fact that the algae eaters in Lake Malawi are a different species from the algae eaters in Lake Tanganyika is not particularly significant to someone who believes in the God of sudden creation (possibility 1). God, one may propose, just chose to make a different set of species for each lake. However, it is not as simple as that. There are various ways of showing that all of the cichlids in Lake Malawi are closely related to each other. The algae eaters of Lake Malawi have certain trademarks (discussed below) that indicate they are closely related to the insect feeders in the same lake. Indeed there is absolutely no doubt that the algae eaters are much more closely related to the insect feeders of the same lake than they are to the algae eaters in Lake Tanganyika. The reason for that is simple. They both descended from the same cichlid species that populated the lake to begin with. As time has gone by, they have become diversified into separate species, each adapted to a particular lifestyle.

Various types of evidence indicate that all three hundred to five hundred cichlid species in Lake Malawi are descended from a single species. The most foolproof evidence, however, comes from analysis of their DNA. Just as you inherited your DNA from your parents, and thereby it is virtually identical to theirs, so also these fish inherited the DNA that came from the parental fish that populated Lake Malawi. There has been time for it to change, but it is still clear that the DNA of all the cichlids in Lake Malawi comes from a common lineage and that it is different from the DNA of the cichlids in Lake Tanganyika. This is not consistent with possibility 1, because the DNA similarities make it clear that the all the cichlids in Lake Malawi, no matter how different

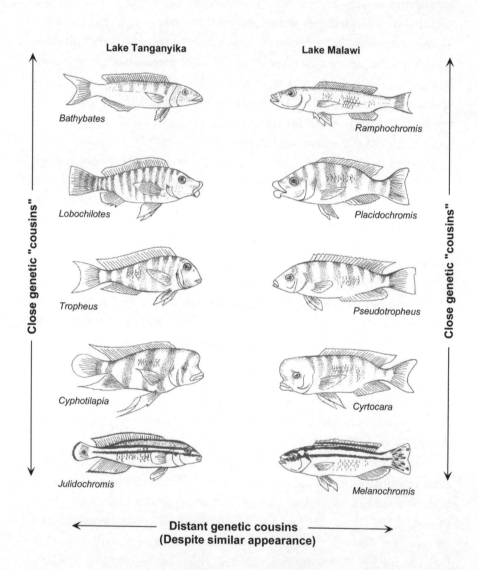

Figure 5.1. Cichlid fish of Lake Tanganyika and Lake Malawi

their appearance, are related to one another. Similarly, those in Lake Tanganyika are related to one another. The species in the two lakes are all still cichlids, so they are certainly related, but they are much more distantly related—they are distant cousin species (many times removed).[3]

We have discussed two ways in which organisms have become isolated. In one case the isolation came on newly formed islands; in the other it occurred in newly formed lakes. In each case the secluded confine possesses its own particular set of species found nowhere else in the world. Not only that, but the species present bear trademarks indicating they have descended from a small number of colonizers that subsequently diversified into many new species. God's creation command results in modification and adaptation of the founding species (possibility 2 or 3, but not 1).

OTHER EXAMPLES OF GEOGRAPHICAL ISOLATION

Islands and lakes that are not interconnected are obvious examples of physical isolation. Are there other, not-so-obvious barriers that can result in physical isolation? The answer, as the question implies, is yes. Consider the fur of a particular species of mammal. In the wild most mammals have little insects or other arthropods in that fur. We do all we can to remove fleas, ticks and other small organisms that can affect the health of our dogs and cats. We may dust our pets with powder and provide regular baths. On occasion we may even take them to the vet to be "deloused." In the wild mammals do not have that advantage. Indeed some tiny insect species are found nowhere else on earth but on a particular species of mammal. Lice are not like fleas, which are provided with the springlike ability to jump. Nor are lice like flies, which can readily take to the air in moving from one food source to another. Lice do have little legs, of course, but they live their entire life wandering around in the furry forest of a single mammal.

---

[3]Lake Victoria, the youngest of the lakes, has about five hundred species, most descended from a small number of progenitor species in the past hundred thousand years. Indeed this lake almost dried up about fourteen thousand years ago, and many of the new species have been formed since that time. E. Verheyen, W. Salzburger, J. Snoeks and A. Meyer, "Origin of the Superflock of Cichlid Fishes from Lake Victoria, East Africa," *Science* 300 (2003): 325-29.

Studies have been done on various species of pocket gophers and the lice that are found in association with them.[4] Some gopher species share many features and thus are closely related to each other, whereas other species are clearly dissimilar and more distantly related. The notion of creation by gradual change (possibility 2 or 3) implies that the gopher species that most closely resemble each other have been derived from a single ancestral species in the fairly recent past, whereas a pair of dissimilar species share a common ancestral species that dates back much further in time. If descent by gradual change is correct, then one might expect that the parasites that spend their whole lives in the fur of the gopher would be changing as well. Consider, for example, two gopher species, which we shall call species A and species B. Let's say they resemble each other in many respects even though they are members of different species and therefore will not successfully interbreed. One might expect, if species A and B are closely related, that the louse species that inhabits the fur of species A will also closely resemble the species of louse on species B. Why? The lice know only one existence; they are passed from mother gopher to baby gophers down through the eons of time. In a sense a particular species of gopher is the equivalent of an island. A single louse species resides on that "island," and since the gophers of species A never mate or interact in other ways with species B, it is not possible for one louse species to move from one "island" to the other. The two furry forests never come in contact with one another, and so the lice species are also isolated from one another.

When one examines the lice that populate species A, it is possible to show that they are indeed a different species from those that populate species B. This might seem to be no surprise, even to those who believe in possibility 1. Perhaps God instantaneously just made a different louse species for each type of gopher, they might say. However, one telltale sign is significant. Consider a gopher species we will call C, one very different from A and B. If one examines the lice on species

[4]R. D. M. Page, "Temporal Congruence Revisited: Comparison of Mitochondrial DNA Sequence Divergence in Cospeciating Pocket Gophers and Their Chewing Lice," *Systematic Biology* 45 (1996): 151-67.

C, one finds an amazing parallel: like the gophers in whose fur they reside, the lice on gopher species C are only distantly related to their cousin lice species that live on gopher species A and B. The gopher species have been changing over the time, since they had a common ancestor. A long period of time has meant lots of changes. A short period of time since two species descended from a single ancestral species has meant fewer changes. Interestingly the changes in the lice species parallel almost perfectly the changes in the gopher species. In other words, if the gophers are close cousin species, the lice that each carries are also close cousins of one another. On the other hand, if the gopher species are only distant cousin species, the lice that each carries are also distant cousin species. Why? The longer the time since the two species had a common ancestor, the greater the opportunity for change.[5]

It is important to note that there is not a great deal of subjectivity in determining which species of gophers and lice are most closely related to each other. Analyzing the language of the genes, DNA, clearly shows which species are closely related. Just as your DNA came from each of your parents and thereby is virtually identical to theirs, so also it is almost the same as that present in a specific great-great-great-great-grandparent. Since DNA does not change much in just five or six generations, it would still be almost the same. But it does change, and because of elapsed time, there would be differences—slight differences, but larger ones than those found when your DNA is compared to that of your parents.

Geneticists can tell how closely related organisms are by examining a particular section of DNA. The more similar a specific segment is, the shorter the length of time since that DNA was in the common parent. The more specific portions of a DNA molecule differ, the longer has been the time since the two organisms had a common ancestor. Gophers that are closely related have similar DNA. Distantly related go-

---

[5]For clarity, I have focused on only three species in this discussion. The detailed study by Page, "Temporal Congruence Revisited," evaluated fifteen different species of pocket gophers and seventeen species of lice. The correlation between the relatedness of the two sets of organisms was remarkably consistent.

phers have less similar DNA. The same is also true for the lice that each gopher species carries.

I want to be sure that the evidence for common ancestry beyond the species level for pocket gophers is clear. It is not just that they have similar DNA and similar physical features; the real clincher is that there is a second independent set of organisms hitching a ride during this journey of gradual change into distinct species. If gradual change is true, then one would expect that the "hitchhikers" would be changing over time in parallel with their "ride," the gopher species. The fact that both change in tandem points clearly to possibility 2 or possibility 3—new species are created, not from scratch, but by gradual change from preexisting species. New species of gophers come from a single ancestral species, and new species of lice also come from their own single ancestor. This is just one of many reasons why Christian biologists like myself are convinced that possibility 1 (creation of each new species from scratch) is not the way in which God's creation command was carried out.

The phenomena I have been describing (Hawaiian bats, birds and flies; the cichlid fish in African lakes; and the gophers and lice of North America) are just examples of the changes that take place over relatively "short" periods of time—hundreds of thousands of years. In each case the founding organisms may be thought of as prototypes. Studies like those I have summarized provide indisputable evidence that change occurs, but the studies are confined to a single prototype. Possibility 2 states that there is a limit to change. It can occur within a prototype, but organisms of different prototypes do not share common ancestors. If possibility 3 is correct, so that all of creation is produced through modification of lineages, then we should be able to see much greater effects of geographical isolation when examining the effect of millions of years of isolation instead of the hundreds of thousands of years that we have been dealing with. Let's see if that expectation is realized. Before doing that, however, I want to digress to discuss what we know of God's action in the world by our personal experiences as believers in Jesus Christ. I will then relate that to the Creator God and what we have been learning about how God apparently acts in creation.

WHERE IS DIVINE ACTIVITY IN THIS STORY OF THE GEOGRAPHIC DIVERSITY OF LIFE FORMS?

One of the most fundamental theological truths is that God has not created human beings to serve as robots. God does not preprogram every activity of our lives. God is not the immediate and direct cause of every seemingly good or bad event that happens to us. If God were, we would be nothing more than his puppets. Consider, for example, Paul's statement "We know that in all things God works for the good of those who love him, who have been called according to his purpose" (Rom 8:28). What does this mean to the Christian? Recently one of my personal heroes, my father, led a devotion for his fellow seniors at church. In his devotional he made the parallel between the pilot of a seagoing ferry and God as the pilot of our Christian lives. In relating it to one of his own personal experiences on a ferry trip near Vancouver, British Columbia, he talked about the pilot navigating his vessel through a blinding fog. My father described his feelings, upon being piloted out of the murky mist, at seeing the deep blue sky and verdant green forest as their island destination came into view. The point of my father's devotional is foundational to evangelicalism: God, as our pilot, is personally involved in guiding us through the uncertainties of our lives. Hovering in the background, almost invisibly, God brings us through the fog in our lives to a final destination—beautiful beyond description. God works all things together for good.

It is important to emphasize the subtlety of the ferry pilot in my father's analogy. The analogy he chose to illustrate God's Presence was not that of a puppeteer pulling strings on a marionette. Although God is always at the controls in our journey, "the Lord is the Spirit, and where the Spirit of the Lord is, there is freedom" (2 Cor 3:17). That particular scripture goes on to point out that we are free to be transformed into Christ's likeness and then goes on further to talk about the fact that we can expect to be hard pressed, perplexed, persecuted and struck down, but because of God's Presence in our lives, we will ultimately endure. There is no sign of God pulling strings in scriptures such as this. Instead the analogy is made to a beam of light. God's Presence is implied to be all-pervasive. His light shows the way. His love is overwhelming. He has become our wisdom, "that is, our righteousness, holiness and redemption" (1 Cor 1:30). He is an ever-present help in trouble (Ps 46:1), but he is not the continuous manipulator of the strings of our lives. There is no scriptural support for this. God wills that we live our lives in his Presence, but always within the freedom of the circumstances of our particular situations.

If this is the case, then we must be careful to allow that God may grant liberty to other aspects of his creation as well. There is freedom implied in the recorded words of creation, *"Let* the water teem with living creatures, and *let* birds fly above the earth across the expanse of the sky," and *"Let* the land produce living creatures according to their kinds" (Gen 1:20, 24). There is nothing to imply here that God built each individual creature in the way that a puppet builder builds his or her puppets. On the contrary, the keyword of God's instruction to creation is "let." The implication is clear that it happened at God's command and that all that happened occurred within God's Presence and under God's authority, but the notion of a puppet builder of millions of individual species is a human notion, not a scriptural one. If we want a scriptural one, we should turn to statements like the "hovering" of God's Spirit (Gen 1:2) or "the light that shines in darkness" (Jn 1:5). These sorts of verses imply an omnipresent God who is not coercive but rather a God who lights the way of our lives and lights the way for creation. We are told in Hebrews 13:8, "Jesus Christ is the same yesterday and today and forever." If so, and if Jesus is a reflection of the Father, then is it not reasonable to draw analogies of Christ's character and manner of working to the Creator's manner as well? After all, they are one and the same, unchanging. Is it not possible, then, that there is a much better analogy for how God has guided the course of creation than the analogy of a master designer—a sort of divine watchmaker? The analogy of hovering Spirit and guiding light is biblical, while that of master engineer is a product of modern society and the industrial age.

Much that happened in creation may well have occurred in the liberty that God gave to creation, just as much that happens in my life occurs in the freedom of my choices and those of others. I am never removed from God's Presence and am constantly mindful of God's command, but I live my life in freedom. It would be in keeping with God's character if God gave that same sort of liberty to creation as well. We now look further at some of the ramifications of that freedom.

LONG-TERM ISOLATION: THE RAMIFICATIONS OF CONTINENTAL DRIFT

The examples chosen in the earlier sections of this chapter demonstrate the effect of geographical isolation on species formation over hundreds of thousands of years but not many millions of years. This "short-term" isolation produced what some would consider only minor alterations, albeit alterations that led to different species. If, as asserted in the previous chapter, possibility 3 (all creation by gradual change) is correct and not possibility 2 (gradual change, but only within prototypes), it might be possible to see more pronounced evidence of the effect of geographical isolation if separation is many millions of years rather than hundreds of thousands of years. Possibility 3 predicts that changes observed over the short term would become increasingly pronounced over long periods of time.

When I was very young, my father (who is not a geologist) pointed out to me that South America and Africa look like interlocking pieces of a jigsaw puzzle. He also told me about the theory of continental drift: the two continents had previously been joined but had slipped apart through the eons of time. Actually, as good as the match between South America and Africa is to you and I as we peruse our world map, it is not a perfect fit. The reason for this less-than-ideal fit is not that the theory of continental drift is wrong. Rather there has been erosion and changes in sea level over the 100 million or so years since they drifted apart. Since the eroded material is still present below sea level on what is known as the continental shelf, a more accurate way to match the two pieces of the puzzle is to include the submerged, eroded land. This can easily be done using maps that include the submerged shelf around a continent, and the result is an almost perfect fit, mile by mile between the two continents.

The evidence that continental drift has occurred goes well beyond the fitting together of continents on a map. There are, for example, fossils of a snaggletoothed reptilian organism that can be found in the rocks in only two world locations: the eastern edge of South America and the southwestern side of Africa in a region that matches quite precisely its South American complement. Moreover, distinctive, matching rock formations are found on each side of the Atlantic in the appropriate complementing regions.

It is possible to measure the speed at which continental drift occurs. When iron-containing molten lava erupts from the earth, iron-containing minerals will orient themselves toward the magnetic poles just like a compass. As rocks form over the eons of time, they contain, in essence, frozen compasses pointing to the magnetic north pole. Occasionally the magnetic north and south poles have reversed themselves through time. Without going through the technical details, it is possible to make use of the magnetized minerals and the regular shifts in the magnetic poles to determine the speed with which the continents are drifting apart.[6] Depending upon the area of the world, a typical speed for separation is in the vicinity of five centimeters (two inches) per year. This seems like a snail's pace, and it is, but over 100 million years, that corresponds to a distance of three thousand miles—the approximate distance that separates Africa and South America.

Measuring the speed of continental drift by the changes in the orientation of the magnetized minerals is an indirect way of plotting the movement of continents in history. It would be even more convincing if we could track the movements of continents now, in real time. Indeed, using two independent techniques, it has been possible to determine the speed at which differing locations on the earth's surface are moving apart from one another. The first technique involves firing laser beams at a satellite and then measuring with extreme accuracy the length of time that it takes for the beam to bounce back to earth. Using this technique, it has been possible to show that an investigative site in Maryland is moving away from one in England at the speed of 1.7 centimeters per year. The second technique is a totally independent mechanism that involves measuring signals from distant quasars in space.

---

[6]For a fine overview of the method of determining the speed of drift by various techniques, see E. J. Tarbuck, *Earth Science* (Upper Saddle River, N.J.: Prentice-Hall, 2000), pp. 199-205.

By measuring differences in the time of receiving two identical signals at two different sites, and then comparing those differences in a similar experiment at a later time, it is possible to measure the speed at which those two sites are departing from one another. Amazingly, both of these independent techniques give the same speed of drift. It varies a little depending upon which regions of the world are being compared, but both techniques give values that are in the same range as those obtained by studying magnetic fields in rocks.

Not only do these three methods provide convincing evidence for continental drift, but significantly they provide independent confirmations of the ancient age of the earth. If Africa and South America, for example, really were one continent in ancient history, we have three totally independent ways of estimating approximately how long it has taken for them to reach the point where they are today—roughly 100 million years. If there was only one piece of data that pointed to this time frame, we might be able to claim that scientific knowledge was incomplete and possibly in error. However, when there are three independent means of arriving at an answer and all give the same answer, it becomes clear that the conclusion is correct. Recall that chapter three discussed methods of dating the age of rock formations using radioactive isotopes. They point to an earth that is over 4 billion years old. This was followed by a discussion of a totally independent means of estimating the age of the universe using the tools of astrophysics. It leads to age estimates of billions of years. Now, in this section on continental drift, we have followed one event by several combined mechanisms and find that it all leads back to a time in ancient history—much, much further than six thousand years. Indeed it leads back tens of millions of years.[7]

---

[7]Individuals interested in arguing fine points would be correct to point out that our estimates of the speed of continental drift today need not accurately reflect its speed in the past. They would also be correct to point out that measurement of rates of the drift in the past depend upon the assumption that decay rates of radioactive isotopes have been constant. As mentioned in chapter three, all nuclear physicists are in agreement that the latter is true (that is, decay rates have not changed in the last 100 million years). The real point, however, is that the independently derived numbers (current rates of drift and estimates derived from magnetized iron ore) *are* in agreement, and both point to a time frame that is about ten thousandfold greater than six thousand years.

Although we have been discussing the breakup of Africa and South America, other events can be followed as well. The mechanisms of tracking their movement go well beyond simply fitting the pieces of a puzzle together as we have discussed above. One particularly interesting aspect of the story is the breakup of South America, Antarctica and Australia. Antarctica was not always the polar icecap that it is today. Fossil data indicate that it supported a rich flora and fauna in earlier years when the world climate was much milder than it is today. Indeed these three continents were connected until about 50 million years ago. However, at that time Australia drifted off on its own and remained almost totally isolated, biologically, from other landmasses until the arrival of humans. Fifty million years is a very long time for organisms to live in isolation. If the scriptural command "God said, let . . . ," which is repeated eleven times in the first chapter of Genesis, really does imply that God granted freedom to his creation, and if the process initiated and sustained by God really does result in gradual change, then there can be a great deal of gradual change in such a long time. In Hawaii we saw that isolation over 5 million years resulted in new species of Drosophilid flies, birds and bats, along with many other changes. In the lakes of eastern Africa we followed changes leading to species formation (speciation) in the cichlid fishes, and on the fur of gophers we saw the gradual change that resulted in speciation in lice. The time frame for these changes was, at most, hundreds of thousands of years. If God really has built freedom into his creation, and if creation really does occur by gradual modification of preexisting species, then it will be particularly interesting to follow the results of living on an isolated "island" for 50 million years.

THE ISOLATION OF THE ISLAND CONTINENT, AUSTRALIA

The story of Australia actually begins a "while" before 50 million years ago and is closely related to the separation of South America from North America and Africa about 100 million years ago. At the time of that breakup, dinosaurs still were the predominant large life form on the earth. Mammals were present, but they were mostly small and nowhere near as diverse as the mammals of today. There were two major groups of mammals. One group, known as *marsupials,* bore their young fairly soon after conception and incubated them in a special exterior pouch attached to the mother's abdomen. The other group, known as *placental mammals,* had a special nutritive device (the placenta, of course) that allowed the young to be nourished within the mother's body. At the time of the breakup, according to the fossil record, South America did not have a very diverse array of placental mammals. For example, it had no placental carnivores, insectivores or rodents. We will return to a discussion of South America later, but it is important to note this reduced variety of the early mammals compared to what was present in other sections of the world. Marsupials, on the other hand, were much more prevalent in South America than they were elsewhere. At that time the southern tip of South America was still connected to Antarctica, which in turn was connected to Australia, and Antarctica had a much milder climate than it does today. Although the fossil record of the mammalians present in Australia at the time of the breakup is extremely sparse, it appears that it was primarily marsupial. If placental mammals were present, they died out fairly early, because there is an extensive Australian fossil collection that represents the organisms that were alive 15 to 25 million years ago, and this consists exclusively of marsupials.

In the discussion of the Drosophilid flies of Hawaii and the cichlid fish of the African lakes, you were introduced to the concept of an ecological niche. Each organism is adapted to a particular lifestyle. Some flies are adapted for feeding on flowers; others, for living on decaying fruit. Some fish are adapted for scraping algae off of rocks; others, for scraping the scales off passing fish. The fact is, though, that both sets of fish and both sets of flies maintain certain distinctive characteristics— trademarks showing they are related to one another. The time since their origin has been relatively short compared to the entire history of life on earth. The flies still all maintain enough of their ancestral characteristics that they can be identified as Drosophilids, and the fish all maintain enough of their original characteristics that they can still be recognized as cichlids. The time since the Australia-South America separation, however, has been greater (about ten to twenty times as long), so if the notion of creation by gradual change is correct, we might expect greater change. Longer time would provide more opportunity for change than that observed in Hawaii, the lakes of Africa and the fur of gophers.

In the previous examples the characteristics of the organisms that developed depended upon two primary factors: the founding species and the ecological niches that developed for those founding species. Life in Hawaii was founded in part by a small number of Drosophilid flies that by chance were carried on air currents to their new island home. As we survey the situation in Australia, we will limit our discussion to mammals. Just as fish can become adapted to exploit the different ecological niches in a lake, so mammals become adapted to exploit the niches that occur on land. Moreover, just as the same sort of ecological niches develop in two different lakes, so also similar niches develop on different continents. The fact that North America and Australia are separated by thousands of miles is irrelevant in this respect. Australia has grassland plains and forests just like America does. In North America one mammal that was ideally adapted to life on the plains (until humans took over) was the buffalo. In Australia it has been the kangaroo. Although the same niches may develop in different world areas, the founding members will determine which organisms arise to fill those niches. If, for example, the mammalian species that were present in Australia in its early years had pouches, then over the 50 million years of gradually changing life forms, all the organisms that develop may well have pouches also. If the founding organisms have a placenta, then the organisms that are produced by gradual change may all have a placenta. Nevertheless, since the ecological niches will be similar, we might anticipate that a similar array of organisms will arise to take advantage of those ecological niches.

In Australia a mammal called *Myrmecobius* has a long, pointed snout ideally suited to sniffing out the soil for ant colonies. It has a reduced number of small, flat teeth that are specialized for its one simple food supply, and it has powerful front limbs that are ideally suited for digging in mounds of earth. Its body form is strikingly similar to the anteater of the western hemisphere, *Myrmecophaga*. It is about the same size, has an extremely long nose and has dentition that is strikingly similar to that of its Australian counterpart. There is, however, one major difference between the two—the former has a pouch, whereas the latter does not.

Many other examples of parallel features in body structure appear when comparing the mammals of the two continents (figure 5.2). In Australia a mammal called the wombat is adapted to the lifestyle of what is called a fossorial herbivore. This means that it is adapted for burrowing through the soil and that it eats only plant material. The wombat looks much like its counterpart in North America, the groundhog, except for one important difference. If you were to turn a female wombat over on her back, you would note that she has a pouch where the groundhog would have a navel. Australia also possesses squirrel-like animals, including some that are adapted for gliding from one tree to another—flying squirrels. Other parts of the world also have flying squirrels. The difference, of course, is that the Australian one is a marsupial, with a pouch and no navel. Until extinction in the twentieth century, Australia had its own wolf, named the Tasmanian wolf. It was adapted to the same lifestyle as our wolves and at first glance looked much like its North American counterpart. The difference is that it arose from the tiny marsupial mammals that inhabited Australia at the time of the breakup, and they had pouches. Australia has small rabbitlike herbivores, a variety of marsupial mouse species and moles, and in former times it had catlike carnivores. All are characterized by one fundamental difference from similar American species, and that difference points strongly to a message about their ancestry—they all have a pouch.[8]

One major body form is conspicuously absent from the Australian fauna. There are no hoofed animals roaming the plains. Instead there is a different type of organism occupying the niche that, in the rest of the world, is occupied by ungulates (animals with hoofs). Australia has a diverse variety of kangaroo-related species. Instead of walking on

[8]For more details on the Australian mammals, see D. W. Walton, ed., *Fauna of Australia* (Canberra: Australian Government Publishing Service, 1989); and Ronald Strahan, ed., *Complete Book of Australian Mammals* (Sydney: Angus & Robertson, 1983).

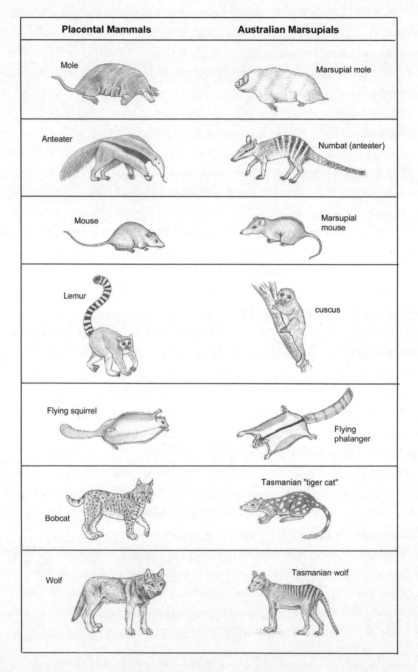

Figure 5.2. A comparison of body forms of mammals with a placenta to counterpart body forms in the "pouched" mammals of Australia

hoofs, they hop on two legs and a powerful tail that has almost become a third leg. The same grassland niches exist, but in this case God's natural world at work has come up with a different body plan—one that works well to exploit the available ecological niche.

Thus the rule of convergence (similar body structures for similar niches) is not hard and fast. Similar body forms *have* developed in this area of the world, but they are not identical and sometimes they are even very different. But the nature of the diversity of life in Australia compared to the rest of the world points dramatically to one thing. Just as it is possible to identify humans that are clearly related to each other by some feature such as a big nose or a bald head, so in Australia it is possible to conclude that almost all the mammals are related to each other because they all have the same trademark trait: where the mammals in the rest of the world have a navel, they have a pouch.[9]

Exceptions to the rule are often the most revealing of all. Imagine that you were introduced to an African family with ten beautiful children. Nine of them have black skin, kinked hair and dark brown eyes. The tenth, however, is different. She has blond hair that is wavy instead of kinked, blue eyes and fair skin. You would not need to be a terribly astute observer to suspect that the blond-haired child had a family history that was different from that of all of the other children. You may or may not inquire about how this child happened to become a part of the family, but one thing is for sure: you would know that she had arrived into the family by a different means than did the other nine children. In examining the family of mammals that inhabits Australia, we can tell that they are almost all related to each other because of the features they share. However, there are two groups of long-time members of the family that stand out as being different. These members are missing the trademark pouch, and in its place they have a navel.

Just as with the little blond child in an African family, we are prompted to inquire how it happened that these two groups of crea-

---

[9]There is a single exception to the rule that only placental mammals occupy the rest of the world. The exception is the opossum family, which originated in South America and migrated up into North America after a land bridge formed between the two continents. An interesting story about the history of marsupials in South America is discussed below, and the existence of the opossum is a reflection of that history.

tures happened to become part of the family of Australian mammals. In each case it is a trait other than the underside of their belly that gives us the clue as to how they became adopted into the Australian family of mammals. The first has a trait unlike all other mammals on the surface of the earth. It has one telltale feature that explains how it arrived to join its Australian cousins. It is the bat, and it has wings.

In thinking about the second group, one needs to examine the geography of the region. Australia, unlike the Hawaiian Islands discussed earlier, is not located a huge distance from the nearest land. In fact many islands are strung between Australia and the nearest continent, Asia. Given millions of years, it is conceivable that small animals such as mice and rats could end up drifting the relatively short distance from one island to another, eventually traversing the distance between Asia and Australia. This is exactly what has happened. Hence, not surprisingly, Australia does have some small placental rodents whose ancestors are believed to have arrived several million years ago.

The mammals of Australia are an isolated group. Certain features (the pouch is only one) make it clear that almost all the members share a common set of ancestors. Those ancestors occupied the land at the time of breakaway from South America and Antarctica more than 50 million years ago. But over the course of 50 million years, they have changed. There are no other species exactly like them anywhere on the surface of the earth. Created life is a product of its history, and given a very long time, body forms change. However, the telltale signs of that history remain, and today we celebrate the results of God's command. God said, "Let the land produce living creatures according to their kinds." So the land did. It obeyed God's command, and in response to God's Presence, we have a spectacular array of "kinds." So spectacular is this array that even God, in all of his majesty and greatness, looked upon it and declared it to be good. In fact, in the words of Genesis 1:31, God saw all that he had made, and it was "very good"—very good indeed.

FITTING INTO A NICHE
As we have discussed, the key to the diversity of life forms is the variety of niches that exist in the world of biology. Each organism becomes

adapted to a particular lifestyle. If an organism specializes in eating meat, it would be best if it has some sharp teeth for tearing the meat off the bone. Organisms that do not have sharp teeth will have less chance of surviving to reproductive age if all of their "cousins" in the species have teeth that are long and pointed. On the average, over a long period of time, organisms that are not good at tearing the meat off the bone will get less than their share when food is hard to come by.

Wherever there are animals, there will be an ecological niche for carnivores, and one of the rules of the world of biology is that, given enough time, carnivores will develop. Furthermore, in general, there will be subspecializations. Anteaters are a type of carnivore, but they are adapted to a much different lifestyle than that of a lion. Foxes, hyenas and sea lions are carnivores too, but again they have their own unique subspecialty.

The world of biology is not unlike the world of economics. Certain economic niches have spread all over the world as a result of changes in the lifestyle of human beings. One hundred years ago, no one knew what a gasoline service station operator was. With the advent of the automobile, a whole new set of economic niches opened up. Today you would be able to travel to Sweden and find people who pump gas (or at least will accept your money while you pump your own gas). The odds are high that the person who operates the service station will have fair skin and light-colored hair. Wherever there are highways, there will be a niche for people who operate service stations. In the far north of Canada the attendants will generally have dark eyes and skin that is not as fair as that of the operators in Sweden. If you pull in for gas in Kenya, you can expect that the individuals who fill the niche of service station attendant will have black skin and other features that make them distinct from those you would meet in Mexico City. The niche exists everywhere highways are found, but the features of individuals occupying it vary.

It is not a difficult task to find someone who can fill the gas station niche. In a matter of less than a day, the attendant will learn the fundamentals, such as opening and closing the station, filling out the appropriate paperwork, operating the cash register and perhaps even (heaven forbid!) pumping gas. At the end of that day, as long as the individual has certain important features like honesty and a friendly smile, he or she would be a full-fledged service station attendant. Service station attendants who are dishonest, constantly grumpy or sloppy about closing correctly would not last long. However, as long as they have the basic features, they may operate the service station for the duration of the niche's existence at that particular location. Now to the important point: the niche exists all over the surface of the earth, but the physical nature of people who occupy it is limited by the history of the region. People with very dark skin operate service stations in Kenya because people with those characteristics are the long-term residents. Furthermore, the specific manner in which the niche is filled will vary with regional culture and history. Recently I was in Japan, where not only do the people who occupy the service station attendant niche look a little different from their counterparts in San Diego, but they also carry out the task much differently. In Japan we were welcomed to the station by two young men in spotless white uniforms. They guided us toward an open pump, making us feel important. They pumped our gas, washed our windows and checked fluid levels in the car. When all was done, they walked in front of us to the road and told us when it was safe to reenter the traffic. The final touch was visualized by a glance into the rear-view mirror, where I saw them bowing repeatedly in appreciation for our having chosen their station. Hence, not only does the niche exist all over the world, and not only do people who fill the niche have different physical features, but they also have different approaches in successfully filling the niche. I suspect that a service station who attempted to operate in Japan the way they operate in San Diego would not be in business long.

The reason I have taken this diversion to discuss economic niches is, of course, because it is closely related to the biological story of life on earth. The same ecological niches exist in Australia as exist elsewhere on earth, but the physical characteristics of the organisms that occupy those niches, as well as their behavioral adaptations, are a reflection of the history of the region. In ways that are clear and unmistakable, one can account for the characteristics of the organisms on the basis of which organisms were there as the niche began to open up. Just as the opening up of highways worldwide resulted in new niches (service station operator is only one) filled by whomever happened to live in the region, and just as the niche took on idiosyncrasies appropriate for that region, so also organisms arose to become ideally suited to fill ecological niches. Which organisms filled those niches was a function of "who" was there in the early days.

ABSENCE OF NICHES NORMALLY OCCUPIED BY MAMMALS IN NEW ZEALAND

Many other fascinating stories demonstrate how the characteristics of the species that inhabit a region are a function of the history of the region. We will look briefly at a few more, just to be sure that the generality of this observation is clear. Unlike Australia, New Zealand did not have any mammals (except for its own species of bats, of course) until the arrival of humans. However, it did have birds. A number of these birds are members of the group known as the *ratites,* of which the emu and the ostrich are the most familiar to us. In New Zealand there were (until the arrival of humans in the first millennium) about sixteen different species of moas, ostrichlike birds. Some of the moa species were gigantic, up to ten feet tall and weighing as much as 150 pounds. All went extinct with the arrival of humans, undoubtedly a result of overhunting. It is not just a coincidence that there should be such a diverse array of flightless birds in a land that has no mammals. Indeed part of the reason for their success may be that until that one great mammal—the human—came along, they had few natural predators. The other reason could well be that the ecological niches that would normally have been occupied by mammals were free and available—in this case to birds. It is sad that we cannot see these impressive birds, but they made good meals, we can be sure, for the Polynesian islanders who visited and eventually inhabited New Zealand. All we have today are their bones.

However, one group of ratites did survive the human onslaught in New Zealand. Still today there are three different species representing this group—the kiwi.[10] Each species is closely related to the others, and

---

[10]See W. A. Calder, "The Kiwi," *Scientific American* 239, no. 1 (1978): 132-42.

none of them is found anywhere else in the world. It is interesting that this bird lives a mammal-like existence in a world where there were no mammals to occupy the niches. The kiwi's feathers are different from those of most birds; in fact they are shaggy and almost furlike in appearance. The kiwi has no tail (in flying birds the tail is important for balance during flight), and its wings are little more than stubs that cannot be seen unless one digs for them in the furlike blanket of fine, downy feathers. Its legs are strong and serve for burrowing and fighting. It is an aggressive little bird, like a feisty weasel or mink. Its principal food supply is the earthworm, which is particularly abundant in the rich and moist New Zealand soil, and it almost looks like a little anteater as it roots through the soil in search of worms. In parallel with this, it uses a highly developed sense of smell—a mammal-like characteristic for which birds are not well known. Like mammals, but unlike birds, the female kiwi has two functional ovaries. Indeed so much like a mammal is this bird that one biologist has only half jokingly awarded it the status of an honorary mammal.[11] The point of this is that ecological niches arise and that organisms present become genetically altered over time, enabling them to become better suited to live in that environment. Today, as biologists examine the organisms, they find the trademarks that point back to the history of the region. In this case there were no mammals, but there were birds, and thus the birds became increasingly adapted to a mammal-like existence.

THE FLEET-FOOTED CARNIVORE NICHE OF SOUTH AMERICA

The story of birds occupying niches normally occupied by mammals is not unique to New Zealand. Another island is particularly noteworthy in this respect—an island that we think of as a continent. South America has had a rich history in geological time. After the breakup with Africa, it continued to be connected to North America until about 65 million years ago, at which time the two continents parted ways. They remained separate until fairly recent times (as geological history goes). About 2.5 million years ago, a major fall in sea level due to the

---

[11]Ibid.

formation of a polar icecap, combined with an uplifting in the land-mass at what we now know as Panama and northern Colombia, re-sulted in a reconnection. The long period of isolation resulted in a dis-tinctive array of mammals on each of the two continents. As already mentioned, it appears that South America had few if any placental carnivores at the time of the breakup; thus, following its separation, the large carnivore niche was initially occupied by two different sorts of animals—marsupials and birds. As with Australia, marsupial cat-like and wolflike animals arose in South America. The wolflike ani-mals were especially noteworthy, with species varying in size from that of a skunk to certain species the size of a bear. There was even a large saber-toothed marsupial predator, similar to its placental equiv-alent, called the *saber-toothed tiger*. (The latter roamed North America until it was probably hunted to extinction by humans.) All of this is consistent with the sort of story that was presented in the discussion of Australia—similar ecological niches develop the world over, and organisms become similarly adapted to fill these niches. The chief lim-iting factor is which organisms happen to be present at a particular world location as the niches develop.

There is one fundamental difference, however, between the marsu-pial carnivores of South America (and Australia, for that matter) and the placental carnivores in the rest of the world. The marsupial carni-vores did not have long legs, nor did they have the specialized skeletal adaptations that are associated with high speed. Thus it seems as though the really high-powered carnivore niche, which thrived on at-tacking high-speed herbivores such as horses, was occupied by a dif-ferent sort of organism altogether. What was that organism? Many fos-sil samples of a large group of ratite birds have been found in South America in rocks as old as 62 million years and as "young" as 2.5 mil-lion years. They are known as terror birds.[12] They were about ten feet tall and had a head that was over three feet long, with a throat that would open up to a diameter of eighteen inches. They had extremely strong legs and gigantic, sharp-clawed feet. There is good reason to be-

---

[12]See L. G. Marshall, "The Terror Birds of South America," *Scientific American* 270, no. 2 (1994): 90-95.

lieve that they could reach speeds of forty miles per hour—fast enough to keep up with many of the fastest herbivore species. It is thought that in the chase they would reach up with their powerful leg in order to knock the target animal off balance. Once that had been done, the terrified animal would be torn apart by the gigantic, powerful beak and claws. Like the moas of New Zealand, the terror birds of South America had small stubs for wings, and they probably used them for balance in the high-speed chases.

Hence, in South America, the large, fast carnivore niche was occupied by birds and not by mammals. Indeed even the marsupial catlike and doglike animals eventually went extinct, quite possibly because of their inability to compete with the powerful, speedy ratites. The story does not end there, of course, since these birds are no longer in existence. What happened to them is a matter of speculation, but it is closely tied with the reestablishment of the land bridge connecting North and South America. In rocks dated at less than 2.5 million years, fossils of North American carnivores can be found in South America. None are found in rocks older than that. Biologists believe that the simultaneity of the disappearance of the terror birds and the sudden appearance of the fleet-footed carnivores from the north is not a coincidence. They believe there may have been competition between the two groups of organisms (terror birds and fleet-footed mammals that occupied similar ecological niches), with the mammals winning. An alternative (and not necessarily mutually exclusive) possibility is that the terror bird chicks were especially vulnerable to attack by the newly arrived carnivores. A third possibility is that the eggs of the terror birds, which had been safe on the ground until then, were suddenly open to attack by the new organisms that migrated southward. Whatever the cause, terror birds went extinct at about the same time as the formation of the land bridge, and North American carnivores took over the southern continent.

WHEN REPTILES PLAY THE LEAD ROLE

To complete this analysis of the tie between geographical history and the history of species, we now return to Australia. I have already addressed the absence of placental mammals in Australia and how marsupials filled many of the niches occupied by placentals in other world areas. The fact is, however, that there were a limited number of marsupials in Australia that played the role of major carnivore. What animal fed upon the largest kangaroos? What animal occupied the throne at the top of the Australian food chain? The answer is as interesting as it is surprising. Until just several thousand years ago, the top Australian carnivore niche was filled not by a mammal nor by a bird but by a reptile—in this case a giant dragon lizard. The lizard, *Megalania*, was fifteen feet long and weighed in at close to a thousand pounds, or the size of a Kodiak bear.[13] Since all we have are fossils, we know little about it, but its monstrous jaws and sharp, curved teeth certainly made it a formidable enemy. The notion of a slow, lumbering, cold-blooded reptile at the top of the food chain may seem surprising to us today, but we need to remember that for a long time (prior to the current age of mammals) reptiles, in the form of dinosaurs, really were the dominant organisms all over the earth. Hence, perhaps it would not be surprising if, given the absence of a powerful mammalian carnivore, a reptile could develop that would take on this lifestyle.

In fact the notion of huge reptiles in the carnivore niche is made particularly germane by the existence of an organism on which we have more than fossils to go by: the Komodo dragon.[14] Once again it is noteworthy that this unusual organism should develop in an island environment in which there are no fleet-footed mammalian carnivores, namely islands off the coast of New Guinea. A sort of a blown-up version of a monitor lizard, the Komodo dragon can reach a size of up to ten feet in length and can weigh about as much as a lioness. Not being particularly fast (running up to twelve miles per hour for short bursts), these creatures lie in wait until one of their favored prey, a deer, comes bounding past. They then tear at the deer's flesh. If the deer escapes, which is not unusual, it has probably been infected by unusually toxic bacteria that the Komodo dragon harbors in its mouth. Hence, at a later time, either the killer itself or one of its Komodo "cousins" will be able

---

[13]See C. Ciofi, "The Komodo Dragon," *Scientific American* 280, no. 3 (1999): 84-91.
[14]Ibid.

to feast upon the bounty, immune to the bacterial infection that has killed the deer.

Once again the same theme is played out for us. When there are no organisms occupying a particular niche, the niche will be filled in a manner that is determined by history. Which organisms fill the niche is largely a function of contingency—the particular array of organisms that happen to be there at the time.

CONCLUSION

The purpose of all of this has been to illustrate that species really do come and go in the history of life and that our theology must not be based upon a view of God that prohibits this. We must be careful not to make God into some type of master engineer—the great tinkerer in the sky—who made the billion or so species that have inhabited the earth just because it was a hobby of his. The Bible does not give us a reason to believe in this type of God. If we read carefully, we see that although the Bible has specific things to say about the creation of humans, it simply speaks of life's appearance as being a response to the command of God. Hence the view of God as the engineer-designer of species one by one has come from our own minds and not from God's holy Word. Life appeared at the command of God, and the parade of life was always under his control. Both the Bible and the biology are entirely consistent with this view of life.

6

TRACING LINEAGE BY TRACKING GENES

THE PRECEDING PORTION OF THE BOOK laid emphasis on the fact that
the Bible does not provide many details about the mechanism of creation.
Genesis speaks of God's command "Let the waters bring forth . . . ," and
the Gospel of John speaks of the Word of God "through whom all things
were made." However, when it comes to the details, we leave the realm
of biblical *declaration* and enter into the domain of *interpretation.* Where
details *are* provided (for example, reference to six creation days), is the
language figurative or not?

Augustine, one of the founding fathers of Christianity, had some
words of admonishment for us about interpretation of Scripture. We
would be wise to pay heed to them:

> In matters that are so obscure and far beyond our vision, we find in Holy
> Scripture passages which can be interpreted in very different ways with-
> out prejudice to the faith we have received. In such cases, we should not
> rush in headlong and so firmly take our stand on one side that, if further
> progress in the search for truth justly undermines our position, we too
> fall with it. We should not battle for our own interpretation but for the
> teaching of Holy Scripture. We should not wish to conform the meaning
> of Holy Scripture to our interpretation, but our interpretation to the
> meaning of Holy Scripture.[1]

---

[1]Cited in Alister E. McGrath, *The Foundations of Dialogue in Science and Religion* (Oxford, U.K.:
Blackwell, 1998), p. 119.

Moving from the distant past to the present, consider the words of a leading spokesperson for biblical inerrancy, J. I. Packer: "It should be remembered . . . that Scripture was given to reveal God, not to address scientific issues in scientific terms. . . . It is not for scientific theories to dictate what Scripture may and may not say, although extra-biblical information will sometimes helpfully expose a misinterpretation of Scripture."[2] Both of these men, who have been helpful (in different eras) in aiding us to formulate our faith, advocated a high degree of caution in making conclusions about how to interpret passages of Scripture that are open to more than one interpretation. They both said the same thing: sincere extrabiblical searches for truth may helpfully inform us of our own misinterpretations of Scripture. Augustine warned that Christianity should not allow itself to be put in a position whereby it stands or falls on a particular interpretation that is not fundamental to faith. Packer, in the above quote, was summarizing the position of approximately one hundred scholars at a 1982 biblical inerrancy conference.[3] He emphasized that the purpose of Scripture is not to address scientific issues and moreover, that outside information is a valid source of data to help inform us about the meaning of certain scriptural passages.

Much of evangelical Christianity today has taken the position that either possibility 1 (creation of each new species from "scratch")[4] or possibility 2 (creation of new prototypes from "scratch," followed by minor modification)[5] represent the best way to interpret the creation account. One goal of this book has been to lay out the reasons why the gradual creation perspective (possibility 3) is an extremely likely alternative.

Certainly the data of nuclear physics, geology and astrophysics lead virtually all individuals with doctorates in these disciplines, both

---

[2]J. I. Packer, *God Has Spoken: Revelation and the Bible,* 3rd ed. (Grand Rapids, Mich.: Baker, 1993), pp. 167-68.

[3]The quotation cited in the previous footnote is from Packer's summary of a 1982 meeting of the International Council of Biblical Inerrancy, a meeting of approximately one hundred scholars whose purpose was to achieve a consensus and practice of biblical interpretation. Although Packer drafted the statement, he has indicated that his statement had the broad approval of almost all participants.

[4]Henry Morris, *History of Modern Creationism* (San Diego: Master Book Publishers, 1984).

[5]Phillip Johnson, *The Wedge of Truth* (Downers Grove, Ill.: InterVarsity Press, 2000); Jonathan Wells, *Icons of Evolution* (Washington, D.C.: Regnery, 2000).

Christian and non-Christian, to conclude that the earth is very old. Furthermore the fossil record leads virtually all paleontologists to conclude that new life forms of increasing complexity have made a gradual appearance throughout earth's history. Finally the geographical distribution of distinctive organisms is consistent with the notion that species in one part of the world are formed by gradual modification of founding species. Although this tidal wave of scientific data lends strong support for the third possibility, it is important for us to further explore what the data coming from God's world have to say about how God's Word and God's ongoing Presence brought living creatures into being. The goal in this is that we, alongside all of God's creation, will be able to look heavenward in a more meaningful manner as we bow in worship to Abba, Father, the source of our being.

GENETIC LANGUAGE AND WHAT IT TEACHES ABOUT THE MECHANISM OF CREATION

A collection of genes serve as an instruction manual. If we are going to be able to understand, even in broad outline, how God created life, then we need to know about genes. Genes carry the instructions on how to make a living organism, and by studying them, we are in essence reading from the manual of life. Since the author of that manual is God, it is an awesome privilege to be able to understand its language, to be able to pick it up and read it and see what it teaches about how God chose to bring living creatures into being.

All organisms from the simplest bacteria (so small that they cannot be seen under a light microscope) to the majestic blue whales have a set of genes. Collectively, genes are the blueprint for the construction of bodies. Genes dictate how each of the parts within a cell should be organized; they cause individual cells to arrange themselves into tissues; they provide instructions enabling tissues to form organs; and their instructions orchestrate the body's organs, enabling them to function as a unit.

The instruction that each gene carries is the message of how to assemble a particular protein molecule (or portion thereof). Proteins are the workhorses of life's processes. For each task associated with being alive, there is at least one protein necessary to ensure that it takes place.

The task of delivering the oxygen we breathe to the tissues of our body is one example. A specific protein—hemoglobin—binds to four oxygen molecules in the lungs, transports them through the blood to a particular tissue, releases them, then quickly returns to the lungs to repeat the cycle. The instructions on how to build hemoglobin are found in two genes. Those genes provide details that dictate the exact shape of each hemoglobin molecule and the precise properties that will enable it to carry oxygen.

The clotting of blood is another task for proteins. When you cut your finger on a piece of glass, blood comes oozing out of the damaged vessels. If there were not a way of sealing off the damaged vessels, you could bleed to death. Fortunately a clot forms almost as soon as the injury occurs. Certain proteins patrol the bloodstream, seeking out sites of damage. When they find such a site, they stop, assemble into a complex net that seals off the injured area and thereby prevent continued blood leakage. Genes provide the directions for making these blood-clotting proteins. The genes dictate the precise shape of the proteins, ensuring that they have the properties of correctly assembling into nets at sites of damage (figure 6.1).

For each of the processes of life, there is a protein or a set of proteins responsible for the task, and it is genes that tell the body's cells how to make them. Humans have about thirty-five thousand genes. Hence there are a lot of proteins, which comes as no surprise, because there are also a lot of tasks.[6]

The key to what each protein molecule does is its shape. Consider hemoglobin, for example. Why can it transport oxygen? Simple. It carries oxygen because it has four little cavities, each of which has a binding site to which an oxygen molecule sticks. Each cavity and its binding site must be precisely fashioned so that only oxygen will fit and then stick. If the shape of the hemoglobin protein is distorted even slightly, the binding sites may be altered, destroying hemoglobin's ability to transport oxygen (figure 6.2).

---

[6]In some cases, two or more genes may participate in providing instructions on how to make a single protein molecule. Hemoglobin is one such example. Two genes, one called *alpha* and the other *beta*, are needed to make our hemoglobin molecules.

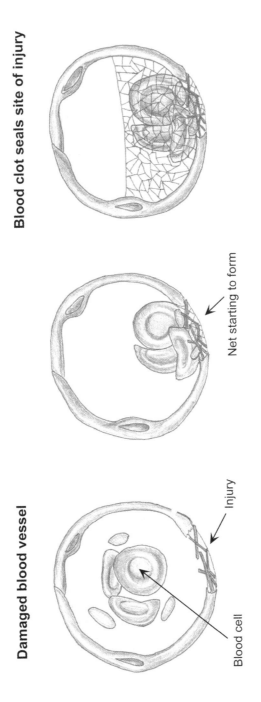

Damaged blood vessel

Injury

Blood cell

Blood clot seals site of injury

Net starting to form

Figure 6.1. Certain proteins have structural properties that cause them to assemble into nets at the site of blood vessel damage.

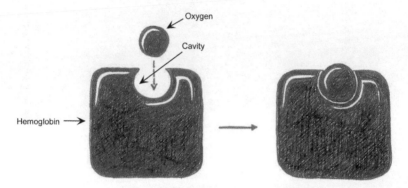

Idealized diagram of hemoglobin molecule

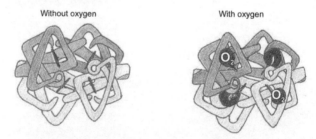

More accurate diagram of hemoglobin molecule

Figure 6.2. Each type of protein has a specific shape that enables it to carry out its function. In the case of hemoglobin, its function is to bind to oxygen.

I will make analogies throughout this part of the book to put scientific concepts into everyday imagery. This is fairly easy to do for proteins. Proteins have particular shapes that enable them to carry out their task, just as do the objects we use every day. A portable car seat, for example, is designed to carry babies. Its contours and overall shape are perfectly designed to fit a baby. A bookcase is designed for books, and a pencil sharpener has a cavity that is perfectly contoured to receive pencils. For each of these objects, someone has drawn up a set of plans, and those plans, if followed correctly, provide information on how to construct the object. So also one or more genes provide the plans on how to build a particular protein molecule.

The nature of the instructions of a gene. We now turn to the question of how a gene's instructions for making a protein actually work. The plans are in the form of a code that the cells in our body can understand. Let's begin by thinking about the nature of any message, regardless of whether it is found in a cell or on a printed page. For example, I am now going to write a sentence that conveys a message you will be able to understand:

Put down this book, go to the refrigerator and fix yourself a strawberry sundae.

That sentence contains twenty-one different letters, sixty-five in all. The twenty-one letters are arranged in a manner that conveys a message to you, and you (and your appetite!) understand exactly what it means. Genes are analogous to such a message. Instead of having twenty-one letters, genes speak in a language that has only four letters. The letters (called *bases*) are actually four different molecules strung together just like letters in a sentence. The four molecules have names: *adenine, guanine, cytosine* and *thymine* (or A, G, C and T, for short). I am now going to write a different sentence:

ATGGTGCACCTGACTCCTGAGGAGAAGTCTGCCGTTACTGCC.

That sentence means nothing to you, but to a cell inside your body, the string of A, G, C and T molecules bonded together in this specific order means something. Just like you would go to the refrigerator in obeying the earlier sentence, so your cell might respond to this instruction by making a portion of hemoglobin. Genes contain a code. The code is in the form of four different molecules strung together in a specific sequence known as DNA. The cell "reads" the order of these A, G, C and T bases in a DNA molecule in a manner that is analogous to how your eyes and brain read and perceive the letters on a page.

Different ways of expressing the same genetic message. Now we come to an important point. There are multiple ways to say the same thing. For example, the above sentence could be rewritten with slightly different wording:

> *Put down the book you are reading, head over to the refrigerator and prepare a strawberry sundae for yourself.*

The message is the same, though it is said differently.

I am now going to record another genetic message, which also means the same thing to the cell as the one you were given earlier:[7]

*ATGG**T**TCA**TT**A**A**CACCAGAAGAAAAAAGC**G**CGGGA**A**CGGC**T**.

These instructions could be read by the cells in your body to make the same portion of the hemoglobin molecule. They mean precisely the same thing to your cells. They would make the same portion of the protein and assemble it in exactly the same way.

Several years ago my wife and I found a good sale on bicycles—so good, in fact, that we bought two identical bikes, one for my wife and one for our daughter. The bikes came unassembled, so I loaded the boxes into our car, looking forward to a not-so-exciting afternoon of reading through the instructions and trying to assemble two bicycles. As I opened each box, sure enough, I found that each of them contained the paperwork that would allow me to put the bikes together in a step-by-step fashion. There could have been many different ways of telling someone how to assemble those bikes. However, it will not surprise you to learn that the two sets of instructions were identical. The wording was precisely the same, word for word. The diagrams for both sets of instructions were identical and were placed at the same position on each page. The two sets of instructions would not

---

[7]Differences between this message and the previous one are shown in **bold**.

have had to have been identical to get their message across. The reason that they were the same, of course, is that they were duplicated from a single source.

Let's get back to biology. As mentioned above, there are many different possible ways of expressing the instructions for making the hemoglobin in blood. They all would work equally well. In spite of this, the instructions in the cells of the body of a specific chimpanzee are exactly the same as the instructions the chimp inherited from its parents. Of course they are the same, we reason; they are exact copies that were passed into the chimp's body from the sperm and egg of its parents. Just as the two sets of instructions on how to build the bicycle were identical because they were duplicated from a single source, so a duplicate of the instructions on how to make hemoglobin was placed from the chimp's mother into her egg and from its father into his sperm. Those instructions from the parents were, of course, duplicates themselves—from the grandparents and their parents before that.

Actually, even though there are many ways of expressing the instructions for making the same portion of the chimp hemoglobin molecule, the chances are good that they are exactly the same in two different chimps, even if the two are not related. Although there are many ways of "wording" those instructions, each would have almost the same "wording" because they have been faithfully copied generation after generation, century after century, from the original plans in a common ancestor. Just like the instructions for my two bicycles, two chimps carry the same instructions despite the many other ways genes could say the same thing.

The near identity of the genes for hemoglobin in two different chimpanzees tells us that the copying mechanism must be amazingly efficient. Apparently it can be copied for thousands of years with almost no changes. Indeed this is true, but like all copying systems, this one is not perfect, and it is the minor changes that are the most powerful tool in tracing lineages.

Chimpanzees are not the only organisms that have two genes with the instructions on how to make hemoglobin. Orangutans have them too. In fact, because the lineage of all orangutans could theoretically be traced back to a small number of ancestors, they also use a similar set of instructions on how to make hemoglobin. Even though there would be many, many ways of "wording" those instructions, the "wording" is almost exactly the same for all orangutans on the surface of the earth. Similarly the genes of each of the gorillas that my wife and I love to watch at the San Diego Wild Animal Park use the same "wording" on how to make their hemoglobin as do the genes of their cousins back in the jungles of Africa. The reason is that their ancestral lineage could be traced back to a common set of parents. The instructions within a species are almost the same, even though there are many different ways of "wording" those instructions.

Copying the genetic message: do mistakes ever occur? The reason for the near-identical set of instructions for gorillas, orangutans and chimpanzees is the accuracy of the copying mechanism. Experimental investigation has enabled geneticists to determine the faithfulness of this process, and although it is clear that mistakes are almost never made, they do happen on occasion.[8] Let's assume, for the sake of illustration, that it has been twenty-five thousand years since two chimps in different parts of Africa had a common ancestor. Let's also assume that throughout the intervening time each of their ancestors was, on average, about ten years old when the next generation was conceived. This means that the gene has been copied about twenty-five hundred times since it was present in the single ancestor that both chimps share in the distant past. So accurate is the copying mechanism that an error preserved in the lineage would occur during these twenty-five hundred duplication events at the rate of about one mistake for every four thousand "letters" of the genetic code copied per twenty-five thousand years of running the "copy machine." Although this is an amazingly faithful process, over exceedingly long periods of time, the fact that changes do occur becomes extremely significant to those of us who want to understand details about the time frame for God's creation.

---

[8]It is beyond the scope of this book to explain in detail how one determines the rate at which copy errors occur. Suffice it to say that the approximate rate is known with a very high level of confidence. See M. W. Nachman and S. L. Crowell, "Estimate of the Mutation Rate per Nucleotide in Humans," *Genetics* 156 (2000): 297-304.

The mistakes point to a common lineage even for members of different species. The reason that all chimps look so much alike is because they share a common lineage. If we could go back far enough in time, we would find a common ancestral population from which all chimps are descended. If genes can be used to trace lineage, then now we come to the central theme of this story. Do they point to lineages that cross the species boundary? Most biologists think that, just as different chimpanzees are so similar because they share the same ancestors, so also the reason chimps and gorillas resemble each other is because they also share a single set of ancestors. The only difference is that it has been a longer time since the single ancestral group was alive. If this is the case, then this would mean that the genes of the chimps and the genes of gorillas have been copied and passed on to each generation many, many times through their two separate lineages since the days when they had a common ancestor. In fact biologists estimate that the genes have now been copied over a million times since the days when their common ancestor was alive. Now we come to the most amazing part of our story. There are many ways of "wording" the instructions on how to make hemoglobin, but chimps and gorillas still "word" the instructions in an almost identical manner. What if we consider organisms that are clearly related but have not had a common ancestor for an even longer time—the chimp and the macaque monkey, for example? In this case, again, the instructions in the gene are *almost* identical, but there are additional differences. The instructions say exactly the same thing, but the wording of the instructions has changed.

The key point is this: the "wording" for the instructions is *not* exactly the same; there *have* been some changes over the years—precisely what one would expect if rare changes occurred during the many copying events. Just like my two sets of bicycle instructions were worded and diagrammed in the same way because they were duplicated from a single source, so the genes of chimps and macaque monkeys are nearly the same and thereby point to a single original ancestral species. There is one important distinction, however, between the bicycle plan analogy and the plans for hemoglobin in chimps and monkeys. Unlike the bicycle plans, the chimp/monkey plans are only similar, not identical.

Let's reexamine the bicycle plan analogy in this light. Pretend the in-structions for bike 1 said, "The nut A should be threaded onto bolt A," but the instructions that came with bike 2, omitting the initial word, "the," said only, "Nut A should be threaded onto bolt A." Other than that, suppose the instructions were identical, not only word for word, but diagram for diagram, with everything positioned exactly the same on each page. If that had been the case, no one would doubt that the two sets of instructions had a common source. Without question all would agree that initially one set of plans had been drawn up but that this had been followed by a minor change somewhere in the drafting process, and thus I was given two slightly different versions of a single initial plan.

It is fifteen years since I bought those bikes, and they are both old and rundown now. In fact I really should replace them. Let's pretend that I go back to the same store and find that they still make that same bicycle. Furthermore, because we liked the other two so much, I decide to buy the same model again. After all these years, it is still the same— not a single change anywhere. Hence I buy it, bring it home and start to assemble it again just like I did on that Saturday afternoon fifteen years ago. In fact I think I still have those old plans, so I decide to ex-amine them to make a comparison. Not surprisingly, I note that the plans are still virtually the same. But there are some changes. Ten lines down from the sentence about threading nut A onto bolt A, I note that where it used to say "Place the chain upon the sprockets," it now says "Place the chain on the sprockets." The old version of the plans used the word "upon," whereas the new version uses the word "on." In-deed, as I examine the plans further, I find that there have been several other changes, all similarly inconsequential. The bike is still exactly the same bike; the only difference is that the plans have changed slightly in a manner that has no impact on how the bicycle is assembled.

It is the same with genes. Just as a single set of bicycle assembly in-structions can be modified slightly to say the same thing, so a genetic message can be altered slightly and still provide the same message on how to assemble a protein. The protein end product may be identical, but the slightly altered way of telling the cell how to make that protein points to a common set of plans that have been altered ever so slightly over the eons of time.[9]

I need to make absolutely certain that you understand the ramifications of two genes in two different species having slightly different ways of saying the same thing. There are many different words for the object you are holding in your hand and from which you are currently reading. You call the object a "book." People in your country have been continually calling it by that name for hundreds of years, and you have inherited that tradition. In France a different name gets passed on from one generation to the next for that same object. In France it is called a *livre,* and in Spain it is called a *libro.* For each of these names a lineage can be traced back through the centuries. There is more than one name for the same object, and your calling it a "book" is a reflection of your personal history. It is the same with genes. Because of ambiguity in the genetic code (different ways of saying the same thing), there are thousands of different ways of specifying each of your proteins.

You will have noticed the great similarity in the words that the French and Spanish use for "book": *livre* and *libro.* It may even have occurred to you that it is not just a coincidence that two neighboring countries call the object by similar names. In theory, any combination of letters from the twenty-six-letter alphabet would have sufficed for naming this object. If someone in France had decided long ago that she wanted to construct a language from scratch, and if somebody in Spain had independently done the same thing, then the words they would have chosen for "book" would have been different from each other. The fact that the arrangement of letters to make these two words is almost the same points to a common ancestry of the two words. So it is with the "language of the genes." If chimps and gorillas really do have a common ancestor, then it would be predicted that in both species a

---

[9]The reader may wonder if I am implying that the copying mechanism only makes errors that result in different ways of saying the same thing. The answer to that query is no. Errors created by the copying mechanism are quite random, and this means that they certainly do change the message on occasion. Usually, however, changing the message is detrimental to the health of the organism and such changes are not efficiently passed on to subsequent generations. Hence, the changes that are tolerated and preserved in the lineage are primarily those that do not change the message.

gene that makes a given protein would utilize almost, but not quite, the same "genetic language." Just as *livre* and *libro* leave an indelible trace for us today of a common ancestral language base, so it is for the genes of chimps and monkeys.

Although our example has focused on the genes with the instructions on how to make hemoglobin, organisms have thousands of genes. Each of them exhibits the same phenomenon. If two species are closely related, each of the genes say the same thing using almost exactly the same "language." If, on the other hand, species are further apart (for example, chimpanzee and monkey rather than gorilla and chimpanzee), then when the instructions say the same thing, the "language" they use to say it is more dissimilar. This phenomenon is repeated over and over for thousands of genes in all species examined.

Recall possibility 1—creation of each new species from scratch. If this were indeed God's way of carrying out creation, then one is left with an intriguing dilemma. When God's instructions are saying the same thing, why is it that the wording is virtually identical for closely related species, a little different for species that are not so closely related and very different for species that are even more distantly related? In each case it is the same thing being said. Why would God alter the way of saying it in a manner that so perfectly parallels what we find when we trace the origin and gradual change of languages? Words are similar because they have a common ancestor. So it is with genes.

FOLLOWING MARKED GENES THROUGH THE EONS OF TIME

Some time ago my wife and I attended a reception at which a friend whom we had hardly seen in thirty-five years was present. We knew that this friend's son, now in his twenties, was also going to be present. So closely did this son resemble the father of thirty-five years ago that we spotted him in the crowd well before we spotted our gray-haired friend of long ago. The son had the same nose and other facial features that had characterized his father, and his voice sounded exactly like that of his dad's thirty-five years ago. The lineage from father to son was "marked" by distinctive features, and one did not have to be particularly perceptive to know whose son this young man was. The distinctive features gave it away.

Sometimes, if one looks closely at photographs of family reunions, it is possible to trace the lineage of certain distinctive genetic features. Indeed, if a collection of photographic portraits of grandparents and great-grandparents (and beyond) exists, and if there are distinguishing facial characteristics, it may in some instances be possible to track lineage back a century or more. The analysis of facial features in photographs is, however, a somewhat crude tool for tracing gene lineage. Its lack of refinement stems from the fact that one is attempting to trace features that are the product of gene activity rather than the genes themselves. With the tremendous advance of molecular genetics, it is now possible to use much more sophisticated tools—we can analyze the inheritance of the genes themselves, and it can be done with awe-inspiring precision. These techniques allow us to trace lineages through much more than dozens of generations. Now, by following uniquely "marked" genes back through the eons of time, it is clear that lineages of what are now two or more distinct species can be traced back to a single ancestor that both species have in common. I will now describe the nature of these traceable genes.

Gene duplications. The average human chromosome has about two thousand genes. Frequently a given gene is represented on the chromosome only once. Occasionally, however, certain genes get duplicated, so that two copies of the same gene come to reside adjacent to each other on a chromosome. There is no reason to go through the technical details of how this occurs, but it is a process that is well understood, something called *unequal crossing over*. When it happens, both genes are usually active, since both carry a functional set of instructions for making a particular protein.

In order to make the next genetic concept clear, I will turn to an analogy. Suppose that you are a parent of two beautiful children, a boy and a girl. As a typical parent, you prepare a photo album of their childhood years. You lay out all of the pictures into an album, but by mistake you insert two copies of the same photo (pretend it is the picture of your little girl with her fingers in her first birthday cake) on one page of the album. Upon noticing your error, you make the decision that a blank spot in the album would look worse than having two identical photos side by side, so you allow the duplication to remain. When your children grow up, you decide to give a copy of the album to your children as graduation gifts, so you take it to a high-quality copy center and have it copied. Thus each of your children inherits a copy of the photo album, complete with that page that has two identical pictures side by side. In fact, pretend that this eventually becomes a family tradition, so that long after you are gone, grandchildren and great-grandchildren are still getting copies of your photo album, each with that first birthday duplication that you never bothered to remove.

Just as two identical photos can be placed into an album, the same sort of thing can happen to genes. When the genes are copied so that they can be passed on to the next generation, the duplicate is copied also. In fact the extra gene, just like the extra photograph, gets passed on from generation to generation. Now we come to the important point. If there is really a continuous lineage from one species to the next, as the theory of gradual creation suggests, then these unusual duplication events will be passed through the lineage so that not just members of one species inherit the duplication but members of closely related species inherit it as well.

Genetic investigation of organisms has turned up a multitude of cases of this sort. As an example we will consider one thoroughly documented study of the fly *Drosophila*.[10] There is a group of different species known as the *repleta* group that are closely related to each other, based on various physical characteristics. Almost all the genes within these species are present in only one copy. However, some years ago, David Sullivan, Phil Batterham and others at Syracuse University discovered a species within the *repleta* group that had two copies of the gene with the instructions for making a par-

---

[10]I like to choose *Drosophila* for my examples because I am, by background, a *Drosophila* geneticist. I choose this particular example because much of the data was obtained by colleagues, located one floor up from my lab, during my years at Syracuse University.

ticular protein referred to by the name *alcohol dehydrogenase.*[11] As their investigations continued, they discovered that this duplicated gene was a characteristic only of these closely related flies. Those species that were physically quite different from the *repleta* group had just the standard one copy of the gene. Since gene duplication is a rare event (just like the insertion of a duplicate photo into an album), and since this is found only in a closely related group of species, it is clear that at a particular point in time an extra copy of the gene was generated by accident.[12] Ever since that event, the duplication has passed on through the lineage that has diversified into many different species, all of which have descended from the fly in which that duplication occurred and all of which still have the duplication in their chromosome.

In case you are tempted to conclude that this simply demonstrates microchanges within a single prototype, that is, flies (this, you may recall, has been termed possibility 2), it is important to emphasize that this is a general phenomenon. Distinctive duplicate genes are found within all lineages. Chimps and gorillas (ape prototype) share certain telltale duplicate genes with monkeys, perhaps the most noteworthy being genes with the instructions for making the oxygen carrier, hemoglobin. In fact one of these duplicates—that for a version called *delta globin*—is specifically found in all monkeys and apes. If you are tempted to place monkeys and apes into a single prototype, read on; the story of marked genes runs much deeper than that.

Pseudogenes. It is important to explore the concept of duplicate genes a little further. The fact is that two identical genes on the same chromosome are not necessary for the life of the organism. The duplicate is redundant even though it is being passed on through the lineage from generation to generation. Because of its redundancy, the duplicate can accumulate mutations without affecting the viability of

---

[11]L. E. Mills, P. J. Battherham, J. Alegre, W. T. Starmer and D. T. Sullivan, "Molecular Genetic Characterization of a Locus That Contains Duplicate ADH Genes in *Drosophila mojavensis* and Related Species," *Genetics* 112 (1986): 295-310.

[12]Based upon analysis of flies preserved in amber, the *repleta* group probably began as a distinctive lineage about 10 million years ago.

the organism.[13] Usually mutations are deleterious.[14] They cause a specific protein to fold abnormally, and since the function of that protein is necessary for life, the organism will die or at least be less efficient at reproducing. The result of this is that defective genes are eliminated from the population. However, if the organism has a duplicate gene, then mutations in one member of the duplicate pair can be tolerated without any negative impact on survival. Thus the duplicate gene is passed from generation to generation with mutations freely tolerated as it passes through time. Mutated duplicate genes of this sort are called *pseudogenes.*

To be sure this concept is clear, I want to return to the analogy with the photo album. Remember that you had your album photocopied and passed it on to each of your children as a graduation present. Let's assume that one of your children eventually has a daughter of her own—a granddaughter for you. Furthermore let's assume that this granddaughter is handy with crayons. One day she gets into the precious photo album and scribbles on one of the pictures, specifically the picture of her mother with her fingers in her first birthday cake. If it had been any other picture, the scribble would have been removed or the picture replaced because of the high value the mother (your daughter) placed upon that picture. However, this one is okay, because it is present in duplicate and one good copy of the photo remains. The ramifications of that fateful day, however, are passed on in perpetuity because, within the lineage of your daughter, all of her descendants will receive a copy of the album that has the scribbled-over duplicate. The lineage of your other child (remember you had two children, each of whom received a copy of your photo album) will not contain the damaged duplicate unless at some time one of his children or grandchildren, being equally handy with a crayon, gets a hold of his family's prized copy of the album. Even if he did, however, the markings would be distinctive, and a

---

[13]Mutations change the code in a DNA molecule, often causing the gene to make a slightly altered product. Usually such alterations will reduce the ability of the gene product to function properly.

[14]Although they are usually deleterious, this is by no means always the case. Indeed sometimes mutations produce novel characteristics that are beneficial to the organism's chance of survival.

distinctive lineage of his photo album would be established.

Just like the damaged duplicate photo, pseudogenes are passed on from generation to generation in the same manner as ordinary genes, and their distinctive lineage can be followed.[15] There are many examples of pseudogenes. However, for the sake of illustration, we will consider one found in goats that makes the point in an especially succinct manner. The pseudogene we will examine is a mutated relative of the gene with the instructions to make the protein hemoglobin. Hemoglobin, as you will recall, is required for oxygen transport. The sequence of the code of bases (A, G, C and T) has been determined in this pseudogene so that it can be compared to the natural, unmutated gene. Just as it is possible to retrace the movement of the child's hand as it passed over the duplicate photo, so it is possible to trace the mutations that have occurred in the gene. One of the abnormalities is especially noteworthy. It is a deletion mutation that resulted in the removal of a specific portion of the code. The reason this deletion is noteworthy is that cows have a pseudogene for hemoglobin as well, and their pseudogene has this same deletion.[16] Deletions are very rare, and thus the notion that the same deletion could have occurred independently in both the cow and the goat is virtually unthinkable. It is analogous to proposing that two children independently marked up exactly the same picture and that the path followed by their scribbles was identical at the microscopic level. Just as the photo in the albums distributed throughout your daughter's whole lineage will have exactly the same marking because it is faithfully copied by the photocopy machine, so the cow and goat have exactly the same deletion in their nonfunctional pseudogene because they inherited copies of it from a common ancestor. Clearly the mutation occurred in an ancestor, and through the ages this pseudogene, with its telltale dele-

---

[15]One might wonder at this point why the cell does not just cut out the defective gene and remove it. The fact is that there is no such mechanism inside of cells for recognizing these abnormal genes. But there is no need for such a mechanism since such genes do not cause the organism any problem by sitting in the chromosome.

[16]D. G. Shapiro and M. Moshirfar, "Structure of the Goat psi-beta-Y Beta-globin Pseudogene: Analysis of Goat Pseudogene Evolutionary Patterns," *Journal of Molecular Biology* 209 (1989): 181-89.

tion, has been passed on to its descendants, which include both goats and cows, and probably further tests would show that it is present in other hoofed animals as well.

What about other groups? Do they also show marked pseudogenes that leave telltale signs of common descent? Consider a specific pseudogene DNA sequence in the primate lineage.[17] The sequence of As, Gs, Cs and Ts (discussed earlier in the context of genetic language) is virtually identical in all of the primates examined. However, there is a small deletion of eleven bases that are missing in chimps, gorillas, orangutans and gibbons. In all other primates examined, from macaque monkeys to lemurs, the sequence CCACG(Cor T)GCTGA exists at this location. According to the thinking of virtually all biologists, the above stretch of eleven bases was deleted in a single common ancestor to the great apes.[18] They all now carry the deletion because they inherited it from that ancestor. On the other hand, the organism in which that deletion occurred was not ancestral to macaque monkeys, lemurs, spider monkeys and so on, and thereby they do not share the marked gene. People who hold to possibility 1 might be tempted to suggest that the reason why God put a deletion into the ape lineage is because it would make the gene more ideally suited to carrying out its purposes in apes. That might well have been a valid argument if this was a functioning gene. However, it is not. The gene has no function. It is a remnant of an old gene duplication event, now badly marred due to accumulated damage and tolerated because of the existence of a functioning duplicate.

Two examples of uniquely marked pseudogenes have just been discussed. Both occur within single prototypes (the former within hoofed animals, the latter within the primate lineage). Can marked genes be followed across the prototype boundary? This is a most important question, since it would provide more data to help distinguish between possibilities 2 and 3. It is to this question we now turn.

---

[17]E. J. Devor, R. M. Dill-Devor, H. J. Magee and R. Wazire, "Serine Hydroxymethyltransferase Pseudogene, SHMT-psl: A Unique Genetic Marker of the Order Primates," *Journal of Experimental Zoology* 282 (1998): 150-56.

[18]Alternatively, it is possible that a single eleven-letter addition occurred in a single ancestor of the monkeys.

Retroposons. As discussed above, genes carry instructions as to how to make each of the many proteins in a cell. Each protein molecule then folds in a manner that allows it to take on a specific function, such as carrying oxygen molecules. About twenty-five years ago it was discovered that the DNA instructions for making a protein molecule are punctuated by stretches of meaningless gibberish. Remember that earlier message: "Put down this book, go to the refrigerator and fix yourself a strawberry sundae." I used it to make a parallel between the language of genes as it is read by cells and the way in which we humans communicate with each other. The parallel is almost perfect—almost, but not quite. Unlike human language, genetic messages are frequently interrupted by meaningless gibberish. A more accurate way of making the analogy between a human instruction and the message of a gene is as follows:

> *Put down this book, abcdefgjruhgufiurjfujurikkffyrjriofhjkluvwxyz go to the refrigerator and fix yourself a strawberry sundae.*

A stretch of gibberish, when it occurs within a gene, is termed an *intron*. The cell is able to recognize signals that represent the start and end of the intron. (In this example, those hypothetical signals are "abcedefg" and "uvwxyz," respectively.) Once the cell sees these "start of gibberish" and "end of gibberish" signals, it ignores all the blather in between.

With this as background, a more accurate depiction of a human cell's instructions on how to make a portion of the hemoglobin molecule might read as follows. In this example, the sequence in lowercase bold is a set of bases—A, G, C and T—that the cell is able to recognize as meaningless blather.

ATGGTGCACCTGAC**ggacttgcatcc**TCCTGAGGAGAAGTCTGCCGT-TACTGCC.

This is exactly the same sequence you were given earlier, except for the inclusion of the section of gibberish. Almost all genes have these introns, although they are generally a little longer than this hypothetical one. A signal at the start ("gg" in my hypothetical example) tells the cell that it is about to read gibberish, and another signal ("cc" in the example) tells the cell that it has reached the end of the gibberish.[19]

Since the sequence within an intron has no meaning to the message, it can change freely without affecting the message. Hence, if I change the message you read earlier to read,

> Put down this book, abcdefgzzzzzzzzzzzzzzzzzzzzzzzzzzzzzzzzzzuvwxyz go to the refrigerator and fix yourself a strawberry sundae.

you will still be able understand the message perfectly. As long as you know the start and end signals for the gibberish, you would soon find yourself in front of the refrigerator door, should you wish to obey the instructions and follow your appetite. The lettering inside the gibberish section is irrelevant.

Keep all of the above in the back of your mind as I move on to briefly discuss a second bit of background information. In studying the parallel between genetic instructions and human instructions, you are learning that the parallel is not perfect. Genetic instructions contain stretches of gibberish called introns. But there is another sense in which the two differ. DNA has "floating gibberish," one example of which is something that biologists call *retroposons*. This "floating gibberish" can insert itself into genes, including the intron section of a gene. Once inserted, it is copied faithfully by the cellular "machinery" generation after generation.

Consider some floating gibberish, "tuttuttuttuttuttut," and pretend that it gets inserted into the "intron" in our message. If that happens, we would have a new message:

> Put down this book, abcdefgzzzzzzzzzzzzzzztuttuttuttuttuttutzzzzzzzzzzzzzzz-zzzzuvwxyz go to the refrigerator and fix yourself a strawberry sundae.

You and I have no problem reading this message because we see the signal "abcdefg," which tells us that we are coming to gibberish, and the signal "uvwxyz," which tells us that this blather is about to end. The fact that floating gibberish has moved in makes no difference to our ability to read the message.

---

[19]The actual signals are longer and more complex than this, and the blather often goes on for hundreds or thousands of As, Gs, Cs and Ts, but for the sake of illustration, this makes the point.

This is exactly like what happens to genes. The sequence we showed earlier may occasionally have a retroposon move into it. As long as the retroposon moves into an intron, the message can still be read without a problem. For example,

ATGGTGCACCTGACG**gga**cccaaccaaccaaccaaccaa**ttgcatcc**TCCTGAG-GAGAAGTCTGCCGTTACTGCC

can still be read by the cell without difficulty because the insertion of the retroposon (*"ccaa"* and so on) is within the section that the cell knows to ignore.

How does all of this relate to God's mechanism of creation? When a retroposon moves into a gene, the marked gene is passed to the next generation. There is no mechanism to remove retroposons once they have been inserted, so they are passed faithfully through generation after generation down through the millennia. Each retroposon has a distinctive sequence of the bases, A, G, C and T; hence they can be recognized by geneticists. Indeed they are frequently given names as identifiers. We will consider one particular retroposon that goes by the name SINE CHR-1. It consists of 120 bases (that is, As, Gs, Cs and Ts) in a defined sequence of these DNA bases.

The retroposon SINE CHR-1 is found inside a specific intron of a particular gene in a group of related animals. The fact that this stretch of gibberish is found in the same gene, in the same place, but only in these related animals, suggests to virtually all geneticists that this retroposon entered the intron in one organism many years ago and has been copied faithfully in its new position ever since. Which organisms have SINE CHR-1 in the same gene, in the same intron and in the same position within that intron? On the basis of fossil data, biologists have long believed that whales are most closely related to even-toed ungulates, like the hippopotamus. (The data in support of this became especially strong with some fossil finds in the 1990s. See chapter four.) Cows, sheep, deer and giraffes are also even-toed ungulates. It is extremely significant that all even-toed ungulates, like their cousins the whales and dolphins, have the retroposon SINE CHR-1 inserted at the same position in a specific intron within a specific gene.[20] On the other hand, more distantly related animals, such as the camel and pig, which are not even-toed ungulates, do not.

One cannot argue that the cows, whales and dolphins need to have this retroposon at this place, whereas pigs and camels do not. This is gibberish and it has been inserted into the gibberish portion of a gene (that is, the intron). It is clear to virtually all geneticists that many millions of years ago the SINE CHR-1 retroposon became inserted into the intron of one gene of an animal that was on the lineage to whales, dolphins, hippos and other even-toed ungulates. Camels and pigs, on the other hand, do not share that ancestral history; hence they do not have the same inserted retroposon.

It is important to point out that related animals have many retroposons inserted in exactly the same position in differing gibberish sections of many different genes; SINE CHR-1 is only one example. The more closely related the animal, the more identically positioned retroposons they share.

Recall our three possibilities for God's mechanism of creation. Possibility 2 was that animals share ancestry, but only within prototypes. The retroposon data, like the data from geographical distribution (chapter five) and the existence of transitional fossils (chapter four), are not consistent with possibility 2 but completely consistent with possibility 3. Since gibberish is inserted within the same intron (which is gibberish itself) at the same position in two different species from different prototypes, virtually all geneticists are convinced about the reason: they share common ancestors.

Viruses. As strong as all of the above data are, there is more—much more. Let's look at viruses, for example. Viruses are produced from reading a set of genetic instructions, just like the parts of an animal or plant are produced from reading genes. When a virus invades a cell, it injects a copy of its instruction book, *How to Build Viruses Just Like Me.* The cell into which the virus has inserted the instructions may then read them and proceed to make millions of the minuscule particles, all just like the original invader. Sometimes a "silenced" version of the in-

---

[20]M. Shimamura et al., "Molecular Evidence from Retroposons That Whales Form a Clade Within Even-Toed Ungulates," *Nature* 388 (1997): 666-68.

structions gets inserted into the organism's own instruction book, that is, into one of its own chromosomes.[21] When that happens, it is there forever. This causes no problem for the organism as long as the instructions have inserted themselves in a region of gibberish—the original message can still be read. So, for example, in our message about the strawberry sundae, this would cause no problem as long as the insertion occurred within the recognizable gibberish section:

Put down this book, abcdefgzzzzzzzzzzzzzzzhow to build viruses just like me-zzzzzzzzzzzzzzzzzzuvwxyz go to the refrigerator and fix yourself a strawberry sundae.

In such cases the cell recognizes the start of gibberish signal, "abcdefg," and the end of gibberish signal, "uvwxyz," and having done so, reads the message as though it were not interrupted at all. In other cases the silenced version of the virus instructions are inserted *between* genetic messages, in which case the cell just ignores them.

The point that is most germane to this discussion is that when the silenced virus instructions are inserted into a chromosome, they cannot be removed. Hence they sit there for generation after generation, passed on faithfully through millions of years. Each inserted set of instructions is the result of one event in one individual in the ancient past.

By studying which organisms carry the virus instructions inserted into the identical spot, it is possible to tell which ones share a common ancestor.[22] Thus, for example, Old World monkeys and apes all have a virus insertion, dubbed HERV-K64, whereas New World monkeys do not. This means that this particular virus insertion occurred in an organism that apes and Old World monkeys share as an ancestor. On the other hand, a different virus insertion, HERV-K18, is found only in apes, not in Old World monkeys. Geneticists are certain this means the insertion event occurred later in the lineage, in an individual that was an ancestor to apes but not to monkeys. The previous virus insertion occurred earlier but not so early that it included all monkeys. That in-

---

[21]The way in which a set of viral instructions are silenced is a long story that is not germane to the current discussion.

[22]E. D. Sverdlov, "Retroviruses and Primate Evolution," *BioEssays* 22 (2000): 161-71.

sertion occurred at a time considerably later than the existence of the common ancestral species of Old and New World monkeys.

In describing the evidence for shared lineage as it relates to viral insertions, I have given examples of only two insertions. There are many more. The data are extensive, and there is no good interpretation of these data other than that species that share common insertion points also share a common ancestor in their ancient past.

Putting the inheritance of marked genes into perspective. Prior to the invention of the printing press, books were reproduced by hand-copying every word—a method susceptible to error. If there were three copies of a particular book, all of which had the same minor discrepancy on one of the pages, and twenty others that did not have the discrepancy, would there be any doubt that the three that had the discrepancy shared a copying lineage?

The genetic instruction book is nowhere near as subject to error as the hand-copied manuscripts of long ago. Nonetheless, given the massive amount of information that genetic material contains, changes do take place.[23] The sorts of changes that may take place include errors in the copying process, insertion of a section of "floating gibberish" or the insertion of silenced instructions for building a virus. Today geneticists, molecular biologists and computer scientists have read the genetic instructions for dozens of species, and the number that will soon climb into the hundreds. Because of this recently acquired ability to read the instruction books of a host of species, we are in a new and exciting era. It allows us to compare the instruction books of similar organisms. In so doing we see things that bring us deep into the past, and the things that we see fit extremely well with what biologists have long predicted about the history of life on this planet.

Many telltale signs indicate that the instruction book used to build the bodies of various species of whales and dolphins is derived from the same one used by hippos, cows and deer. Many of the same alterations are found in each of their books. Often the alteration has no

---

[23]If one were to type out the series of As, Gs, Cs and Ts that represent the instructions on how to build and maintain the body of a mouse, the information would fill three thousand volumes the size of this book.

functional significance at all (for example, pseudogenes, retroposons and virus insertions). It is just a case of something that happened. What occurs in the history of life as a whole is analogous to that which happens in the progress of our own individual lives. You, like me, probably have a set of scars on your body, each associated with a specific event one day in your past. For example, when I was sixteen, the cartilage covering the lower section of one of my nostrils was ripped open. I still have a faint scar to show for it. When I was nine, I broke one of my lower front teeth playing football in our front yard. I still have that broken tooth as a memento of that day so long ago. I have other scars scattered around my body, and so do you—each one unique to you, with its own particular story that you might well be able to relate to anyone who asked. Just as you and I suffer cuts, bruises and other insults to our body on occasion, the same sort of thing happens to the genetic instruction book. When it happens, the "scar" associated with the event lasts down through the eons of time.

Are you any less a creation of God because you have a little scar on your knee (or wherever)? Absolutely not. Is the instruction book for how to make a chimpanzee any less the product of God's creation because it carries with it the "scars" of gene duplications, pseudogene deletions, retroposon insertions and old silenced instructions on how to build a virus? Absolutely not! God willed liberty for his creation. In that freedom we humans fall and bruise ourselves on occasion. But also in that freedom gene sequences shuffle, change and become rearranged. Just like each specific scar on your body is a reflection of a specific event in your past, so also the distinctive changes in DNA are a reflection of the past history of organisms—a past that stretches far back into the antiquity of biological time. Just because, in the freedom of our existence, we have fallen while running or had teeth bashed in playing football, that does not mean we have been separated from God's guiding Presence in our lives. So also, just because creation in general has picked up a few scars during its history, that does not mean it has ever been out of reach from the Word of God's command or the Spirit of God's Presence. The God whose Presence remarkably influences the progression of my life is the same God who has always guided creation. God can move suddenly in ways that represent unmistakable miracles, but he also works in subtle fashions, in manners that frequently cannot be detected except through the lens of faith. Which way he chooses (or has chosen) in any particular event or series of events is his call, not mine and not yours.

Your scars, moles and other blemishes are unique products of your personal history. No one else on the surface of the earth has exactly the same set. When you die, your scars "die" with you. In this respect, then, the genetic instructions differ from the surface of our bodies: the genetic instructions *are* duplicated. Hence these "scars" do get passed on, and organisms that share a specific "scarred" section of DNA do so because of their shared history.

Arrangement of genes on chromosomes. Most mammals have about thirty-five thousand genes. Each gene carries a message on how to do something that is important in the life of the body. The genes are not just scattered around the inside of a cell, like thirty-five thousand pieces of paper spread out all over the floor and desk of a disorganized person's room. Rather they are arranged in order into a defined number of chromosomes, almost like pages in a book. You and I, for example, have two sets of twenty-three different chromosomes. Although they vary in size, the average chromosome has about fifteen hundred genes, each one the equivalent of one page.

Chromosomes get passed on from one generation to the next through the sperm and egg of the previous generation. The two sets of twenty-three different chromosomes inside the cells of one of the chimpanzees you saw at your last visit to the zoo are almost perfect duplicates of what she would have received from each parent. Not only that, but if you were able to trace her lineage and go back to the time of Christ, two thousand years ago, the genes in each of her chromosomes would be in exactly the same order in those chromosomes as well. Chromosomes, just like photocopies of that family photo album described earlier, are faithfully copied each generation, and the order of the "pages" almost never gets rearranged. That is how faithful the copying mechanism is.

However, errors may occur on occasion. Let's go back to think about our photo album again. You will remember that you gave one copy of it to your son and one to your daughter, so that they also could pass copies on to their children, and this becomes a family tradition down through the eons of time. Let's say that when your son's daughter (your granddaughter) takes her album into the copy center, she gets a careless clerk and an error is made. The ten front pages get moved to the back of the album and what had previously been the eleventh page becomes the first. After she gets home, your granddaughter notices the error, but she does not worry about it. "What the heck," she says. "All the pages are still there. I'll just leave it the way it is." So she does. However, 150 years from now there will be two distinct lineages of the photo album. One will carry the photos in the original order, but a branch of the family will be passing along a photo album with an order that is a little different from that of the original.

Actually the photo album of each family would be an outstanding way of finding out which of the various cousins (or by this time third or fourth cousins) are related to you through your son's daughter. The lineage of the photo album tells you who is related to whom. A genealogist studying your family would be able to use these photo albums to trace all the people who are related to you and would also be able to use them to break the family down into two branches. As long as the rules had been correctly followed, there is no doubt that all family members would be traced back to you, because they all have the same pictures in the album (your pictures, including that old duplicated photo of your daughter with her fingers in the cake). Nonetheless we can also tell that some members have their own distinctive lineage, all because your granddaughter chose not to put pages 1 through 10 of the album back into the correct order.

It is exactly this concept that allows us to determine that certain species share a common ancestry. Each chromosome has its own particular order of genes, just like pages in a book. Very rarely, however, the pages get rearranged. The rearrangement can easily be traced, exactly like the rearrangement of the ten pages in the photo album. Consider as an example the arrangement of a particular chromosome of a chimp and an orangutan. The same genes of that chromosome are present in the gorilla, but there has been a single rearrangement—a segment of the chromosome has the genes arranged in inverse order. The genes work fine in either order;

it's just that a rearrangement occurred in the gorilla family history.[24]

Rearrangements do not occur often, so it is easy to see when they do occur. Frequently two species share the same rearrangement that another more distantly related species does not. Virtually all geneticists agree that the reason they share the same chromosome rearrangement is because they all spring from the same great-great-great-great- . . . grandparent in which the event first took place. For example, chimpanzees and gorillas share a number of rearrangements that are not present in macaque monkeys. To geneticists, this means that if we could go back in time, we would see that there was a common ancestor to both chimps and gorillas—one that carried the particular arrangement of the genes they share.

By the same token, macaque monkeys, chimps and gorillas all share certain rearrangements that cats do not have. What this means to biologists is that they share a common ancestor (much deeper back in time). However, even cats, monkeys, chimps and gorillas share some rearrangements. The analogy to the photo album carried to its extension leads us deep into the distant past, revealing that God's mechanism of creation has been a gradual process. It is clear now that God did not create each new species from the dirt of the ground or with the snap of his fingers, as some have thought. God did it in his own way. Now, like never before, God is allowing us to peer back through those millions of years to see how it was done.[25]

AUGUSTINE REVISITED: GIVING UNDUE SIGNIFICANCE TO ONE INTERPRETATION OF SCRIPTURE

When you add the information just discussed to all of that presented in

---

[24]Because of the scope of this book I have chosen to mention only one specific chromosome in the lineage to chimps, gorillas and orangutans. This type of analysis has been done for all the chromosomes and is currently being done at an increasingly refined level. For the details see J. J. Yunis and O. Prakash, "The Origin of Man: A Chromosomal Pictorial Legacy," *Science* 215 (1982): 1525-30. For an example of more recent, refined analyses, see A. de Pontbriand et al., *Genomics* 80 (2002): 395-401.

[25]Genesis 1 is quite general in its discussion of creation. It speaks of creation occurring in response to God's command. Scripture deals separately, however, with the details of the creation of humans. Those details are provided in Genesis 2—3. Likewise, this book will deal separately with human creation (see chap 7, "Coming to Peace with Biology," pp. 216-27) and will place it into the scriptural context of these two chapters.

previous chapters, it becomes harder and harder to understand why possibilities 1 and 2 are still serious contenders in the search for truth. At the least, are we now at the point where Augustine's admonition should be heeded? Recall his words: "We should not rush in headlong and so firmly take our stand on one side that, if further progress in the search for truth justly undermines our position, we too fall with it. . . . We should not wish to conform the meaning of Holy Scripture to our interpretation, but our interpretation to the meaning of Holy Scripture."

In reaction to one of the early drafts of this book, I was told by some individuals (none of whom were theologians) that all of Christian theology stands or falls on a sudden creation. This is most certainly not true, but it is this perception that causes some people to take a stand for possibility 1 or 2 against all odds.

Why is it that so many feel that Christian theology is intricately tied to the question of whether God created each new species or prototype from scratch? One answer I repeatedly get to this question is that the Scripture teaches that there was no death until Adam and Eve sinned in the Garden of Eden. Since possibility 3 states that organisms were created gradually prior to the existence of humans, it implies that the death of organisms preceded the Fall. Augustine warned us about rushing headlong into a particular interpretation of Scripture lest we fall with it. Is this a case in point? What does Scripture really say about the entry of death into earth's history?

The Genesis account itself has only one reference to death. Genesis 3:19 states,

> By the sweat of your brow
>   you will eat your food
> until you return to the ground,
>   since from it you were taken;
> for dust you are
>   and to dust you will return.

This specifically refers to Adam and his death, but it says nothing about other living organisms. There is nothing in Genesis stating that no organism died until the moment of the Fall.

So why is this view stressed so adamantly? Why does it seem to some that Christian doctrine stands or falls on the notion that death *in general* entered the world at the time of Adam and Eve's sin? There are three key New Testament Scriptures perceived by some to be central to this position. Romans 5 is the first. The whole chapter is important, but it really revolves around the 12th verse, which reads, "Sin entered the world through one man, and death through sin, and in this way death came to all men, because all sinned." A careful reading of the chapter shows that what is really being talked about is *spiritual* death. If you, as a reader, are particularly concerned about this issue, you might put this book down now, get your Bible and turn to Romans 5. Note that the chapter goes on to talk about Christ's coming to free us from the power of death. What sort of death did Christ free us from? It could not have been physical death, could it? After all, bodies, even Christian ones, have been getting old and dying for the past two thousand years. It is the spiritual side of our existence that has been freed from death by the coming of the second Adam, Christ. Clearly, Paul was discussing spiritual death and life in this chapter; it is the spiritual side of our being that springs to eternal life because of the death of the second Adam—Christ. In the context of this chapter, then, Adam's sin brought spiritual death into the human race, whereas Christ came and freed us from that death. It is also important to note that no mention is made of organisms in general in this passage.

The second New Testament Scripture that has become a foundation stone for this view is 1 Corinthians 15. For example, verse 22 states, "As in Adam all die, so in Christ all will be made alive." Again, consider putting down this book and opening your Bible to this chapter. Note that it is about human resurrection and passage into heaven. Once more Paul made it clear that he was talking about spiritual death and spiritual resurrection. In verse 36, for example, he stated that our bodies do still die, and in preparation for eternity it is only the spiritual seed inside of them that lives on in new bodies provided by God. The second Adam comes to free us from the death that ensued from the first Adam's sin. In other words, it seems clear that Paul was telling us that spiritual death comes to us through Adam and that spiritual (eternal) life comes to us through Christ. If Paul was saying that *physical* death entered through Adam and *spiritual* life entered through Christ, he would be changing topics in the middle of his comparison. Paul was much too careful a communicator to do that. Certainly there is nothing in this chapter to build a whole theology around the notion of grass-eating mountain lions, vegetarian hawks and anteaters that did not eat ants—all because there was no death on the earth during the Garden of Eden era. Where does this notion that Christian doctrine depends on absence of death of all animals, be they deer, mice, or ants, come from?

We have looked at two key scriptures, neither of which mentions or implies an absence of animal death in the early years of the earth's existence. Yet I am frequently told by nontheologians that the doctrine of sin and redemption hinges on this notion that death entered the animal universe with Adam's sin. Why? Apparently Romans 8:20-22 holds the answer:

> The creation was subjected to frustration, not by its own choice, but by the will of the one who subjected it, in hope that the creation itself will be liberated from its bondage to decay and brought into the glorious freedom of the children of God.
>
> We know that the whole creation has been groaning as in the pains of childbirth right up to the present time.

The phrase "subjected to frustration" is taken by many to mean the entry of death into creation as a result of the Fall. But remember how Augustine warned us that there are often alternative interpretations of Scripture and that it is dangerous (let alone unorthodox) to build a whole theology around a single three-verse passage. For example, one could argue that human sin has indeed spoiled the earth of its earlier beauty and that the whole creation is indeed groaning because of our sinful exploitation of the earth. Further, one could argue that the extinctions that are rampant today, resulting in the destruction of so many precious species, are tied to the self-centeredness of humankind. The sinful exploitation of the earth began with human civilization and was surely well under way in the Mediterranean area when Paul was writing. One could argue that way, but that, too, is only one interpretation of what Paul was saying in Romans 8. The fact is, however, that we (Christians in general) learned a long time ago that we must not build an entire theology around a single statement in Scripture. For example, some statements in Scripture imply that we are predestined to accept or not accept God's grace, but there are other scriptures that seem to imply that God's grace is free and available to all. Individuals who are Arminian in their theology believe that there are alternative interpretations of the predestination passages; the Calvinists have a similar perspective on the passages that imply free choice. Arminians do not base their whole theology upon a single proof text. Rather they look at New Testament Scripture as a whole and arrive at the conclusion that they do. The same is true of Calvinists. To say on the basis of this one scripture that Christian theology stands or falls on the notion that there was no death of any sort on the earth until Adam and Eve's sin is an unorthodox way of doing Christian theology. It has never worked that way and should not start now.

7

COMING TO PEACE
WITH BIOLOGY

——

I HAVE HAD THE PRIVILEGE OF SPENDING a good portion of my life as a professor of biology—twenty-seven years, the last nineteen of which have been at a Christian university. Frequently, when I introduce the possibility that God may have created gradually, my students will raise the issue of whether this view is inconsistent with the second law of thermodynamics.

COMING TO PEACE WITH CONCERNS ABOUT THE SECOND LAW

Life leads to increasing order, not disorder. The second law states that the universe is tending toward disorder. Clearly, according to the notion of gradual change toward increasingly sophisticated organisms, the process of life has not been headed toward disorder. It is continually producing cells, and they are nothing if not elegantly organized. Each microscopic cell—so tiny that one would have to stack a thousand or so of them on top of each other in order to reach the thickness of a dime—is equipped with Lilliputian machines that are vastly more complex than all the parts that run your automobile. Each cell, for example, has little "battery packs" that continually convert energy into a usable form. Each also has its own little waste disposal units and a compartment (called the *Golgi*) that is somewhat analogous to a paint shop. The inside of cells is a constant hub of activity, with parts moving from place to place in a highly organized fashion along a trackway that is similar to the moving walkways in an airport. Life in a cell is the epit-

ome of order, and it has become increasingly ordered during the history of life on earth. According to the fossil record, a very long time ago
all life on earth was in the form of single cells. As highly ordered as
those cells would have been, they almost seem to represent disorder,
compared to the highly ordered collection of cells in the body of a
mammal, be it an elephant or a mouse. Here cells become associated
with one another into wondrous structures such as the heart, an amazingly efficient and long-lasting pump; the vertebral column, a won-
drously flexible support beam; and the eye, a photo sensor that is
equipped with an attachment to its own information processor.

But is this inconsistent with the second law? Life is amazingly complex,
and it became more complex as time passed by. However, the second
law of thermodynamics states that the universe is tending toward disorder. Is not this, then, my students ask, a contradiction to the second
law? The answer to this question is an emphatic *no!* Even if there were
no Creator guiding the process, the gradual change that has taken
place in organisms does not in any detectable way contradict the second law of thermodynamics. Beginning students who have asked the
question dozens of times over my years of teaching unfortunately do
not understand what this law states. Oh, that they better understood
physical chemistry! It does state that the universe *as a whole* is tending
toward disorder. It also states that any *part* of the universe will tend to
become increasingly disordered *unless* there is an input of energy.
However, if there *is* an input of energy, it is not unnatural for increasing
order to arise. As a snowflake is formed, for example, it becomes increasingly ordered, but it does so with energy input, and thus it does
not violate the second law. An acorn becomes an oak seedling and then
eventually a magnificent oak tree, but in so doing it does not conflict
with the second law of thermodynamics because there has been an input of energy—the rays of the sun.

I try to tell my students that it is important that they not try to
make the second law of thermodynamics state something that it does
not imply. The notion of changing life forms and the tendency toward
increasingly sophisticated organisms may be amazing, but it is not in
any demonstrable way an exception to the law. Organisms can be-

come increasingly more sophisticated with time because there is an input of energy, and even though the universe as a whole is running toward disorder, subsections of it may well become increasingly ordered as long as there is energy input. The leading spokespersons for the sudden-creation perspective recognize this and make note of it in their writings.[1] Unfortunately a sort of folk science has spread the word that gradual change to increasing complexity is contrary to the second law. This, very simply, is not true.

What about at the very early stages, where life first appeared—is that inconsistent with the second law? The fact is, Christians believe that everything in creation (including, but not limited to, the creation of the first cells) happened in response to God's command. Life took the turns it did because of the command of God and because of God's guiding Presence. When one accepts this, one is saying there was input from the outside that influenced, indeed directed, the order that developed. However, even though I view this as fundamental to the concept of gradual creation, it does not mean that it will ever be possible to *prove* through thermodynamic measurements that the increased order depended upon God's Presence.

There is no question that one of the great mysteries of biology is the origin of the first cells. Those of us who believe in gradual creation would maintain it occurred because of the organizing principle of God's command. However, it would not be fair to point to the scientists who are pursuing investigations of the early stages of life on earth and ask them to prove that the second law is not being violated at those stages. Their theories are simply not developed enough yet to determine whether they contradict it or not. Asking a scientist to determine whether the appearance of the first cell is contrary to the second law is sort of like taking a frozen snowflake to a tribesman in the New Guinea highlands and asking him to explain why the formation of that snowflake is not contrary to the second law. He simply does not know enough to answer the question. He does not even know what a snowflake is and certainly has no idea of how it is formed. Scientists are in that position

---

[1] See, for example, Duane Gish, *Creation Scientists Answer Their Critics* (Santee, Calif.: Institute for Creation Research, 1993).

with respect to their studies on the origin of life. It is true, unfortunately, that many of them think there was no God influencing the process, but their ideas about what did happen are immature and they certainly cannot yet address the topic of how that relates to the second law.

The second law and Christian apologetics. If scientists ever discover how the first cells arose, the finding may point to the hand of God. But it is also possible that it may not. If any lesson has come out of biology, it is that God works in subtle ways. God clearly uses natural forces to accomplish God's purposes, and often we see God's hand only when we look back in faith at the finished product. In doing so we worship God for a finished product that is awesome indeed.

Do not think it is foolish, however, to propose the possibility that even if scientists have worked out many of the details of God's creation, the movement of God's hand has been so subtle that it might not be recognizable to those analyzing only the individual "brush strokes." It is certainly conceivable that by focusing on individual strokes alone, scientists may not be able to recognize that there was a hand guiding the brush.

Let's think for a while about what the Scripture tells us about the activity of God. Although God clearly desires that all humankind will be drawn to him, I am not sure that God is in the habit of using the "magic" of miracles to draw humankind to God's being. I do not see this as being God's style. When Jesus (who was God) healed anyone, he often told the witnesses to tell no one (e.g., Mt 12:16; Mk 7:36). He wanted individuals to follow him, but not because they were attracted to his power over nature. The most poignant example of God's revealing himself to humankind was on the hill of Golgotha. This event Jesus did not want kept secret! God chooses to draw humankind to himself through that aspect of his character best pictured in the form of a suffering servant. It is this he wishes humankind would focus on. Paul wrote beautifully of this attribute of Christ throughout his epistles. Consider these words, as an example:

> Jews demand miraculous signs and Greeks look for wisdom, but we preach Christ crucified: a stumbling block to the Jews and foolishness to Gentiles, but to those whom God has called, both Jews and Greeks, Christ the power of God and the wisdom of God. For the foolishness of

God is wiser than man's wisdom and the weakness of God is stronger than man's strength. (1 Cor 1:22-26)

It is through faith in the resurrected Christ, who was first of all the crucified servant, that we come to God. When God wanted to reveal himself to humankind, he

made himself nothing,
> taking the very nature of a servant,
> being made in human likeness . . .
> and became obedient to death—
>> even death on a cross . . .
that at the name of Jesus every knee should bow,
> in heaven and on earth and under the earth. (Phil 2:7-11)

I am convinced that it is through faith in Jesus that God wants us to come to him, not through some scientific "proof" that the creation of cells is contrary to the second law of thermodynamics. If God had so chosen, he could have established a kingdom in which his Presence would have been so obvious that all people would live in fear of his awesome power and Presence. One of the three temptations of Jesus was to establish such a kingdom (Mt 4:9). Moreover, the disciples kept assuming that such a kingdom was forthcoming. When Jesus told them he was going to die, Peter actually rebuked Jesus, so contrary was this view to Peter's vision of what was forthcoming. This was not Peter's idea of a coming king. Kings do not die in order to become king. Peter was expecting a human kingdom complete with power, majesty and overthrow. When Peter rebuked Jesus for talking of an immanent death, a perturbed Jesus said, "Get behind me, Satan! You do not have in mind the things of God, but the things of men" (Mk 8:33). It is significant that in one of the only two times when we have any hint of Jesus feeling that he was being impacted by a Satanic influence (the first was his temptation in the wilderness) it comes in the context of a temptation to set up a kingdom based upon his majesty. There is something about Jesus, mirroring the character of his Father, that is most consistent with a kingdom based not upon majesty but upon servanthood.

It is possible that God may have chosen to work in creation in subtle ways because he wants humankind to be drawn to his servanthood more than to his majesty. Frankly, however, I doubt that this is the key to God's subtlety in creation. I think the basis for God's subtlety in creation is more profound than his devising the most appropriate way to draw humankind to God's self. More likely what we see in biology is just God working in ways that characterize who he is. We are indeed drawn to God because of the essence of God's character, but the inside of a beautifully organized cell has little to do with how God wants to get our attention. Much more significantly, the pathway to God points to a lonely hillside where he died as a servant for us all, that is, upon the tree that eventually became the tree by which we find life—a form of life that is much more significant and meaningful than the hub of activity that is the cell.

So do not look for God through a calculation of an exception to the second law of thermodynamics. God works in nature, of course. All of nature is a reflection of God's command and guiding Presence. But just as Peter would be disappointed if he looked to Christ as the builder of a human kingdom, so also we will be disappointed if we try to prove God's existence by examining cells or the history of life on earth. God worked in subtle ways in creation, and he wants scientists to come to him not because they see him in their test tubes but because they see him dying on the cross for their sins, a servant enduring a suffering that is proportional only to his love for them. God does not want us to be distracted from that message, for it is that which brings us life. Real *life* is not to be found in studying the test tubes that are teeming with living cells. *Real* life is not to be found in magically reproducing RNA molecules that are believed to represent the beginnings of the first cells. *Real life* is found only by kneeling at the foot of the suffering servant's cross in acknowledgment that we want *our* old lives to die too. It is only in dying that we come to live; it is only in giving up all that we come to possess everything.

COMING TO PEACE WITH THE SLIPPERY SLOPE REALLY BEING A HEAVENWARD CLIMB

The slippery slope to scientific respectability? If I have heard my students ask me dozens of times about whether the notion of gradual creation is contrary to the second law of thermodynamics, I have heard their second objection hundreds of times. "If we begin to believe that God created gradually and that there is some figurative language in the account of creation, then are we not sliding down the slippery slope toward a liberalism that will lead to rejection of the whole Bible? How are we to decide what is figurative and what is literal? If we give in here, is there any reason to assume that it won't lead to rejection of the resurrection?"

My students almost always ask good questions, and that question is a particularly germane one, because they can point to history where that is precisely what did happen. The movement toward liberalism over one hundred years ago began that way. Liberal theology developed out of scholars trying to make Christianity compatible with experience. "Experience," in this sense, includes test tubes and scientific data, but it does not include miracles or resurrections. Hence, in the theology of the liberals, much of classical Christianity went the way of the Tasmanian wolf and the dinosaur. Is there anything different now, one hundred years later, or are we once again on the slippery slope of discrediting the Bible in the name of trying to make Christianity scientifically respectable?

At this point I would like to make one point as clear as possible. The reason for my writing this book is not so that it might influence evangelical Christianity to head down the road to scientific respectability. Orthodox (traditionally accepted) Christianity holds many tenets that are beyond the realm of scientific testability. Let's explore some of these, and then I will return to the question of why I feel it is so important for all Christians to acknowledge that God could have created gradually and not suddenly.

Scientific respectability and belief in the resurrection. First and foremost, Christians believe that Jesus Christ died and rose again. If this is taken away, what is left is really not Christianity. Christianity is the belief that Christ is God, and the strongest evidence for this is that, as God, he rose again and is still alive. Take away the resurrection and one is left with Jesus as a great teacher—but not as the God of the universe. The view that Christ is not God is contrary to the heart of Christianity, and I would maintain that if that is taken away, then what is left is a different religion.

Faith in the resurrection is thus the single most important belief that Christians hold. Is it scientifically credible? Think about it. The essence of Christianity is the belief that after Jesus' heart had stopped and his brain had ceased its activity, even after the decay process had set in, the same body came to life again. All the experimental data that we have and probably will ever have indicates that in the normal day-to-day world in which we live this would have been impossible. There is no way we can massage the notion that a resurrection from the dead is scientifically credible. It is not. Yet this is the position we hold. Furthermore, if we ever cease to hold it, then we have ceased to be Christians, because the resurrection is the most fundamental of all Christian tenets.

As a scientist, how can I hold the view that a body could come to life again after dying? The answer, very simply, is because I believe that there is good reason to accept that the Creator of all of life visited this earth in the form of a human being. Given that belief, anything is possible, including a suspension of laws that he put in place to begin with. Nevertheless, to a scientist working in the lab with his or her gels and test tubes, there is nothing that brings this into the realm of anything the scientist can explore. Scientists can only test events that follow natural laws. Hence science is silent on the question of whether it would be possible for the Creator of the universe to visit the earth in the form of a man, die and be raised to life again. Testing that claim is beyond the reach of the tools of science and probably always will be. Thus, to a scientist who believes that what he or she sees is all there is and ever was, the belief in a risen body is irrational. If, however, there is more to life than what can be seen at the scientists' lab benches, more to life than what we experience in everyday existence, then it is not irrational at all. One thing is for certain: since it is a singularity, it is beyond the realm science can explore.

Scientific respectability and belief in the Holy Spirit. A second belief of Christians is the existence of the Holy Spirit, whose presence is manifest in today's world. For someone engrossed in the world of test tubes and things we can see, touch and measure, this is a strange idea. However, the fact is that we believe this, and if that belief is taken away, we are left with something very different from the traditional Christianity of the past two thousand years. Christianity has long maintained that God did not just create the universe and then step out of it. It has long maintained that not only did Jesus die and rise to life again but also that he sent his Spirit to dwell among us, to comfort us and to provide new life. Take away the belief in the Holy Spirit and you are no longer left with Christianity.

Is it possible to massage the doctrine of the Holy Spirit to make it scientifically respectable? I remember when I first became an evangelical again after a period of skepticism. On Sundays, after spending my week in the lab doing experiments that gave concrete answers to carefully posed questions, I would go off to be with God's people and would sense God's Presence in and through them. People in the church talked all the time about the Holy Spirit's impact on their lives, and to my mind this experience was evidenced continually by the joy in their faces that was radiating out from God's Presence in their hearts. One time I took my graduate student, who did not know God but desperately (in my opinion) needed God's Presence in his life, to church. For him, it was like walking into a scene on another planet. People were praising a God he did not know anything about and talking as though that same God was actually living inside of their being. Having lived in the world of experiments, amid things you can see in the here and now, my graduate student thought what he saw was utter foolishness, and he never came to church with me again.

There is no scientific way of testing for the existence of a Spirit who cannot be seen or measured with instruments, let alone prove the Spirit's Presence in the life of a person. So why do we hold this view? And is it a rational one? We come to the view initially because we accept by faith that the Bible is God's Word to us, and the Bible speaks of the Holy Spirit and of the Spirit's indwelling Presence in the life of a believer. This is confirmed by our own observations. Christians really live as though we have God's Spirit inside us. We have seen the change and accept that the basis of the change is God's Presence. Nevertheless we must not pretend that there is anything scientifically respectable about the belief in the Holy Spirit of God, nor will we ever be able to make it so. We believe in it because we believe in a God who communicates with us. His ultimate communication was the sacred visit of God's Son, but in addition, we believe by faith that the Bible is another form of that communication.

Scientific respectability and belief in the power of prayer. A third belief of Christians is the possibility of meaningful prayer. We actually believe that, when we utter words with our voice, a Being hears those words. Not only that, but we believe that we do not even have to voice our prayers out loud. We can whisper them or even just formulate them as thoughts in our mind, and the Creator of the universe "hears" those prayers. We even believe that it is no problem for God to hear millions of prayers being offered simultaneously all over the earth. The belief in prayer is a fundamental tenet of Christianity—if this were ever taken away, we would be left with a religion considerably different from Christianity.

Can we massage the doctrine of prayer in a way that would make it scientifically respectable? Perhaps, but I doubt it. True, evidence from the field of medicine suggests that prayer really makes a difference. But in the world of test tubes and instruments, I predict that prayer's success will be attributed not to some external force (that is, God) but rather to the placebo effect. It will be said that the very act of believing that prayer will work causes it work. The notion that the Creator can hear millions of prayers all at once and respond as he wishes is hardly an idea that is acceptable to someone who restricts his or her life to the realm of the here and now and only in matters that are subject to the tools of science.

This does not in any way imply that belief in prayer is irrational; it only means that there are various ways we can come to know something, and sometimes those ways of knowing lie outside the realm of science. Once we believe that the Bible is one of God's primary ways of communicating with us, and once we experience the power of prayer in our lives, then it is ultimate reality to believe that the Creator of the universe has no problem hearing all those prayers even when they are formulated merely as thoughts in our mind.

Scientific respectability and belief in life everlasting. A fourth tenet of

Christians is the belief that we will live forever in some type of a new, everlasting body. Scientifically, this is an incomprehensible possibility. Science points to the seeming inevitability of death, annihilation and decay. The notion that there is some part of us that lives on or is brought to life again at some later point in time will never (so far as we can see into the future) be scientifically testable. It is a world inaccessible to the tools of science, and there is nothing we can do to massage that notion in order to make it scientifically respectable. From the scientific perspective, it is simply unthinkable. Nevertheless we believe it, and that belief cannot be classified as irrational. Once one accepts that a God visited this earth in human form, that there is a Holy Spirit whose Presence is at the center of our being and that we can communicate with the Creator of the universe through prayer, then the issue of immortality almost becomes a given. Nevertheless it is not a belief that is scientifically credible. Its credibility comes from outside the scientific method.

The purpose of the foregoing is to make it clear that belief in gradual creation must not be a slippery slope that leads eventually to un-Christian beliefs. The fact is that Christianity has core beliefs that are not accessible to the scientific method. If any of a host of those core beliefs (I have addressed only a few of them here) are taken away for the sake of compatibility with the scientific method, then what is left is very different from Christianity. It is highly possible that core Christian beliefs will always be outside of the realm that science is able to investigate, and any attempt to bring them into line with each other would be futile.

Listening to God's voice and looking for the movement of God's hand. Evidence for God creating gradually is much different than the sorts of Christian phenomena addressed above. The resurrection, existence of the Holy Spirit and immortality are all beyond the realm of scientific testability. Even testing the power of prayer will probably not bring scientists to their knees. The history of life on earth, however, is in a much different category. It *has* been possible to explore this using scientific methods. Prior to the burst of knowledge that has come from the sciences, there were two equally legitimate ways of viewing the Genesis account. The first is that there is some figurative language in the scriptural revelation of origins. Conceding this as a possibility is not a major concession, since we already know that the Bible contains figurative language. Contrary to a literal interpretation of Job 38:22, there are not literal storehouses for the hail, and in contrast to a literal reading of Psalm 139, God did not knit us together in our mother's womb with knitting needles. Many of us will even acknowledge that when John wrote of the pearly gates of heaven in the book of Revelation, he was simply trying to put the beauty of heaven into an image that was humanly understandable. We know the Bible has figurative language. Thus the idea that the Genesis account contains figurative language has always been a possibility, and as such it was accepted in that light by one of the greatest Christian figures of antiquity, Augustine. The second possibility is that the account was meant to be taken as historical. Hence there have always been two interpretations, both of them perfectly compatible with Christianity.

So which is it—gradual or sudden, figurative or literal? For the past century and a half, thousands of scientists from disciplines as diverse as physics, geology, astronomy and biology have amassed a tremendous mass of data, and the answer is absolutely clear and equally certain. The earth is not young, and the life forms did not appear in six twenty-four-hour days. God created gradually. However, that need not, indeed must not, be considered a revolutionary statement. The heart of Christianity does not in any way relate to the time period of creation. If any of our human-made theology depends upon that notion, then that theology needs to be modified. However, the fact is that there is no centuries-old theological concept that hinges on the notion of sudden creation. No tenet revolves around it, and accepting it need not be the first step of a downhill journey away from the core concepts of Christian faith. In fact the reverse is true. We now know more about the nature of divine action. We now know a little about how God created life, and any time we understand something new about the activity of God, it brings us one step closer to God. The "slippery slope" is really not that at all—it is part of a journey that leads heavenward.

Recognizing the limits of scientific tools. I have tried to make it clear that taking the step of believing that there is some figurative language in the Genesis account is a fundamentally different step from questioning long-held tenets of Christianity. I will conclude with a final illustration, which demonstrates why accepting a gradual creation has a basis very different from concluding there was no resurrection or no such thing as a Holy Spirit at the center of our being.

This morning I glanced at the weather page of my local newspaper, the *San Diego Union-Tribune*. "The high temperature yesterday was quite cool," I noted to my wife. It had been fifty-nine degrees—a chilly day by San Diego standards for early March. In making that conclusion, I trusted an instrument of the science of meteorology, a trust made even more credible by my observation that all of the various localities in and around San Diego gave about the same reading. Not only that, but since I had been working in the garden most of the day, I knew that it really had been quite chilly.

The instruments of science also tell us that life appeared gradually. All of the instruments, each viewed from its own perspective, relay the same message. Life has appeared gradually. I have spent the past thirty years out in the "garden" of biology exploring those instruments, and I am satisfied that they are working fine and that God did really create by a gradual process and not a sudden one.

If I had opened up the newspaper and read about a different sort of finding from meteorology, there would have been legitimate reason to be skeptical. Let's say, for example, that I read an article entitled, "Meteorologists Search Atmosphere for Evidence of Spiritual Being." The fact is that the meteorologists can bring out the most elaborate and expensive equipment known to humans, and they could use that equipment to thoroughly analyze every component of the earth's atmosphere, but no matter what they did, they would be unable to comment scientifically on whether the Holy Spirit was penetrating the atmosphere of earth with God's Presence. Science cannot address that question with meteorological instruments. So also science is unable to address the question of the resurrection. Scientists can say that it would need to be a dramatically different sort of event from what they have ever seen before, but they cannot say it could not have happened. Put simply, science does not have the equipment to measure whether such a singular event could have happened in the past.

Believing in gradual creation is the equivalent of trusting the instruments of science that yesterday's temperature was really fifty-nine degrees. It is hard for some of us to trust those instruments because it seems to us that there is so much at stake. Nevertheless, after careful consideration, we must trust them—they are legitimately measuring what they were made to measure. Accepting this, however, need not be the first step down a slippery slope. Taking the step of doubting the resurrection or other tenets of our faith has nothing to do with the instruments of science. Scientific tools are silent on the issue of whether the resurrection occurred, just as meteorology is silent on the issue of whether God's Holy Spirit can penetrate our atmosphere. There may be a slippery slope away from God, but it is not belief in gradual creation that is the first downward step. The remaining steps are of a fundamentally different kind, because they are not grounded in the tools of science. Furthermore, I would maintain that coming to a realization of gradual creation is not a downward step at all. At worst it may be a step sideways. However, if it leads one closer to an understanding of God's activity—closer to his truth—it is more than a step sideways: it is a step upwards. It brings us one step closer to understanding the action of God in his universe, one step closer to understanding the role of God's activity (through the Holy Spirit) in our own lives.

COMING TO PEACE WITH HUMAN CREATION

The two complementary accounts of human creation. In our discussion thus far, we have focused primarily on creation events related to the first chapter of Genesis, and we have noted that this chapter speaks of the creation act as a series of commands from God. It does not give specifics about the processes that occurred as a result of those commands. It only tells us that when each stage was completed, God was pleased with the result. Even the story of the creation of humans is left in the same vague format in Genesis 1, although we are given one extra detail: humans were created in God's image. We are told nothing in this chapter about how God carried out this magnificent task, nor are we told what it means to be created in the image of God.

Beginning in Genesis 2:4, we find a complementary account of creation. This account has a much different tone to it—a more personal tone. It gets quickly to the point: the creation of humans. In this account the creation of the universe is almost incidental and the narrative draws the reader almost immediately to the picture of God creating humankind. The two accounts are not contradictory; rather they have two different purposes. The first account is the creation of the cosmos from a viewpoint above the earth. In a sense it is the view from God's perspective—humankind-for-God. The second account is the view from the earth—God-for-humankind.[2] It is not a picture of a majestic God who created all that is and all that there ever will be; the narrator has a different point to make here—he wants to make it clear that this God is knowable. From within the garden, this God is a Father who bends down and picks up a lump of earth to personally create the first human. This God breathes his own breath into the nostrils of his beloved creature. This God plants a garden and puts his beloved in the center of the garden. This God knows that the man is lonely and creates a helper for him, putting just as much individual attention into the creation of the helper as he had for the man. This account does not want us to think about God as being from a distant universe—majestic and untouchable. Rather this is a God who, when it comes to his relationship with human beings, can best be thought of as Abba, Father. He walks in the garden, and it almost seems like the couple can reach out and touch him.

There is wonderful beauty in the two accounts of creation. God wants us to know who he is. On the one hand, God is the eternal being whose greatness is beyond our imagination. But on the other hand, there is every reason for us to think of God as our own personal Parent who brought us into the world and wishes nothing but joy, peace, companionship and love for us. What a magnificent thought! And what a

---

[2]Dietrich Bonhoeffer, *Creation and Fall* (1937; reprint, Minneapolis: Fortress, 1997).

magnificent way for God to begin that which turns out to be, in essence, an almost two-thousand-page (in my Bible) love story of God for humankind.

If ever there were proof for the Bible being God's Word, this story—the story of Genesis—must be among the clearest of proofs. Could the most creative Hollywood producer or playwright tell such a profound message in a simpler, more poignant manner than this? The two companion pieces reach a climax when the Creator of the universe comes down from on high—from his "throne" in a distant universe—and tenderly breathes life from his Being into the nostrils of man. Man—created in God's image with the breath of God inside—thereby comes to life. This is truly a message for the ages, and so it has been. It is a message inspired by God himself, and as such it is the greatest of all possible truths.

The historicity of the second account. Is it possible that God put this in story form because this is the only way we could grasp its real truth? Is it possible that its message is so true that the only way its truth can be comprehended is if it is told in an almost poetic manner? Alternatively, could it be a historically accurate account of what really happened and its beautiful message to us has come through real events that actually did happen precisely as they are told? Perhaps God really did reach down and grab a handful of dust from which he fashioned the first man. Perhaps God really did cause the man to go into a deep sleep, during which he removed a rib and then fashioned it into Eve. Let us make one thing clear: if we accept that God could raise Jesus from the dead and give him a transformed body, it is not a major leap of faith to accept that God could make a woman from a rib. If we believe that some aspect of our being never dies, when we know full well that our bodies suffer decay in the ground or disintegrate in an incinerator, then the notion of God's bending down and making a man from the earth need not be particularly difficult to accept. Christianity holds the view that some unnatural possibilities are the essence of reality, immortality being just one of them. Given this, the issue of the unnaturalness in accepting the second account of creation as real history need not concern the Christian. If we are Christians, we must all acknowledge that we believe, to the heart of our beings, in the unnatural.[3]

Nevertheless the question remains: is this event a story told to make the essence of God and his relationship to humanity clear, or is it actual, real-time history? I have tried to demonstrate why I believe that God created organisms in general by a gradual mechanism. The Bible speaks of the creation of life forms in terms that imply little more than that they are the result of God's command; hence I feel it is clear that the gradual appearance of life in general is totally consistent with Scripture. The second account, however, has a different tone. Since it is a personal account of the Father's love and care for man and woman, it cannot—no, must not—speak in terms of an "impersonal" God uttering commands in a detached fashion. The only way God can make his message clear to us is in a manner that is in the same vein as the personal message that permeates the New Testament. The great God of the universe comes down to where we are going to be and fashions us into his image. Just as Scripture shows God breathing his breath into our body in the initial creation event, so the great God of the universe removes his breath from his dying Son so that we might know how much he loves us—*our* new-creation event.

Earlier I mentioned that Romans 5 speaks of Jesus as the second Adam. Paul did this, in large part, to show us the dichotomy of the acts of the two men. By Adam's one act, death entered the human race, whereas by Jesus' one act, new life arose. By Adam's one act, humankind was banished from the garden, whereas by Jesus' one act, we begin the journey back to the garden again. The ramifications of that analogy, a picture painted for us by God through Paul, are tremendous, because as I have mentioned earlier, it is really a

---

[3]C. S. Lewis put this especially poignantly:

> When the author of Genesis says that God made man in His own image, he may have pictured a vaguely corporeal God making man as a child makes a figure out of plasticine [Play-Doh]. A modern Christian philosopher may think of a process lasting from the first creation of matter to the final appearance on this planet for an organism fit to receive spiritual as well as biological life. But both mean essentially the same thing. Both are denying the same thing—the doctrine that matter by some blind power inherent in itself has produced spirituality. (C. S. Lewis, *God in the Dock* [Grand Rapids, Mich.: Eerdmans, 1970], p. 46)

picture of the church as God now intends it to be. Just as Adam is the bridegroom of Eve, so Jesus is pictured throughout Paul's writings as the bridegroom of the church. Adam and Eve are pictured as being one flesh—a beautiful image of marriage as God intended it to be. However, there is an even deeper message than that here, for the imagery of Adam and Eve clearly leads us to the church, the bride of Christ.[4] We in the church are all one body, the bride of the second Adam. Recall that on the night before Jesus' crucifixion he was praying for the church (Jn 17). He prayed that it might be one as Jesus and the Father were one, and although Jesus never mentioned it in his prayer, it is for us to notice that it is also as Eve and her bridegroom, Adam, were one. Indeed they *were* one flesh—"bone of my bones and flesh of my flesh" (Gen 2:23). Not only did Paul often speak of the church as being the bride of Christ, but because of our unity with Christ, Paul also told us repeatedly that we are Christ's body here on earth. The most sacred of all acts of Christians the world over is our reminder of oneness with him and with each other—the act of Holy Communion. Many Christians believe that when we drink the wine we are literally drinking Jesus' blood and partaking of his body. Others believe the act is symbolic. Regardless of whether the act of Communion is symbolic or literal, the fact is that it signifies that we are the body of Christ—"bone of my bones and flesh of my flesh."

Adam gave of his body in the creation of his bride, Eve, just as Christ gave of his body for the creation of his bride, the church. Just as God created the bride of the first Adam, at the expense of a part of Adam's own body, his rib, so God created the church from the body of the second Adam—a church created literally at the expense of the body of Christ.

This section becomes deep with imagery, but it is sacred imagery that points out to us God's plan for marriage and his plan for the church. It could not have been done more poignantly than in the story of Adam and Eve. There is no other way that God could tell the story

---

[4]Bonhoeffer, *Creation and Fall*, pp. 22, 82, 83, 100.

of his love and desire for the church than to show us the imagery of his reaching into Adam's side, removing it and creating Eve. It points toward the new creation, for this is exactly what he did to his own Son when he reached down into the Son's bleeding body and at the expense of that body created the church. Just as the rib coming from Adam's side became the life of Eve, so the blood that came out from Jesus' pierced side became our lifeblood. By the act of the first piercing, life began for Adam's bride. By the act of the second piercing, life began for the bride of Christ.[5]

Hence there is a good reason for God's putting the creation of Adam and Eve into the form he did. The story of Adam and Eve is our story. It is not simply the story of an ancient couple who lived in a garden. If that is all we see, we are missing a gift that God gives to us. He wants more than anything to tell us how much he loves us, and the story of Adam, Eve and a garden is the story of Jesus, you and I, and life in God's Presence.

The story of Jesus is real history. We accept that. There is an element of faith in our acceptance of it, but it quickly becomes certainty as we spend life walking in his Presence. We also accept it because of real data.[6] The Gospel accounts have been traced to manuscripts written within a generation or two of the time of Christ. No one could have written with the heartfelt passion of Paul unless there was a genuine belief in what was being written about. It is real history that occurred in real time.

But what about Adam and Eve? Did God literally make Adam from the ground, or did he put it before us in the manner of a story to illustrate his intricate involvement in our creation, both the new as well as the original? Did God really reach into Adam's side and create Eve from a rib, or is it told in the form of a story so that we might see God's expectation for marriage and the church? One thing must be remembered above all else, and that is that regardless of the historicity of

---

[5]Karl Barth, *The Doctrine of Creation,* vol. 3 of *Church Dogmatics* (Edinburgh: T & T Clark, 1958), p. 321, cited in Henri Blocher, *In the Beginning* (Downers Grove, Ill.: InterVarsity Press, 1984), p. 102.
[6]See Lee Strobel, *The Case for Christ* (Grand Rapids, Mich.: Zondervan, 1998).

Adam and Eve, their story is our story and the truthful meaning of the story comes from God.[7]

We do not all have to believe the same. It seems to me (and to others) that on this issue the evangelical church must allow diversity of opinion and work through it in much the same manner that Paul guided the early church to work through a similarly controversial matter in his day.[8] Let's digress for a moment to explore this issue and God's Word on how to handle it. Those early years soon after the death and resurrection of Jesus were tumultuous for the church because it was breaking away from its heritage in the Old Testament laws. There were people who felt that the rules of what to eat and what not to eat should still come from the Law and that the way in which the Sabbath was observed should be based upon Jewish tradition. Opinions on this were splitting the church, breaking apart Christ's sacred body at a time when it was just an infant and was needing all the nurture it could get. The church survived that period and went on to revolutionize society in a manner of which we are still the benefactors today. If the right thing had not been done at that time in history, we probably would not be Christians today and the world would be a much different place. So what was God's word to his people in this time of ominous potential for divisiveness? Let's read for ourselves:

> One man considers one day more sacred than another; another man considers every day alike. Each one should be fully convinced in his own

---

[7]Michael Lodahl said,
> We are the sinners in the garden; we do well to remember that the name Adam means literally "humanity." Thus to read of Adam's fall is indeed to read of our own. Truly the narrative of the Fall in Genesis 3 is "your Story and Mine." In fact to make it the story only of our first parents is to foist the problem of sin, *our* sin, onto others as though we had no responsibility and they had it all. Such projection may itself, in fact, be a manifestation of sin, since sin often involved the abdication of one's own responsibility, one's own answerability, for one's actions. (Michael Lodahl, *The Story of God* [Kansas City, Mo.: Beacon Hill, 1993], p. 75)

[8]Consider, for example, these words of C. S. Lewis:
> Does this mean that Christians on different levels of general education conceal radically different beliefs under an identical form of words? Certainly not. For what they agree on is the substance, and what they differ about is the shadow. When one imagines his God seated in a local heaven above a flat earth, where another sees God and creation in terms of Professor [Alfred North] Whitehead's philosophy [process theology], this difference touches precisely what does not matter. (Lewis, *God in the Dock*, p. 46)

mind. He who regards one day as special, does so to the Lord. He who eats meat, eats to the Lord, for he gives thanks to God. . . . For none of us lives to himself alone and none of us dies to himself alone. If we live, we live to the Lord; and if we die, we die to the Lord. So, whether we live or die, we belong to the Lord. (Rom 14:5-8)

God's word to us is that we should think through the controversial issue carefully, make a decision if we can and then offer that decision to God. Regardless of what we decide, it should be adopted with a spirit of worship, because all for which we live and die is for God's kingdom—it must never develop into *our* kingdom.

Let's further consider God's word to us:

Let us stop passing judgment on one another. Instead, make up your mind not to put any stumbling block or obstacle in your brother's way. As one who is in the Lord Jesus, I am fully convinced that no food is unclean in itself. But if anyone regards something as unclean, then for him it is unclean. . . . For the kingdom of God is not a matter of eating and drinking, but of righteousness, peace and joy in the Holy Spirit, because anyone who serves Christ in this way is pleasing to God and approved by men. (Rom 14:13-14, 17-18)

Finally, as this discussion draws to a close, the admonishment is especially germane to us today: "May the God who gives endurance and encouragement give you a spirit of unity among yourselves as you follow Christ Jesus, so that with one heart and mouth you may glorify the God and Father of our Lord Jesus Christ" (Rom 15:5-6).

If this is God's word to us, one might wonder why a book like this is even being written. I have, after all, strongly advocated the view that God's mechanism of creation of the various life forms is gradual, not sudden. That position hardly sounds like a position that will engender unity in the church, because there are many who will, no matter how clear the argument, be unwilling or unable to accept this view. If that is the case, so be it, because through all of this God's command of unity stands above all else. We must recognize that we are permitted diverse opinions, but in that diversity we must be able to put our arms around each other, bonded together in love. But if the topic is potentially divisive, why has this book even been written?

First John 4:1 states that we are to "test the sprits to see whether they are from God." It has been my task, as someone who has spent his life studying biology, to write about why there is no doubt in the minds of most biologists that new life forms appeared on this earth gradually. Those of us who are Christian biologists, of course, believe that it happened at the command and under the guidance of the Creator. Out of respect for the 1 John mandate, I have felt it important to give you opportunity to "test the spirits." Now that we have thought together about the reasons, regardless of how each of us personally ends up believing, it is extremely important that we allow for people of both creation persuasions, sudden and gradual, to exist side by side in Christ's body. One of my primary goals in writing this book has been to lay before the church the reasons why almost all scientists (including Christian ones) believe in the gradual appearance of life on this earth. It is hoped that, having done so, we will be able to go on in unity and love, despite the diversity that still exists. It is God's kingdom, and we need to heartily follow God's rules, not ours.

Are the scientific data related to creation of humans different than for other organisms? Now back to the issue at hand. Is the account of God reaching down and creating Adam from the dust of the ground, and God reaching in and creating Eve from the rib of Adam, real history or figurative language? The genes on our chromosomes are arranged in almost the same order as the genes in the chimpanzee and gorilla. Geneticists are convinced that this specific gene order is not particularly important: the genes can be rearranged and put into different orders that would work just as well.[9] The similar order, geneticists believe, is a reflection of our shared ancestry. The same is true for the language of the genes. The genes in our cells use the same "dialect" in providing instructions on how to make proteins as the genes in chimpanzee cells. The "dialect" has changed some, but the change, geneticists believe, is what one would expect if it has been a while since we had a common ancestor. Humans have many of the same marked genes as the great apes. We have many retroposons and silenced virus genes inserted into

---

[9]J. G. Hacia, "Genome of the Apes," *Trends in Genetics* (2001): 637-45.

introns in the exact same position as chimpanzees and gorillas. There is no "break" in the genetic data that implies that the human body was created in a manner that is different than the way in which God created other living creatures.

The fossil data is especially poignant. It indicates that creatures with intermediate characteristics were on the earth at about the time when one would expect them to be if the notion of gradual creation holds for humans as well. The fossils have been found, and they turn out to be the expected age—several million years or less.[10] The age of those fossils is closely correlated with how similar they are to modern humans: the closer the structural similarities, the younger the fossil. We even know there were creatures on this earth (Neanderthals) that had bodies much like ours (albeit clearly distinctive). They lived here alongside of us until about forty thousand years ago. A small amount of the DNA from one of these creatures has, amazingly, been obtained.[11] The analysis of that DNA suggests it was a different but closely related species. The fact is, then, that there is nothing about our own history, viewed through the eyes of scientific investigation, that would lead us to believe that God did not create us gradually too.

Hence it seems likely that when God's Word to us shows God reaching down to the ground and making Adam, it is telling us that God created humanity from the dust of the earth, but not necessarily in an instant. Moreover, when it tells us that Eve was created from Adam's rib, it seems likely that it is telling us that husband and wife in God's kingdom are one flesh and that they must live their lives that way. Given the notion that Eve is Adam's bride, just as the church is the bride of Christ, so God's Word to us also foreshadows the fact that the church itself is one body, derived at the expense of Christ himself.

Created in the image of God. The story of Adam and Eve is an inspired message that comes to us as revelation from God, told for our edification. Even if humans were created gradually at the physical level, it

---

[10]Robert J. Blemuenshine et al., "Late Pliocene *Homo* and Hominoid Land Use from Western Olduvai Gorge, Tanzania," *Science* 299 (2003): 1217-21.
[11]Igor V. Ovchirnikov et al., "Molecular Analysis of Neanderthal DNA from the Northern Caucasus," *Nature* 404 (2003): 490-93.

certainly is still possible that Adam and Eve were real individuals who
lived in real time. If that were the case, the creation account might be
viewed as the creation of humans as spiritual beings, and Adam and
Eve would simply have been the first humans to experience what it really means to live in the image of God—in full communication with
God as God. If so, then in a historical *and* figurative sense, their story
becomes our story.[12] They sinned. We have sinned. Their action resulted in them becoming separated from the Presence of God. Our sin
resulted in our separation from God. They were *not* restored, but we
(through Jesus) bring completion to their story, for we are able to enter
the garden of God's Presence again. Hence, regardless of whether it is
historical *and* figurative, or purely figurative, their story becomes our
story—a story for all humankind.

No matter how we interpret its historicity, humans are spiritual beings created in God's image and able to know God and love him because of his revelation to us through his written Word, the Bible, and
his living Word, Jesus.[13] Moreover God continues the act of revelation
to members of Christ's body through the living Holy Spirit. The ongo-

---

[12]Perhaps C. S. Lewis expressed the mythical dimension of Scripture best:

We must not be ashamed of the mythical radiance resting on our theology. . . . We
must not, in false spirituality, withhold our imaginative welcome. If God chooses to
be mythopoeic—and is not the sky itself a myth—shall we refuse to be *mythopathic?*
For this is the marriage of heaven and earth: Perfect Myth and Perfect Fact: claiming
not only our love and our obedience, but also our wonder and delight, addressed to
the savage, the child, and the poet in each one of us no less than to the moralist, the
scholar, and the philosopher. (Lewis, *God in the Dock*, p. 67)

[13]Scottish theologian James Orr, one of the authors of *The Fundamentals* (1910–1915), wrote the
following over one hundred years ago:

It is not rightly put to say that the doctrine of the Fall rests on the third chapter of Genesis. The Christian doctrine of Redemption certainly does not rest on the narrative of
Gen. iii, but it rests on the reality of the sin and guilt of the world, which would remain
facts though the third chapter of Genesis never had been written. It would be truer to
say that I believe in the third chapter of Genesis, or in the essential truth which it contains, because I believe in sin and Redemption than to say that I believe in sin and Redemption because of the story of the Fall. (James Orr, *The Christian View of God and the
World as Centering in the Incarnation* [1891; reprint, Grand Rapids, Mich.: Eerdmans,
1948], p. 182, cited in Bernard Ramm, *Offense to Reason* [San Francisco: Harper & Row,
1985], p. 57)

Leading Princeton theologian B. B. Warfield, another author of *The Fundamentals*, "allowed
for large-scale evolution from one or only a few original life forms as a way of explaining
God's way of creating plants, animals, and even the human body" (Mark Knoll, "Ignorant
Armies," *First Things* 32 [1993]: 45-48).

ing message of the entire Bible is that God reaches out to individuals as individuals, in the real time of singular events. Biology and study of the history of life on earth can tell us nothing about humankind's initial creation as spiritual beings. Certainly it could have been an event initiated by God's interaction with two unique individuals, a man and a woman who were brought into the paradise of God's Presence at a unique point in history. Psychology and anthropology can tell us nothing about the initiation of humankind's spiritual journey. As Christians, we believe that we are spiritual beings able to communicate with God in response to God's reaching out to us. That communication process must have begun at some time in history. By all means, one legitimate view of the scriptural account is that it began with two historically real individuals into whom God breathed his breath—the breath that gives real life. However, an alternative view is that God inspired the picture of Adam, Eve and the garden in story form simply to make the above points clear to humankind in a manner that will be understandable through the millennia of time. There needs to be room for both views in evangelical Christianity. Let us not ever allow the acid test of one's Christianity to become one's view of whether Adam and Eve are figurative alone or historical *and* figurative. It is the message itself, and belief that the message came from God, that is central. Let us allow diversity on its historicity so that we can move on in unity to more important issues.[14]

---

[14]Some believe that the historicity of Adam's sin is so central to the doctrine of sin's origin that Christianity will stand or fall on the historical Adam. Conservative scholar Bernard Ramm argued strongly against this view in *Offense to Reason*. So did Michael Lodahl (see *Story of God*); Conrad Hyers (see *The Meaning of Creation* [Atlanta: John Knox Press, 1985]; Dietrich Bonhoeffer (see *Creation and Fall*); and (by implication) C. S. Lewis (see *God in the Dock*, footnote 12). Roman Catholic theologian Jerry Korsmeyer writes the following:

If you ask a Scripture scholar today, most will inform you that there is not "fall," as Augustine describes it, in Genesis. In fact Adam's story, which some today see as the heart of the Christian message because it explains why God became human, is hardly mentioned anywhere else in the First Testament. There is hardly any mention of him in the Prophets. What is even more striking is that there is no mention of Adam's sin in the Gospels. As historian of original sin Henri Rondet, DS.J. noted, "Obviously the evangelic doctrine of the redemption is not based primarily upon the need to make reparation for Adam's sin. Jesus came 'to seek and to save the lost,' to wrest us away from evil, to restore us to life Luke 19:10 and John 10:10." (Jerry Korsmeyer, *Evolution and Eden* [New York: Paulist, 1998], p. 24)

COMING TO PEACE WITH THE FACT THAT THE BIBLE IS NOT EXPLICIT ABOUT GRADUAL CREATION

The purpose of this book has been to explore the story of creation in light of what we know from science. From science we know that new life forms have appeared gradually over billions of years. Hence, for Christians, this means that God must have created gradually and that the scriptural account needs to be interpreted in that light. My students frequently ask me, why, if God created gradually, does not the Word of God specifically tell us that? The answer to that question resides in two considerations. One is the timeless nature of Scripture. God's Word to us today was also God's Word to civilization thousands of years ago. His Word is timeless and has needed to speak in an understandable manner down through the millennia. The fact that it does is a miracle in its own right. However, as we saw in chapter five, perhaps there *are* elements of the gradual creation story in the account. The Word could have simply said that God created all that is and have left it at that. It could have said it all in a single verse. Instead the Word points us to a God creating in stages. A close examination raises the possibility that there are two parallel accounts of gradual creation in the first chapter. The first occurs over the first three days and begins with creating light and the expanse in the sky, followed by dry land and finally plants. It occurs in stages, with each stage being accomplished at God's command. The second occurs over days four through six. It starts off with light again (this time by referring to specific sources of light) and proceeds in stages to discuss God's command as it relates to the animal world. In both of these sections we are shown a picture of God preparing the earth for his creatures—plants in the first case, animals in the second. It did not *have* to be told in the form of a gradual unfolding of God's work in creation, but it was. The message is timeless. It was understood four thousand years ago, and it can be understood in even more detail by us today, because we have the fruits of scientific investigation telling us more about the results of God's command. God's Word did not inform us of all the details. Given the timeless nature of the Bible, that would have only brought confusion. However, God did give us the minds to piece the details together, and as we learn that we can trust those minds sometimes, we will be brought closer to under-standing reality—God's reality.

The second consideration in thinking about why the Bible does not provide more detail about the mechanism of creation relates to the pur-pose of Scripture. The Bible, above all else, is a story of God's plan of salvation, and as such it is a story of God's desire to enter into relation-ship—the love story I talked about earlier. In a sense, then, how God created our bodies is incidental, and God chose not to go into it in de-tail because it is a side issue that would detract from the central pur-pose of the story. Readers down through the ages would have become lost in the technical details and missed the real point of the story if it had been told in any other way. Hence God simply told us that we, like animals, are created from the dust of the ground. And that, as you know, is the heart of the gradual creation story—no biologist could put it more succinctly than that. That allows God to get to the essence of his message to us—the fact that he created us in his image and that we have been designed for entering into relationship with him.

COMING TO PEACE WITH THOSE IN THE FAMILY OF GOD WHO THINK DIFFERENTLY

We now return to the real purpose of this book. My hope is that it is now clear that it is possible to be an evangelical who accepts Christ as his or her personal Savior and accepts Scripture as the inspired Word of God but who nevertheless also holds a gradual creation view. There are logical reasons for holding this position. My purpose has not pri-marily been to present the view of gradual creation so that others will adopt the view as their own. If that happens, it would be fine, but it has not been the purpose of the book. Rather its purpose has been to help the church understand that this needs to be accepted as a valid position for an evangelical to hold. I have laid out some of the many good rea-sons for accepting the legitimacy of this belief and have tried to show that it is not inconsistent with the foundations of our faith.

As I began the book, I described it as the personal story of a biolo-gist's attempt to bring unity to his faith and the knowledge that he has gained from the world of biology. I want to conclude by returning to the personal aspect of this story, and I do so not because there is any-thing special about my personal spiritual journey. It is no more special than anyone else's. Nevertheless I think it illustrates a lesson that comes to the heart of the reason for writing this book. Upon my return to Christ (which I described in an earlier section), I was not ready to re-turn to evangelical Christianity. I longed to do so, because I knew that in essence I was an evangelical. I believed in Christ as my personal Sav-ior. I believed that we are able to communicate with God and that God communicates with us. I tried to live my life by walking in Christ's footsteps. Nevertheless certain things kept me from returning to evan-gelicalism at the corporate level. One of the biggest deterrents was my impression that I could never become part of an evangelical fellowship because of my belief in gradual creation. It is important that you see how great a deterrent that was, because unless the church begins to downplay the significance of believing in some variety of a sudden cre-ation (possibility 1 [every species] or 2 [just prototypes]), there will continue to be thousands of individuals (including, in some cases, our own children) who will be denied true fellowship in God's kingdom. They will, in effect, feel denied of fellowship, not because of their re-fusal to accept Christ as Savior but because they believe the church doors are not wide open to someone who believes in gradual creation. Such individuals will associate Christianity with a particular view con-trary to the entire world of science. As Christians, we simply must not allow that to become a barrier to belief. The fence must come down and we must stop presenting the view that belief in the Bible creates a war between the data of modern science and biblical faithfulness.[15] If many Christians want to hold the view that God created suddenly, then so be it. But as a church, we must discourage them from claiming that belief

---

[15]To the extent that scientific investigators advocate the absence of God in the history of life, there is spiritual warfare. To the extent that this absence-of-God philosophy permeates other academic disciplines, again there is spiritual warfare. Having spent eighteen years as a student, postdoctoral fellow and professor in secular universities, I am fully aware that this philosophy is pervasive. However, the data are not at fault. The cause of the spiritual warfare is the interpretation of that data in a manner that excludes God's involvement. On this I am in agreement with Phillip Johnson and his colleagues. See Phillip Johnson, *The Wedge of Truth: Splitting the Foundations of Naturalism* (Downers Grove, Ill.: InterVarsity Press, 2000).

in sudden creation is fundamental to faith.

I am in an unusual position compared to many scientifically trained individuals. I grew up in an evangelical church, and hence I knew the beauty of Christian fellowship firsthand. Upon becoming a Christian again in young adulthood, I yearned for that sort of fellowship once more, but I did not expect that it would ever happen—the bridgeless gulf for people who thought like I did was simply too great. One of my most vivid memories of this period occurred on a Sunday afternoon at a southern California beach. As my wife and I and our two little girls arrived at the beach that day, I saw a Sunday school bus that, judging from the lettering on the side, was from a church of the denomination in which I grew up. That brought back vivid memories of my favorite times growing up as a child. Fellowship in the church had been the greatest joy of my life, and it was the picnics that I enjoyed most of all. This church family, I reasoned, was having a picnic, just like I used to love so much. Now I was an adult and I had my own two young children alongside me. As I mused that afternoon at the beach about the richness of my own heritage and looked down at my own children playing on the beach in front of me, I felt they were being deprived of the richest part of my own heritage. I longed to go back, if only for the sake of my daughters. But I could not go back—the chasm that separated us was too great. One of the widest sections of the gulf was my belief in gradual creation.

The fact that I made it back two years later is the biggest—and best—surprise of my life. It is a surprise because my wife and I decided to take the plunge after all, but it is also a surprise because the small evangelical church we found opened their collective arms to us, despite our hesitancies about the distance that separated us. That church—God's gift to us—built a bridge to us and welcomed us just as we were, gradual creation perspective and all. It has been more than twenty-five years since that happened. The little girls playing in front of me on the beach are grown, and now they have passed the age I was when I had the "beach experience." It turned out that my expectation that day was wrong. Our girls did grow up to experience all that I had experienced in church fellowship—and much more. But the message of this book still stands. We made the plunge back into the evangelical church as a last resort, fully expecting that we would not stay. In today's atmosphere of increased polarization and increased tendency for evangelicalism to be synonymous with sudden creation, I am afraid that many who think as I did then would not even try. If a Christian would hesitate and quite possibly not even try to enter into a church community, how much more would that be true of a well-educated person who does not yet have a budding faith?

Hence the reason for this book. I expect that many persons in our churches will read this book and put it down still believing in sudden creation. From my perspective, that will be fine. After all, few are biologists, geologists, physicists or astronomers, and it is hard to sort through all the details after this single reading of one person's perspective. However, my prayer is that each person who reads it will come to an understanding that evangelical Christians need no longer feel that sudden creation is one of the canons (or for that matter, cannons!) of their faith. I hope that they will respect that one should be able to be accepted as an equal partner in Christ's body even if he or she believes that God created gradually. I hope that such people will not be called "semicreationists" just because they believe in a gradual creation. I also hope that the days of calling the belief in gradual creation a "compromise position," as though that made it less true, will stop. Finally I hope that Christians will stop insisting that the sudden creation view be taught in the science classroom. If there is any lesson in this book, it is that the sudden creation view is not compatible with scientific data. If the most predominant version of sudden creation were true, the sciences of nuclear physics, astronomy, geology and biology would all be utterly wrong. It cannot be taught in a science classroom because it is not science. It is contrary to almost all of science. (Chemistry may have been spared.) It is something different, namely a particular view of Scripture. It is religion.

Please do not misunderstand these comments. People who believe in gradual creation must make a special effort to love—really love—those with a sudden creation perspective. There are a lot of reasons why this is more important now than ever. First of all, we are all members of Christ's body. Second, we must not expect that all Christians will be well versed in science. God does not call us to a life of studying science—he calls us to a life of following in Christ's footsteps. Hence we must be patient with each other and allow each other to follow truth as we see it in Scripture. We must recognize that we will never reach the point where we all see Scripture the same way. Although you may be absolutely certain that God created gradually, this does not mean that you are somehow less obligated to love and care for someone who is equally certain that God created suddenly. We are one body and we must nurture and care for each other, all the more so when we think differently on some points.

My desire is that we will all work at building the bridge. It is my hope that evangelical Christianity will welcome Christians and those who are not yet Christians of both perspectives and that it will make clear that there is room for both perspectives in the family of God. Christians who believe in gradual creation must not be made to feel like prodigal children anymore. By the same token, those who believe in gradual creation must not look down on those who hold to a sudden creation view, as though they are somehow less intelligent. Most of the people who hold this view are not scientists, with a scientist's understanding of his or her discipline, but this has virtually nothing to do with intelligence. On occasion the two schools of thought may want to dialogue with each other about why each believes as it does, but dialogue must always be in the spirit of love and always just to keep each other on track, so that together we might make sure that the nonessentials are not beginning to seem like essentials in the family of God.

PEACE AT LAST

At the conclusion of any meaningful discourse, we like to identify a "bottom line." In a sense the Bible is the record of a centuries-long discourse between God and humans. In looking for the bottom line to this discourse, we can legitimately turn to the last page of our Bibles. Here we find that the book of Revelation ends with this message: "Whoever is thirsty, let him come; and whoever wishes, let him take the free gift of the water of life" (Rev 22:17). The bottom line is that God's love is the answer to humankind's thirst for meaning. When there is division in the church, it will be difficult for the thirsty to find their way to Jesus. Let us refuse to pass judgment on each other. Let us just love each other so that the thirsty will feel comfortable crossing the bridge to drink of the water of life.

Just as the final words of the Bible inform us about what God wants us to appreciate as the bottom line, so the final words of Jesus are equally informative. Not long before his arrest, Jesus was on his knees saying these words: "May they [his followers] be brought to complete unity to let the world know that you sent me" (Jn 17:23). Let us never forget that these were among Jesus' final words to the Father before being carried off, bound in rope, to the trial that would lead to his death. Moreover, just before he ascended into heaven, he told his disciples, "You will be my witnesses in Jerusalem, and in all Judea and Samaria, and to the ends of the earth" (Acts 1:8). Then he was gone. The rest was left to us by the power of the Holy Spirit.

Reaching those who do not have God's eternal life is our mandate, and it is clear that anything that splits us apart prevents us from being the body of Christ to a hurting world. Let us not allow a particular interpretation of a tiny section of God's precious Word to become so central that it creates a gulf blocking the access of any individuals to the experience of God's love in the church. I almost missed out, so wide did the distance seem to me. Thank God for a church that built a bridge, opened its gates wide and took my family into its family without even asking if we believed that creation was sudden or gradual. The church did not seem to care and virtually never mentioned it during our seven wonderful years there. May that spirit characterize the whole church, so that with one voice we may call out to the world, "Whoever is thirsty, let them come." Then, having come and having tasted of the living water, may they find nourishment for their souls that is not tainted by a hint that they will be second-class Christians unless they adopt a particular view of God's mechanism of creation. With that, they too will know peace at last.

Index